Service Clubs in American Society

Service Clubs
in American Society

Rotary, Kiwanis, and Lions

Jeffrey A. Charles

University of Illinois Press

Urbana and Chicago

© 1993 by the Board of Trustees of the University of Illinois
Manufactured in the United States of America
C 5 4 3 2 1

This book is printed on acid-free paper.

Library of Congress Cataloging-in-Publication Data
Charles, Jeffrey A., 1958–
    Service clubs in American society : Rotary, Kiwanis, and Lions /
    Jeffrey A. Charles.
        p.   cm.
    Includes bibliographical references and index.
    ISBN 0-252-02015-4 (cloth : alk. paper)
    1. Clubs—United States—Case studies.   2. Rotary International.
    3. Kiwanis International.   4. Lions International.   I. Title.
    HS2723.C48   1993
    369.5′0973—dc20   93-9803
                                                                    CIP

Acknowledgments

In my last year in high school, I received a college scholarship from the local Kiwanis club. The scholarship had nothing to do with my choosing this book topic, and I cannot say how those Sacramento Kiwanians would feel about this study, which is partially the product of their generosity. Nevertheless, their award proved to be the first of many assistances that club members provided as I went on to research this book. Both Kiwanis International and Lions International responded to my queries for information. I am especially grateful to Rotary International, its secretary, Herbert Pigman, and particularly the director of club service, Paul Bernholdt, who went beyond courtesy to open club archives and who also provided an able staff to assist my research and answer my questions. Club files and correspondence constitute a rich body of historical material, and I emerged from the club archives with a great respect for Rotary and for what Rotarians have accomplished in the United States and the world.

This book began as a doctoral dissertation written at Johns Hopkins University with the help of John Higham. My perspective remains deeply influenced by Professor Higham's multitude of insights into American culture. The more I learn, the more I am impressed by his perception. His suggestions clarified my thinking, and his editorial pen sharpened my writing. At Johns Hopkins, Louis Galambos, Ron Walters, Stuart McConnell, and Peter Kafer read versions of the manuscript and offered helpful suggestions. My close friends Darryl Hart and Dave Watt also read much of the study, and they provided enormous amounts of advice, along with a good-humored fellowship sans joybuzzers. At a time when my confidence in this work was flagging, I had the good fortune to attend an NEH-funded summer seminar taught by Olivier Zunz. He restored my faith in the project, and his thinking had a great influence on the shape of this study. I am extremely grateful.

At North Central College I have had financial assistance from the administration, which gave me a summer grant to pursue research in Illinois and also provided student help. Selina Hoffman did yeowoman's work in compiling club statistics. Even more important at North Central has been the assistance of Barbara Sciacchitano, Clark Halker, and Ann Durkin Keating. Not only have they helped with this work, they have served as role models, as scholars researching and writing while carrying a heavy teaching load.

In the latter stages of my work on the manuscript I received extremely useful suggestions from Lynn Dumenil and Thomas Pegram.

Finally, I have had the good fortune of being born into—and, happily, being married into—families supportive of academic endeavor. My uncle, Paul Glad, contributed counsel and the example of his own distinguished career; my aunt, Katherine Glass, supplied essential library resources; my sister-in-law and brother-in-law Anne D. Hedeman and John Hedeman have helped with source suggestions, publishing advice, and resort-style lodging. My wife, Catherine Charles, is doing work in molecular genetics that is much more important than this book, but she nevertheless has continually sacrificed to help it along. I hope I can repay her in the course of a long lifetime together.

This book is dedicated to my parents, who provided financial support, editorial assistance, and personal inspiration.

Introduction

Round signs depicting a cogwheel, a stylized K, or a roaring lion appear at the edge of towns and suburban communities throughout the United States. They announce the presence there of the Rotary, Kiwanis, and Lions clubs—businessmen's organizations that meet once a week for lunch, fellowship, and community service. Although millions of businessmen and professionals around the world have joined these clubs and continue to do so, to many present-day Americans their signs mean little. The clubs' scholarships, their pancake breakfasts, their sale of chances on a new car for charity—these activities have become familiar features of twentieth-century middle-class life. Still, in many contemporary settings they seem peripheral, anachronistic against the glass-walled office buildings and endless suburban shopping strips that delineate most American communities.

In the 1920s, however, the service clubs were a novel phenomenon, and many regarded them as quintessential expressions of a changing middle-class life. Lampooned and caricatured by H. L. Mencken and Sinclair Lewis, derided by the literati, investigated by Robert S. and Helen Merrell Lynd and other sociologists, the clubs, these observers felt, typified the commercialism and materialism of American democratic society. The intelligentsia of the twenties viewed Rotarians, Kiwanians, and Lions as important but disheartening manifestations of the modern American male, who had evolved into a shallow joiner, booster, and conformist.

For years interpreters of American life have implicitly accepted the twenties' stereotype of the club member. Allowing the shadow cast by Babbitt's plump figure to obscure the significance of the service clubs' sudden emergence, historians and other scholars have virtually ignored the phenomenon that bemused intellectuals in the twenties.[1] Clearly service clubs deserve more than caricature. Not only do they represent a crucial but historically undervalued aspect of American culture—its voluntary associational life—they also reflect vital, often contradictory impulses in

American middle-class experience in this century. This book attempts to qualify the image of the service club member as an other-directed Babbitt cowed into conformity by the forces of materialism and peer pressure. It examines the service club as a complex institution, a sociable association that affected the business, community, and personal lives of hundreds of thousands of Americans.

The first service club, Rotary, was founded in Chicago in 1905. The club grew rapidly and soon expanded to other cities. By 1915 Rotary clubs existed in every major city across the country, and before long imitators appeared, the most prominent of which were Kiwanis and Lions. The clubs' most rapid growth occurred after World War I, when club expansion swept through small communities all across the country and followed American business interests all over the world. In America, town retailers, small manufacturers, doctors, lawyers, and educators eagerly joined these new vehicles for community spirit and breezy camaraderie. The number of clubs went from hundreds to thousands; membership grew from thousands to hundreds of thousands. So explosive was this growth, the businessmen's clubs appeared to be yet another fad of the roaring decade.

Yet the clubs had far more complex roots, and they tapped a much deeper need than playing mah-jongg and dancing the Charleston. Businessmen have always played a prominent role in the voluntary life of America's communities. Whether arising from altruism, community concern, a desire to increase profits, fears of worker unrest, or, most likely, a mixture of these motives and others, the service clubs can all trace their roots to sociable, religious, and civic-minded organizations dating from the colonial era. The pace at which these organizations formed quickened in the nineteenth century as America expanded geographically and industrialization and urbanization transformed society. The men in the business class joined commercial clubs and merchants' clubs to boost their city's business prospects and attempt to prevent ruinous competition; they entered fraternal orders to satisfy sociable and religious impulses; and they sponsored lyceums, athenaeums, and Bible societies for self-improvement. All these organizations helped meet concerns about community loyalty and order.

The service clubs drew on these predecessors as they satisfied business, social, and community concerns. There were no more vigorous promoters of local business prospects than service club members. The informal camaraderie of luncheon meetings—made notorious by Lewis's satire—was for some businessmen the social high point of their week, and they listened to informative lectures at every luncheon. Club service projects demonstrated a concern for community welfare and supported institutions involving youth, including the YMCA and Boy Scouts. Like earlier organizations of businessmen, the clubs offered the additional incentive of status and higher profits from rubbing elbows with other "top men" of the community.

Still, if the service clubs satisfied some of the same motives as earlier clubs, they did so in appreciably different ways—ways that reveal changes within the local business community and American culture as a whole. Though service and fellowship were its main aims, club membership was explicitly chosen on the basis of occupation and thus was much more closely connected to business life than earlier more socially oriented clubs and fraternities. The clubs attracted only those businessmen vitally interested in local economic life and thus appealed primarily to smaller businessmen and independent professionals, whose business success might depend on such informal connections. Men who worked for corporations also joined the clubs if their businesses required direct dealings with local businessmen—railroad shipping agents, suppliers of financial and credit services, insurance salesmen, and utility executives. The clubs functioned as a type of chamber of commerce, bringing together locally interested representatives of the business community in weekly dinners and lunches, helping to ensure consensus and united action.

The need for such organizations was particularly acute in the early twentieth century, when corporate expansion was transforming local economic life. Though the individual community had never been entirely independent, and though it had always drawn on supplies and capital from outside the local economy, in the twentieth century control of growth and progress seemed to be slipping from the grasp of local businessmen. Vigorous—in some cases, frantic—attempts were made to solicit outside enterprises and to ensure that those corporations already present acted in the best interests of the town. The clubs, working in place of or in conjunction with a chamber of commerce, could aid in strengthening the local economy.

Yet if asked about their club, most members downplayed its business function and argued instead that what set their club apart was its charitable service to the community. This theme, too, contained an element of boosterism and involved attempts to strengthen the community in an age of urban centralization. But the clubs' service activities—indeed, the ideal of service itself—extended beyond local interest, reflecting tendencies within the middle class as a whole. At the same time the clubs were rising to prominence, middle-class Progressive-era reformers, shaken by the disruptions of full-scale industrialization and urbanization—massive immigration, labor unrest, and widely publicized squalor—responded with an activism designed to improve conditions, restore social harmony, and reassert middle-class influence.

Though few outside the clubs have taken their service projects seriously, club activity reveals how the progressive response to twentieth-century circumstances resonated throughout the entire middle class. The small businessmen and independent professionals who found club membership most attractive evinced the same sense of middle-class responsibility and shared many progressive values, though as businessmen they naturally preferred projects that ensured order more than those that caused further disruptions in the name of social justice. Echos of progressivism also appear in the idealism that accompanied club expansion overseas. By establishing clubs in other countries in the twenties, the associations attempted to smooth over international complexities and achieve a harmonious world order.

Although their explosive growth in the years immediately following World War I gave the clubs national influence, it also brought derision. By the thirties, members in many local communities experienced the limits of their voluntary activities, first overwhelmed by the Depression and then overcome by government bureaucracy. Foreign expansion, though gratifying in its extent and prestige, entangled club leadership in the thorns of international conflict. Continued growth at home placed clubs in burgeoning suburbs that were similar to small towns in their composition but lacking the economic incentives and sense of residential belonging that had fueled service activities in the twenties. Postwar bureaucratic proliferation and corporate development remained hostile to local interests. Club membership increased, but without commensurate gain in club influence. Service clubs and their constituents, though still a considerable presence in many communities around the world, never achieved the eminence that club spokesmen continued to claim at each international convention.

This book focuses not on the recent circumstances affecting club influence, but rather on its rise and development from 1900 to 1940. It describes the three largest service clubs—Rotary International, Kiwanis International, and the International Association of Lions Clubs. More than twenty national service organizations formed in the early twentieth century. Among the more successful were the Exchange, Optimists, Ruritan, Sertoma, Torch, Gyro, 20/30, and Cosmopolitan, not to mention the distaff service clubs, Soroptimists, Zonta, Quota, and Pilot. But the numbers joining "the big three," as they came to be known, comprised 90 percent of the total service club membership. Further, differences in all the clubs' composition and structure were minor. Membership in Rotary generally carried slightly more status; the Lions expanded a bit more successfully into smaller communities (and are today the largest service organization); but the three service clubs can be treated as a unified group, and as representative of the service club phenomenon as a whole.[2]

This phenomenon makes for a more interesting story than is commonly appreciated. This book relates its details while placing club development within a variety of contexts. Businessmen's service clubs are first viewed within a framework of class transition. Chapter 1 focuses on the decline of fraternal orders as the most popular local association among men of all classes and its fairly rapid replacement by more restrictive service organizations. The shift from fraternity to service as an organizing ideal occurred not just within business interests but also among all groups within the middle class. The emergence of Rotary, Kiwanis, and Lions thus reflects broad changes in the composition and culture of the entire middle class.

The next chapter describes the founding and pre–World War I expansion of Rotary, the first club. Here the focus is on changes within the business culture and the impact of corporate ideology on local business interests. Chapter 3 describes the rapid postwar expansion of Rotary, Kiwanis, and Lions into smaller cities and towns, and it surveys the variety of service projects undertaken by clubs. The context of the local community is the most revealing here. I have chosen for this section of the book to concentrate on the founding and operation of clubs in several selected towns in Illinois—the heartland of the service club movement. Although this focus neglects important regional peculiarities, most significantly the role of service clubs in the complex matrix of race and commerce that developed in the "new South," in other respects Illinois clubs typify the process and local significance of club growth.[3]

The service clubs' rise to nationwide prominence brought them increasing critical attention, and chapter 4 charts their battle with the critics and what that skirmish reveals about both highbrows and lowbrows in this first decade of mass culture. The last third of the book describes some of the complexities the clubs encountered as they continued to develop. The Depression, from which the clubs emerged still quite popular, nevertheless proved a turning point in club life, and in many American communities it signaled the clubs' waning influence. World expansion, one of the clubs' great success stories, further transformed the movement. The book closes with a brief consideration of the clubs in a suburban America. By the sixties and seventies, in the face of urban sprawl the Rotary, Kiwanis, and Lions could no longer maintain the degree of class and community unity that had made for continual growth in earlier decades. Clubs remain active in communities all across the country, but they are associated in the public mind with the small cities and towns in which they operated so successfully in the twenties.

Of the several significant cultural developments the clubs illuminate, this book is particularly concerned with how the clubs emerged as responses to the increasing organization of American economic and social life.[4] Members responded to encroaching bureaucracy with what could be called a vigorous ambivalence. Primarily drawing their membership from a segment of society placed on the defensive in a corporate urban environment, many of the clubs' service activities—attempts to inculcate character in youth, to strengthen their home towns against outside influences, and to restore simplicity and Christian values to their business transactions— revealed an aggressive traditional moralism.

On the other hand, the clubs' informal style and their Madison Avenue– inspired rhetoric smacked of the consumer society. Their obsession with service and efficiency paralleled similar concerns on the part of corporate leaders. And the service clubs' national associations were themselves efficiently run bureaucratic hierarchies, expansive during the twenties, re- silient enough to survive in the midst of the Depression. Service clubs entered small cities and towns as forces of change and modernization, helping to integrate provincial communities into national society.

The dual impulses of club life—to preserve and to progress—reflected choices born of club members' position as local businessmen who valued both their own profits and the quality of their community life. To fight a rearguard battle against social transformation would be to neglect oppor- tunities for business advancement. To pursue individual gain untrammeled by community responsibility would destroy the neighborly relationships members felt were already being degraded by modern life. Instead, the members of the service clubs sought an accommodation that would en- courage economic development but still allow their businesses and com- munities a degree of power and influence.

One might characterize the majority of club members as representatives of an old middle class of small businessmen and independent professionals who were resisting their loss of influence in modern America—but doing so by working in conjunction with corporate representatives and by using tools provided by the new organizational order. In this sense, the history of the development of the clubs documents how the old middle class became integrated into the new.[5] Service club members eagerly adopted organiza- tion, not because their traditional attachments to town and social group had been overwhelmed by corporate and urban expansion, but because they felt it would meet immediate business, social, and community needs. In the process, they created a sociable organization that successfully com- bined fellowship, self-interest, concern for local community, and broader awareness of class standing and worldwide social development. Ironically, however, their attempt to preserve local identity may have aided the stan- dardization of community life. In joining the club, they joined a national organization that then shaped their local aspirations. And thus every town has its Lion pancake breakfast, its Kiwanis ballfield, its Rotary park.

Similar ambiguities concerning traditional identities and new modes of behavior existed in club "fellowship." The clubs' organized sociability reflected twentieth-century middle-class concerns for unity and consensus. The clubs emerged when the American middle class was undergoing what Reuel Denney has called a "transition in sociability."[6] The clubs' mode of discourse—blatantly informal and filled with practical joking—was designed to recapture the camaraderie that members remembered from small-town boyhood. In fact, this element of club life was also evidence of something new—a general openness and informality endemic in twentieth-century life.

The social forces making for this change were identified even by the twenties, when the Lynds, in their study of Muncie, Indiana, observed the new importance of leisure and consumption and the impact of the movies and radio on social life. Later sociologists talked of secularization, the shift from an inner-directed to an other-directed psychology, and the corporate organization–influenced stress on personality and the phenomenon of "keeping up with the Joneses." Most recently, historians have focused on the values emerging from consumer capitalism as the primary propagators of this forced informality.[7]

All these interpretations of twentieth-century sociability contain elements of truth. But if they are applied to club member interaction, these explanations miss an important part of the appeal of club fellowship. If the members' mode of address was evidence of a corporate, mass culture–dominated society, they nevertheless believed that their backslapping camaraderie helped meliorate the personal and community disturbances associated with such modernization. Club members, who found and continue to find their fellowship satisfying, have argued that it countered the impersonality within an increasingly bureaucratic society. Members testified to a degree of success in creating an atmosphere of warm friendliness. When club members spoke of the necessity of cooperative individualism, community spirit, and worldwide fellowship, they sought to establish the continuing relevance of middle-class goals of consensus and order by adapting the familiar homilies of good-neighbor relations to a new age.

Service clubs have been a neglected topic of study partly because they fall into the cracks of a variety of historiographical interests. Despite a recent flurry of middle-class studies, for the most part historians examining social groups have rightfully attempted to redress an earlier neglect of women, blacks, workers, and others excluded from official positions of power and influence. The historical analysis of business organizations has concerned those with a primarily economic function, while work on voluntary associations has focused on associations with a more expressly political or reform purpose. The sociable gatherings of reasonably well-off, native white small businessmen and professionals, which often seemed to result only in expressions of bland optimism or trivial local projects, at first glance hardly seem to merit serious study. For travelers down the wide avenue of American social history, service clubs blend, like their signs, into the background of passed landscape. Their existence and accomplishments deserve to be placed squarely back on Main Street.

CHAPTER **1**

From Fraternity to Service

When the small-town native Paul Harris first opened his law office in Chicago in 1899, he found business slow and friends hard to acquire. "Desperately lonely," he wandered the streets of Chicago but found little solace in the "maelstrom" of streets and beaches. Struggling to build his law business, he envied those lawyers who socialized and did business with the Chicago elite. It seemed to him, as it has seemed to many young job seekers since, that success depended not on what skills you possessed but rather on who you knew. While others were "realizing dividends off acquaintance," Harris had to content himself with "crumbs that had fallen off the banquet table."[1]

Yet Harris was more enterprising than most, for rather than simply scramble for banquet crumbs, he decided to invite others to lunch. He conceived an idea for a club whose members would be businessmen in situations similar to his own. Gathering once a week for food and fellowship, these businessmen would also trade with one another, thus forming a ready-made social and business network. Harris's "Rotary Club"—so named because members at first "rotated" their meetings from office to office—proved an immediate success. Founded in 1905, within four years it had over two hundred members. In one organizational stroke Harris had met both his business and social needs. He had also given initial impetus to a new voluntary association.

With the success of the Chicago Rotary Club ensured, Harris began working for the expansion of the club to other cities, contacting other lawyers and urging all the traveling salesmen he knew to recruit members in their territories. Expansion proved remarkably easy, and by 1911 Rotary clubs existed in every major city across America. The clubs seemed to appeal to men similar to Harris—independent professionals and small businessmen, many of them from small towns—though the club also attracted some middle-level representatives of the corporate world—railway and utility executives, insurance men, and office equipment salesmen. Harris's original emphasis on informality and friendship remained, and a backslapping, first-name familiarity became the trademark of Rotarians in Chicago and elsewhere.

But as the club's popularity increased, Rotary began receiving outside criticism for its insular business practices. Some members felt constrained by the explicit encouragement of trade among members. Harris and others began to realize that this controversy would only increase with growth. And so in 1911, with Harris's urging, Rotary dropped the injunction that members exchange business with one another and stressed instead the opportunities the club provided for charitable activity—for "service." Harris had once again shown an organizational genius, for he had expanded the appeal of the club. Its rate of growth increased, and imitators of Rotary were formed, most prominent among them the Kiwanis Club (1915) and the Lions Club (1917). They too spread from city to town, until by 1920 combined service club membership was over three hundred thousand. By 1930 service club membership was worldwide and numbered in the millions.

Although service club members would later claim that their associations were unlike any that had come before, in fact, Harris, in turning to service, had placed his club in line with trends that had begun before he arrived in Chicago. The story of Rotary and the later service clubs reveals many things about America in the early twentieth century, and the chapters that follow will analyze club expansion in terms of the new modes of business, the changing communities, and the cultural conflicts that were characteristic of a country in the process of rapid modernization. But the story of the clubs begins earlier, before the first Rotary song was sung, before the first salesman claimed service was his business. It begins in the mid-nineteenth century, in the dignified sanctum of a fraternal lodge, and in parlors where groups of housewives earnestly pursued self-education. In these settings was firmly established the middle-class sociability upon which the service clubs tried to build, even though Harris and other service club organizers specifically repudiated some important aspects of these earlier modes of fellowship. To understand completely why businessmen rushed to join Rotary, Kiwanis, and Lions, it is necessary to understand the nineteenth-century appeal of the fraternal order and the emergence of the women's club.

In the nineteenth century millions of middle-class American males flocked to organizations that affirmed, through secret ritual, a symbolic brotherhood. Masons, Odd-Fellows, Knights of Pythias, Redmen, Macabees, Mystic Workers, and Noble Woodmen nightly gathered in elaborate lodge rooms, donned exotic regalia, solemnly recited cryptic locutions, and staged bizarre tableaux, all in secrecy. Outside the secret meetings lodge members enjoyed a fellowship that included respectable members of the working class as well as wealthy professionals, and they cemented their sociability with a system of life insurance and funeral benefits. When a man in late-nineteenth-century America sought companionship and status within the local community, he joined a fraternal lodge.

Fraternalism played an important mediating role for the males of an emergent middle class. While fraternal spokesmen celebrated such bourgeois verities as hard work, thrift, and the sanctity of the home, the lodge offered a spiritual refuge from both the harsh competition of the marketplace and what many men saw as the enervating influence of the parlor.[2]

But the sons of these fraternalists found this refuge less relevant. Many of them joined the lodge but did not attend often; their impulse toward voluntary association sought an outlet appropriate to their new circumstances. Stirred by a sense of urban crisis, their religion had shouldered new responsibilities; shaken by a vigorous assertion of women's prerogatives, their gender roles had assumed new boundaries; reshaped by corporate business, their workplace had taken a more bureaucratic turn.

With each of these changes, fraternalism seemed less appealing, and the ideal of service acquired a new relevancy. For those influenced by the social gospel, service appeared a way to confront harsh circumstances realistically while still retaining the inspiration of Christian idealism. Service projects allowed family men to show a new sensitivity to domestic and charitable responsibilities, and with the rise of a corporate economy, many businessmen and professionals were now supplying services rather than goods. Talk of service, with its connotations of self-sacrifice and stewardship, provided a satisfying and appropriate way of defining the characteristics of their work. For these men, organizing around service was one way of reasserting middle-class influence in an age of labor unrest and corporate power.

The emergence of the businessmen's service club, prompted by the shifting rationale for male association, thus provides a particularly vivid case study of the differences in outlook between the nineteenth-century middle class and that of the twentieth. When most middle-class men—and many women—no longer joined groups where the dominant metaphors were ones of mutuality and kinship and instead became members of groups that spoke the bureaucratic language of service and efficiency, they had redefined their personal lives, and they would soon reshape their communities.

Fraternalism and the Early Middle-Class Voluntary Impulse

"The American has dwindled into an Odd-Fellow," wrote Henry David Thoreau in 1849, "one who may be known by the development of his organ of gregariousness, and a manifest lack of intellect and cheerful self-reliance," and who "ventures to live only by the aid of the Mutual Insurance Company, which has promised to bury him decently." The American male had become a "joiner" by the time Thoreau called for civil disobedience, and the fraternal orders were in the process of reaping (and paying out) the benefits. Yet the multiplication of voluntary associations such as fraternal societies did not primarily indicate, as Thoreau suggested, a laxness in the country's moral fiber due to materialist preoccupations; nor did it necessarily validate another contemporary analyst, Alexis de Tocqueville, when he argued that association occurred in response to democracy's anonymous equality. The flood of voluntarism might better be connected with emerging social stratification and the spiritual and moral manifestations of a developing class and gender system.[3]

The solidification of social classes is reflected in the tiers of association that had appeared in the nation's cities by the 1820s—from the civic and reform organizations joined by powerful urban merchants, professionals, and manufacturers down to the voluntary fire companies and street gangs of the urban laborers. But the process is perhaps best illustrated in the thrust of associations attracting the "middling sort," for these organizations played an important part in crystallizing a previously amorphous class.

In the early nineteenth century small proprietors, clerks, accountants, and professionals responded to changes in their workplace and residence by creating a new class culture. They were no longer as influenced by the communal republican ideology that had been characteristic of colonial artisans. Instead they defined their work world in terms of the individualistic, competitive, small-scale capitalism in which they played an important role. At the same time, they set apart a private domestic sphere with the family at its center. They delimited these spheres by gender with the men expected to shoulder their responsibilities within a competitive marketplace, the women required to cultivate their home as a sanctuary of compassion and nurture.[4]

The culture of this emerging middle class was one of sharp distinctions—between home and business, public and private life, work and play, respectability and irresponsibility—and it veered between cold rationality and lachrymose sentimentality. But helping to bridge some of the gaps, while reinforcing others, were a variety of evangelical organizations, self-help literary clubs, and, above all, temperance societies. Through these voluntary associations the emergent middle class fashioned and transmitted new patterns of behavior.[5]

The interplay between association and class values is well illustrated by the gradual molding to middle-class taste of what was to become America's largest fraternity—and the object of Thoreau's scorn—the Independent Order of Odd-Fellows (I.O.O.F.). The association did not arrive in America until 1819, when Thomas Wildey, a newly emigrated English blacksmith from humble but respectable origins, attempted to recreate in Baltimore the friendly society to which he had belonged in England. Gathering a group of English emigrants—all mechanics or artisans like himself—he formed an American branch of the Manchester Unity of Odd-Fellows.[6] Its English heritage facilitated the spread of the Odd-Fellows in America, as recent English emigrants became the base for lodges in Boston, New York, and Philadelphia. Thus the Odd-Fellows could be considered an early example of the immigrant organizations prominent in late nineteenth-century America, although the fraternity quickly welcomed members of other ethnic groups.[7]

Wildey began the Odd-Fellows mainly as a convivial drinking club. But they soon established a sick and death benefits program similar to that of the Manchester Unity, although less systematized. They also added a secret ritual closely modeled on that of the Masons, America's first fraternal import from England, and an organization closely associated with the founding fathers. With these important elements in place, the Odd-Fellows grew rapidly in their first five years. In 1825 they formed the Grand Lodge of America, with subordinate lodges organized in every state.

Soon after, however, a revealing outburst of moral outrage and political action against freemasonry occurred in the "burned-over district" in upstate New York, where the middle-class evangelical temperament was being forged. Masonry's association with colonial aristocracy, the irreligion of deism, and, most important, its denial of a place for women—in what appeared to its opponents to be an irresponsible repudiation of the influence of domesticity—gave rise to an explosion of antimasonic hostility. Associations dominated by middle-class women attacked Masonry—and indeed all secret fraternities—as antithetical to a Christian republic.[8]

Tarred by the same conspiratorial brush as Masonry, the Odd-Fellows took measures to regain public approval. The Baltimore lodge adopted legislation in the 1820s prohibiting drinking in the lodge in an attempt to allay its Bacchanalian reputation, and the national body reaffirmed this stand in 1835. The Odd-Fellows made sure to disassociate themselves from the Masonic image of idol worship: "we spurn with honest indignation that species of ultraism which denies the legitimate and only proper ends of association—the promotion of man's happiness, the melioration and removal of evil [and] the emancipation of mind from spiritual debasement and degradation." And, in perhaps their most important gesture toward their opponents, they adopted lodge member Schuyler Colfax's suggestion that women be allowed to enter the fraternal fold, though only in auxiliary organizations. "Ladies," in Colfax's opinion, "knowing that Odd-Fellowship apparently exhibits no confidence in them . . . endeavor to induce those related to them to join other, more courteous orders." Forming female auxiliaries would not only "lessen and ultimately destroy the prejudice felt against the Order by many of the fairer sex" but also "assist Odd-Fellowship in cases of brother's sickness," for "she was formed to minister at the couch of affliction."[9]

By deemphasizing conviviality, stressing temperance and charity, and allowing women to join its auxiliaries—the Odd-Fellows acquired middle-class respectability.[10] This process, simultaneously undertaken by Masons and other emerging fraternal orders and completed by the late 1840s, led to a rapid growth of the orders in cities and towns in all parts of the country. Serving as institutions of initiation and training for young manhood, fraternal lodges emphasized family responsibilities. The Odd-Fellows stressed that their death benefits aided bereaved widows and helpless children. Other elements in lodge life verified the entrepreneurial myths of the self-made man. All initiates began at the bottom and had to rise to the top through promotion to a number of ritualistic degrees, each one theoretically requiring additional knowledge of the truths of the order. Odd-Fellows could rise through six of these degrees; the Masons, more than thirty. As lodge spokesmen pointed out, this opportunity was open to all within the lodge, as befitted a democratic society.

But the relationship between fraternalism and coalescing middle-class culture was more complex than one of simple affirmation. The lodge, set off by secrecy and arcane ritual, allowing full membership only to white males, reflected the demarcated Victorian culture. Yet the constitution and ideology of fraternal orders contain elements of opposition to this culture and could allow members to escape the tensions of their workaday world. Without offending bourgeois proprieties, lodge members could experience what Lynn Dumenil has called a "spiritual asylum" from the harsher realities of late nineteenth-century American life. "Here the world is shut-out—you are separated from its care and distractions, its dissensions and its vices," began the ritual of the Odd-Fellowship.[11]

Shutting out the world and defining the fraternal experience was the secret ritual, a set of long recitations and elaborate dramatic tableaux. Fraternal secret rituals combined biblical parables, sage advice, and solemn oaths, parts of them inexplicable to a modern reader (and perhaps also to the contemporary participant). Yet for most American fraternalists, the mystical qualities of the ritual service heightened the sacredness of their

gathering. Indeed, members' attachment to the ritual suggests that fraternalism satisfied the hunger for elaborate religious ceremony in a way the
liturgy of most American churches did not.[12]

Mark Carnes has argued that the pervasiveness of ritualism in male
organizations has deeper roots than an unsatisfied longing for the sacred.
Instead, he sees within fraternal rituals opposition to the feminine influence
shaping morality and religion. While not directly repudiating the pieties of
evangelical Protestantism, fraternalists wrote rituals that pantomimed violence and referred often to death and hardship, ceremonies that had little in
common with the domesticated vision of most mainstream religion. These
explicitly masculine rituals, Carnes postulates, provided a more satisfying sacred experience for fraternalists than feminized evangelical religion.
Participation in these rituals helped men reconcile the tensions between
their upbringing by their mother and their identification with their father's
work world, by initiating them, both in actuality and figuratively, into the
adult male environment.[13]

It is not necessary to accept Carnes's specific formulation of the rituals'
appeal to recognize within the lodge tensions inherent in rigidly defined
gender roles. Leaving the sanctuary of the home for the asylum of the
lodge, members chose, if only temporarily, the succor of brotherhood over
the comfort of female companionship. In their homages to the lodge as a
peerless moral institution, spokesmen did not completely reject Victorian
stereotypes about superior feminine sensibilities but expressed implicitly
their condescension toward the domestic world. At times, however, lodge
spokesmen made explicit the advantages of the lodge as a source of moral
sentiment, openly repudiating what one Odd-Fellow called "the narrow
and feeble effect of the parlor."[14]

Although some women returned the favor and continued to express
their hostility to fraternalism, a great many wives joined the female auxiliaries, the Odd-Fellows' "Order of Rebekah" and the Masonic "Order
of the Eastern Star." Enough women were appeased by membership in an
auxiliary, or reassured by the respectable sentiments expressed by fraternal
spokesmen, that the feminine-dominated antimasonic movement ebbed by
the start of the Civil War.[15]

The Heyday of Fraternalism

The major event of the nineteenth century, the Civil War, worked further
to overcome feminine hostility at the same time that it increased the interest in fraternal organizations among males. With its soldierly camaraderie,
its sacrifice for others, even its dominant "brother against brother" theme,

the war gave birth to new fraternal associations and aided those already established. New general orders such as the Knights of Pythias, founded in 1864 by a Washingtonian, Basil Rathbone, sought to "rekindle brotherly sentiment" with a ritual enacting the friendship of Damon and Pythias. Organizations specifically associated with the war, such as the Grand Army of the Republic, adopted the fraternal model as an appropriate representation of brotherhood under arms. At the same time, established orders capitalized on the era's romantic patriotism. The Odd-Fellows added militaristic regalia and flashy drill to their highly popular "Patriarchal" degree —replete with "Grand Commanders" and "Encampments." Through such adaptations, lodges successfully responded to a more hospitable cultural climate.[16] By the 1870s American males were flocking to lodges representing hundreds of separate organizations and an aggregate membership of several million.[17]

As the sentiments surrounding the Civil War benefited fraternalism, the lodges' appeal was also encouraged by the continuing development of industrial society, which exposed more and more men to the anxieties and brutal effects of economic uncertainty and the impersonality of excessive individualism. Men of all classes turned to the balm of brotherhood and celebrated within fraternalism a mutual aid and artisanal ideal quickly becoming rare in reality. While fraternal ritual appeared crucial to the members of the working class struggling to maintain their dignity, middle-class fraternalists attempted to downplay the divisiveness of economic issues.[18] To some degree both groups were successful; the lodge had a level of class interaction unique among nineteenth-century social institutions. The middle class was dominant, but except for the higher-status Masons, worker participation in lodges appears to have been high.[19]

The moderate class heterogeneity of the orders allowed members, at least while they met in the lodge, an illusion of social equality. This cross-class sociability might have been detrimental to working-class consciousness, thus damaging workers' solidarity in economic struggles. For the lodges' middle-class members, however, the nature of their brotherhood shows a willingness not just to extend an occasional paternal hand but to fraternize weekly with their working-class counterparts.[20] James M. Patton expressed this democratic vision in the magazine of Odd-Fellowship in the Dakotas, the *Odd-Fellow World*. "Odd-Fellowship is a great social leveler, where learned and unlearned, rich and poor meet and unite. . . . It does away with all artificial distinctions of society and each one sees in his neighbor only the man, the brother, and friend."[21]

This leveling effect probably had its greatest impact within smaller communities—towns and cities such as those addressed by Patton in the

Odd-Fellow World. But even in large cities the lodge played a prominent role in promoting a sense of community above class and status distinctions, sponsoring picnics and parades and guaranteeing a large attendance of lodge brothers—if not a large check—at even the humblest member's funeral. In fact, crucial to the lodge's appeal was its local orientation. Although the fraternal orders to which the lodge belonged were national organizations, each lodge had considerable local autonomy in its selection of members, and each set different rules governing members' behavior outside the lodge. In an examination of Missouri lodges, David Thelen argues that membership became a defense of locality against the centralizing forces of the industrial economy. Local ties and personal considerations counted more than occupation in choosing members. Attempting to extend family-type relations and to reinforce loyalty to local community, the lodge brothers were "forging a bond" of mutual protection against the antifraternal intrusions of an expanding commercial order.[22]

Reinforcing this emotional bond was the concrete support of insurance and benefit plans. Of the fraternal orders, only the prestigious Masons did not make fraternal insurance central to their organization, although they did build retirement homes for their aged members. The Odd-Fellows provided both benefits and homes for former members, while orders such as the Royal Arcanum, Woodmen, Macabees, and Ancient Order of United Workmen existed primarily as vehicles for cooperative benefit plans. These groups attracted both working- and middle-class members with a lower-cost alternative to commercial life insurance.

Despite the lower cost, though, participants in fraternal benefit plans were not often making an informed business decision. Many lodges carried an inadequate reserve fund; after several deaths or illnesses, they required extra assessments of their healthy and active members. Some members simply refused to pay these extra assessments, thus "lapsing," or dropping out of the lodge. If enough members reacted this way to assessments, the lodge either went into debt or simply defaulted on its obligation, leaving members unprotected. As a result of these inefficiencies, obscure fraternal insurance orders went out of business as quickly as they formed, and larger orders such as the Odd-Fellows continually scrambled to stay afloat, hoping membership gains offset lapsations and deaths.[23]

If fraternal members had wished to follow sound insurance practice, they had only to follow the example of their English fraternal brethren, who had experienced exactly the same travails before placing their societies on an actuarial and reserve fund basis in the 1850s. Or they could have borrowed the various investment plans being used with great success by the commercial insurance industry, what the lodges called "the old-line companies." Instead, up to the 1890s they continued to ignore the pleas of their secretaries for adequate assessments, even at the risk of losing their own benefits.

It appears, then, that the appeal of lodge insurance differed from that offered by commercial life insurance. The commercial companies successfully played on the desire for individual security amid an uncertain, uncaring society. "If it were practicable, no system of assurance would be so complete as a common brotherhood," commercial insurance salesmen told those weighing fraternal benefits against a commercial policy. But, they went on to argue, such brotherhood "cannot be trusted." A man must "do it for himself" and seek assurance only in the "entirely practical" commercial contract.[24] The fraternal orders made exactly the opposite pitch. Fraternal insurance relied on brotherhood and group support. Cooperation stood as a buffer between the member and the unpredictability of individual chances. "Mutual cooperation against the trials of life" is how the grand secretary of the Odd-Fellows described the order in 1875. Stressing cooperation, fraternal spokesmen downplayed financial self-interest. Only well into lodge addresses did it become clear that such phrases as "mutual relief and protection from want," "the constant practice of charity," and "inculcating higher ideas of duty to your fellow man" referred to cash benefits. More than a disguised materialism, these phrases expressed the values of brotherhood central to fraternalism. In the idealized fraternal vision, insurance served only to reinforce mutuality among the lodge members.[25]

New Middle-Class Values

In its commercial incarnation, however, the insurance industry was helping push a new vision of American life. This vision was shaped by its calculating assessment of occupational risks and life chances, and by its aggressive expansion, which sent agents to remote communities or made local businessmen company representatives.[26] Partly because of this competition and partly because of other influences the insurance companies represented, the character of fraternalism began to change. By the end of the late nineteenth century fraternalism had become a big business, with agents patrolling territories and recruiting members. Most American fraternal orders finally began to follow sound actuarial practice. This change increased the value of their insurance policies but helped undermine their distinctive emotional appeal.[27]

More broadly, insurance and other corporate industries were transforming the middle class in the late nineteenth century. In part this transformation occurred because of the expansion of the middle class's boundaries.

The traditional middle class of professionals and merchants received an influx of white-collar clerks, salespeople, and middle managers. The collar line remained intact, but a new range of occupations now aspired to bourgeois respectability. The large scale of the new business organizations employing these workers also produced changes in outlook. An emerging sense of economic and social interdependence undermined faith in the efficacy of individual effort.[28]

In fact, by the turn of the century the entire worldview of the middle class had been thrown into doubt. With occupation no longer as clear a guide to social standing, men and women sought to affirm—or reaffirm—their middle-class status. Increasingly they turned to consumerism and leisure for social definition. But the crucial social and economic importance of consumerism in the new order produced a new ethic of indulgence and enjoyment, undermining the nineteenth-century middle-class imperatives of work and self-denial. At the same time, the successive shocks of continuing labor unrest and the strangeness of hordes of immigrants gave rise to nativist anxieties and a heightened consciousness of class divisions, and they prompted an attempt to exclude or withdraw from the masses.[29]

This new outlook did not effect simultaneously all the small producers, independent farmers, retailers, professionals, clerks, and corporate managers that made up the middle class in the late nineteenth century, and earlier notions of what constituted respectable bourgeois behavior remained prevalent. Even if the "old" middle class did not immediately become "new," however, all within the middle strata experienced the disturbing turbulence of turn-of-the-century transformations.[30]

Many responded to a shifting middle-class identity by joining new voluntary associations. As the social circumstances of the middle class grew more complex, fraternal sentiments seemed less relevant. The lodges affirmed social mobility by allowing members to ascend through a ritualistic hierarchy. But with middle-class identity in flux, it was more important to confirm status through membership in more selective or occupationally based associations. Businessmen's clubs and merchants' clubs combined sociable pleasures with career interests and attracted attendance away from the lodge. Other organizations with much more restrictive membership policies, such as country clubs, came to shape local social life. The urban upper class had always joined its limited-membership men's clubs, but the growth of these clubs among the middle-class elite of towns and small cities indicated that others less aristocratic now shared this exclusionary impulse.[31]

Often the new clubs were organized around recreation or sports such as golf and tennis. As consumerism influenced middle-class values, recreation and light entertainment appealed more as a way of spending sociable time than the ponderous ceremonies of a night at the lodge room. Fraternalism had its pleasures—it seems likely that a member could find enjoyment as well as portentous meaning in donning a costume and acting a role within a fraternal ritual—but the new leisure valued informality and spontaneity, an atmosphere better promoted by good-natured badinage in the latest slang than by the archaic phraseology of a stern patriarch.

In fact, fewer sought the patriarchal role outside the lodge. Gender role expectations were changing. Women had entered the world of business in greater numbers. Even though they were mainly confined to clerical occupations, these women shook the foundation of the nineteenth-century distinction in gender roles.[32] At the same time, the rise of a more companionate family produced a new vision of marriage for emotional fulfillment and sexual gratification, which redefined male family responsibilities and undermined paternal authority. In a study of turn-of-the-century suburbanites, Margaret Marsh found that in these younger families men showed themselves more willing to share sociable companionship with their wives. Male family responsibilities now included an active presence in the home. In part this was because the new middle-class occupations allowed more time for domestic pleasures and a secure salary with which to provide for them. But the emergence of the "family man" also indicates the extent to which the strictly delineated gender spheres were disintegrating.[33]

Although not all families within the middle class experienced a male domesticity—for some fathers, the decline of patriarchal authority simply meant a further abandonment of family responsibilities—nevertheless, middle-class ideals of masculinity were in flux. Fraternalism, its ideology intimately connected with nineteenth-century gender definitions, began to seem to younger men to be an archaic social activity.[34]

A New Fraternalism

The aggressive recruiting operations of fraternal agents expanded the orders' ranks to all-time highs in the first decades of the twentieth century, but it became evident that the numerical strength of lodge membership was illusory. Complaints of nonattendance at lodge meetings began appearing in fraternal publications. Even more telling, problems began to occur with the center of fraternalism, the ritual. Evidence of boredom with the Masonic pattern occurred not only with the founding of new orders, which stressed "light and pleasing ceremonies," but also within lodges of the more established orders. "Join the encampment," advised the *Odd-Fellow World* in 1890. "There you will find recreation and renewed interest." No need in the patriarchal degree to "turn to any other order for relief from the Monotony of the Subordinate work."[35]

Some within the established orders turned increasingly to elaborate regalia, dramatic presentations, and public displays. Others found relief from monotony in burlesque. As early as the 1850s the members of the Sons of Malta, a fake order, entertained themselves by enticing innocents into participating in an obscene parody of Masonic ritual, but it ran counter to the earnestness with which most members then treated fraternal ceremony. By 1892, however, the Grand Sire of the Odd-Fellows had to caution his order against the burlesquing of its own ceremonies.[36] Also, during the 1890s the Ancient Arabic Order of the Nobles of the Mystic Shrine began to establish its reputation as the "playground" of Masonry, and the Knights of Pythias formed their own fun group, the Dramatic Order of Knights of Khorassan, or the "Dokeys." Levity as well as sacred ritual could promote fellowship, and its existence did not necessarily mean the decline of fraternal feeling. But the joking could mean that an increasing number of members found the allegorical, highly dramatic form of the ritual incongruous. It no longer effectively "shut out the world."

Symptomatic of changes in the context of fraternal association was the new focus of two older organizations—the Benevolent Protectorate of Elk and the Loyal Order of Moose. These orders struggled to survive until they successfully transformed themselves into organizations that suited the turn-of-the-twentieth-century middle-class context.

The Elks began in 1868 as a drinking club of actors—"The Jolly Corks." After changing their name to the Elks, they slowly expanded to other large cities, as a vaguely disreputable order still attracting mainly those in the theatrical profession. By the late 1880s, however, enough non-actors had entered the membership to force an alteration in the order. By raising dues and removing any reference to the theatrical profession in their constitution, the Elks consciously sought middle-class status, just as the Odd-Fellows had done earlier. "Instead of the circus girl jumping through hoops, they will have a Sorosis reading art essays; instead of the minstrel rattling the bones, a drug clerk will be making pills; instead of a tragedian tearing passion to tatters, a dry goods clerk will be selling tape," complained an actor Elk unhappy at the new measures. Despite the complaints of this member and other disgruntled Elks, the order gradually gained respectability.[37]

Unlike the Odd-Fellows, however, the Elks undertook further changes in the early 1900s, reducing their ritual, stressing recreation and conviviality, and sending contributions for disaster relief to Galveston, Texas, in 1904 and San Francisco in 1906. Growth increased dramatically, and by

1910 the organization had reached hundreds of thousands of members. John Willis could write in the *American Elk* that the order was "benevolent, not confining its operations to the membership of the order, but, recognizing no bonds of creed or social station, it has relieved disaster and shown helpfulness to mankind." In 1915 another change in the ritual added what the editor of the *Elk* called "patriotism and a splash of ginger," placing the Elks in position to benefit from postwar Americanism. After World War I, the Elks adopted the celebration of Flag Day as their special provenance, and in the mid-twenties the order built a large memorial to the war dead in Chicago—perhaps also to draw attention to a membership that had reached nearly nine hundred thousand.[38]

With such membership figures, the Elks could afford to build expensive clubhouses—making them not merely lodge rooms but places of recreation and relaxation, incorporating athletic facilities and dining rooms. They also wholeheartedly pursued community service, supporting Boy Scout troops and the Salvation Army, giving money to hospitals and schools, and providing Christmas baskets to the needy. Talk of middle-class stewardship replaced homages to the bonds of brotherhood. "Wealth brings a special capacity for service to humanity," argued an editorial in *Elk's Magazine*. The Elks were not so wealthy that they could establish a hospital, but they could "secure treatment for the crippled kiddie in our community." The ability "to do these little things constitutes the wealth that imposes the obligation to do them."[39]

While the Elks achieved prominence because of their flexibility, the Moose owed their success to the vision of their organizer, James Davis. Davis, who perhaps is best known as Harding's secretary of labor, began as an iron puddler in the steel mills of Pittsburgh and then became a union leader in Ohio. In 1906 Davis saw the opportunity presented by the Moose, a straggling group of local lodges with a total of only five hundred members, and bought "organizational rights" in the order. Guaranteed a percentage of dues from every new member, he became one of the aggressive new salesmen ranging the country, building a new organization. By 1912 the Moose numbered over two hundred thousand. In part this extraordinary growth can be credited to efficient salesmanship. Besides his union experience, Davis claimed membership in a host of other fraternal orders, including the Masons and the Odd-Fellows, and he drew on this experience and these connections in his organizing. Just as significant as Davis's organizational skills, though, was his message. Not only did he promise to put the "fun back into fraternalism" through social events and activities, he also hinted at a broader goal—performing a great service for children.[40]

The Moose's children's project came to fruition in 1912 when the order purchased a large plot of land west of Chicago for an orphan's home. Davis christened it "Mooseheart" and made it the center of national Moose activity, even changing the ritual to end "God Bless Mooseheart." The development and maintenance of the facilities at Mooseheart, Davis felt, moved the Moose beyond "fraternity for its own sake" and into the realm of "practical association." Through Mooseheart, the order worked at becoming "the first beneficial fraternity to devote itself to social service," but it also hoped to contribute to the "science of child caring . . . a specialized form of social work that demands utmost devotion, self-sacrifice, and concentrated effort." Thus the Moose attracted educators such as the Harvard historian Albert Bushnell Hart (who spoke of Mooseheart as "the largest opportunity in the U.S. to prove what can be done by rational education") and the prominent progressives Theodore Roosevelt, Hiram Johnson, and Champ Clark—even William Jennings Bryan, who, when joining, was as "enthusiastic as a high school boy who had just joined his first fraternity."[41]

In their discussion of the children of Mooseheart, Davis and other Moose spokesmen displayed a new understanding of patriarchal duty. Once primarily held responsible for meeting the family's financial needs, as fathers the lodge members now felt the raising of children required a much more active interest on their part. "Suffer the children to come unto me," the Moose initiate recited. Interestingly, the auxiliary, once an important fraternal concession to the women's sphere, was only a minor part of the lodges of the Moose; and the other newly popular fraternity, the Elks, felt little need for a female branch. Davis hoped to recruit women members, for "when the men begin, as the Moose have begun, to study the duties of husbands and the responsibilities of fathers, the women are needed."[42] But in fact the new interest of males in children, while demonstrating the decline of Victorian gender roles, also removed one of the rationales for the operation of female auxiliaries. Members of the new fraternities and service clubs, with their interest in family life well established, felt less need to justify their institution to their wives.

Davis believed Mooseheart took fraternalism to a higher plane, since "man owes no higher duty to God and society than the duty of service to childhood." He also felt Moose principles could be extended to reconcile the post–World War I conflicts between labor and capital. To his job as secretary of labor he brought a vision of fraternal harmony—"conciliation, the spirit of fraternalism, the realization that the best gain for the individual is to work with every other individual in harmony." In the pro-business administrations of Harding and Coolidge, however, this conservative call for "the golden rule in American industry" resulted in a general sacrifice of the interests of labor. Although Davis never repudiated his belief in "labor's rights to organize, to bargain collectively and to be free," he also argued that "Labor provides for today. Property provides for tomorrow. . . . Capital safeguards the future." The "great corporations," said Davis, have acted responsibly since through stock "they were controlled by the American people."[43] Davis might have begun as a laborer, but now, as a wealthy executive, he was attempting to construct a thoroughly middle-class institution. The Moose united to serve children and listened to the financier Roger Babson speak on "What the Moose Can Do for Business."[44]

Service and Middle-Class Anxiety

Organizations like the Elks and the Moose remained male only, but the members often invited their wives to join them at many of their sociable events. Yet the transition to a more heterosocial culture was slow, and not without its anxieties. Complaints about the assertive "new woman" revealed masculine insecurities. These anxieties, too, had their negative impact on older fraternities. The emergence of an influential sisterhood—women active in charity work and community improvement—made the fraternal brotherhood seem embarrassingly ineffectual. Calls for a more strenuous masculine activism appeared in all fields of endeavor, from politics to religion, and undermined the appeal of a sociable retreat into the lodge.[45]

By the turn of the century few in the middle class now sought escape in fellowship; sociability alone appeared to be an inadequate response to the feeling of social crisis that gripped the middle class. Although the fundamental source of this feeling was economic—the depression of the 1890s, labor and agrarian unrest, an uneasiness over industrial consolidation—changes in religious life were also important. Early nineteenth-century revivalism had undertaken reform crusades in the name of individual salvation. By the end of the century mainstream Protestantism was urging social responsibility as part of a struggle to restore social harmony. Liberal theologians and prominent laypeople such as Richard T. Ely began to enunciate what Ely called the "social law of service," urging a self-sacrifice "emancipated from the bonds of a gloomy asceticism." The stewardship urged by Ely and other social-gospel practioners could serve not only as a remedy for social disruption but also as a grounding for a new middle-class identity.[46]

Many middle-class social organizations responded in kind—they claimed new community responsibility. The ideal of social harmony at the center of fraternalism remained crucial, but social redemption required a new type of cooperative activism. These organizations sacrificed the inclusiveness of fraternalism. Yet while the joiners in the middle class were less willing to associate with workers, they proved quite eager to assume the duties of stewardship. Adapting to the dislocations caused by urban change, corporate economic development, and gender transformation, they found reassurance and renewed purpose in the phrase "serving the community."

Women's Clubs and the Emerging Ideal of Service

Service had long been an ideal associated with the feminine sphere, and indeed women's clubs were the first to formulate programs sensitive to the new middle-class concerns.[47] Although the women's club movement is too complex a topic to be given full consideration here, a brief examination of its development shows how women's clubs presaged male service organizations and reveals the extent of the transformation affecting the middle class.

Women had begun forming clubs for "self-culture" in the 1850s, hoping to expand the domestic horizon both through individual study and through association with other women. By the 1880s over nine hundred such clubs had spontaneously formed in communities all over America. Their members paid testimony to the club as "a place of meeting where equality prevails, where the bond of a common purpose above individual life draws all together in the inspiration of mutual effort." These could be the words of a fraternalist describing his lodge, and indeed one prominent early club, Sorosis, aimed in 1868 to "establish a kind of freemasonry among women of similar pursuits, to render them helpful to each other, and bridge over the barrier which custom and social etiquette place in the way of friendly intercourse."[48]

Yet by the time of the first national convention of these culture clubs, held under Sorosis's auspices in 1889, a sizable group of socially active women were going beyond discussions of friendship and culture to community reform. The establishment of a national organization, the General Federation of Women's Clubs, led its new president, Charlotte Emerson Brown, to call for the kind of self-culture that "fits women for useful service in all the broadening avocations that are opening before them." Other leaders called on local clubs to address "the great problem of living" by working for "improvement in our social, civic, and educational institutions." For the thousands of women's clubs soon affiliated with the general federation, practical work took its place alongside self-culture, as members began working for city beautification, building town libraries, and petitioning for conservation and industrial reforms.[49]

Thus associations of women directed social clubs toward civic betterment at least ten years before these activities became prevalent in organizations of male fellowship. In part this precedence occurred simply because women were less attached to the traditions of fraternalism. Fraternal auxiliaries, while they possessed large memberships, followed mid-nineteenth-century practice by consigning women to the subordinate role. The Odd-Fellows' Order of Rebekah, for example, prohibited women from inducting their own members and ruled that a male lodge member must preside over all ceremonies. As Mary Ann Clawson has argued, this did not prevent women from influencing lodge policy. Nevertheless, women could achieve greater autonomy in benevolent and church activities. The Victorian concept of womanhood did allow leadership of charitable endeavors, and women achieved a prominent place in moral reform movements such as temperance. They were thus already inclined more toward a charitable, rather than fraternal, association.[50]

But, in addition, women became the first to adopt the practical form of sociability because late-nineteenth-century dilemmas confronting women in particular made them more sensitive to new problems facing the middle class as a whole. The women's study club had represented a courageous step toward self-development and had expanded the horizons of many women, but it was still well within their traditional sphere. Theodora Penny Martin's sympathetic examination of one such club, the Decatur, Illinois, Art Club, found that the members stubbornly refused to deviate from a program of study and self-improvement. Presided over by Mrs. James Millikin, a longtime resident "devoted to the service of her husband," the club refused to allow "outside" issues to interfere with their cultural companionship. Another women's club in Decatur, founded slightly later, took a different tack. Organized by Mrs. George Haworth, a woman who grew up in New York and Chicago and who taught school before her marriage, the Decatur Woman's Club "supplant[ed] education for self with education for service." The club quickly joined the General Federation of Women's Clubs and became quite active in community affairs.[51]

The story of Decatur was repeated in communities across the country, as younger women pushed into community service. For women like Mary Haworth, varied experiences, better education, and relative freedom from household labor gave them exhilarating glimpses of new roles in the world outside domesticity. At the same time, middle-class women were not ready to abandon the home, and club programs demonstrate great concern about threats to the home and community. Thus these "new" women who presided over homes found themselves in a contradictory position. Conditions that threatened the home, their accustomed sphere of influence, called for new vigilance in their roles as mothers and housekeepers. Yet the increased level of education of late-nineteenth-century women, their new power as consumers, and the example of both prominent and poorer women working outside the home created dissatisfaction with this limited domestic role.[52]

Women turned to the community service of the club as one solution to their dilemma. By founding libraries, improving local sanitary conditions, strengthening schools, and building playgrounds, club women escaped the confines of the home and achieved a satisfying new influence within and beyond the local community. Still, all these activities could be undertaken in defense of home and community. "We have no platform unless it is the care of women and children, and the home, the latter meaning the four walls of the city, as well as the four walls of brick and mortar," said one federation leader in 1908.[53]

Self-consciously expanding the women's sphere, women through service also expressed general middle-class concerns. The clubs made cooperation their keynote and displayed a great awareness of diverse immigrant populations and conflicting interest groups. The general federation's slogan was "unity in diversity." Chicago's club was one of many rather exclusive units that reported "phenomenal good-will" amid a "heterogeneous membership, which brings together every phase of religious, social, and political opinion, and yet harmonizes the whole upon a universal humanitarian basis." Universal, they also felt, was their religion, since their motives, according to the federation's president, Ellen Henrotin, were not "allied to any church or any creed or any nation, but underlying them all." "We must live an applied Christianity," she said. "No greater service can be rendered the world."[54]

Efficiency was another important ingredient in the club women's cooperative, practical idealism. Club members discussed scientific housekeeping and child care, prided themselves on smooth coordination between club departments, and made sure to run businesslike meetings. The women's clubs hoped that being businesslike would dispel feminine stereotypes. But they were also revealing an important aspect of the sociability of service. No symbolic rituals cluttered women's club meetings—in the name of efficiency, most clubs, like that of Indianapolis, Indiana, "followed parliamentary procedure with great strictness."[55]

Perhaps most important for the club members, as both women and members of a service organization, their membership demanded expansive activity, for they were part of a class of women "who are neither forced by the exigencies of their families to work for a living nor are they willing to give themselves up to a life of personal indulgences." "Think how much . . . of educating broadening influence we may give out," said a federation leader, Sarah Platt Decker, in 1896, "if we are only willing to spend ourselves." Decker and other progressive women rejected the fraternal ideal of an insular haven from change. "I grant you that it is much pleasanter to sit in comfortable easy chairs, in a well-furnished drawing room with twenty-five of one's chosen friends . . . rather than to attend meetings where possibly disagreeable subjects will be mentioned." But such security meant a shirking of duty. Women's clubs could not study the fifteenth century "while the problems of the nineteenth are staring them in the face. . . . let us have the unlimited club; it is altruistic, it is democratic, it is American."[56]

Women's clubs at the turn of the century translated this service ethic into a remarkable degree of civic activity. Particularly in the big-city clubs—Sorosis in New York, the New England Women's Club in Boston, and the Woman's Club of Chicago—prominent women could claim significant reforms as a result of their lobbying and direct intervention. Education, settlement houses, better treatment of women and children workers, conservation of natural resources, and pure food and drug laws occupied the attention of their many different departments of reform work. The Woman's Club of Chicago, for example, did not just support several settlement houses. The club's members could also cite its agitation as responsible for improving conditions in the city's jails in 1906. Their lobbying efforts, spearheaded by member Jane Addams, also did much to ensure the passage of child labor laws and ten-hour laws in Illinois. Prominent club women such as Addams, Florence Kelley, Carrie Chapman Catt, and Maude Nathan brought women's clubs into the foreground of the Progressive movement.[57]

Unfortunately, the women's club movement could not sustain its remarkable energy into the twenties. Like the progressive women's movement itself, the clubs suffered from internal dissension and unjust outside attacks.[58] Members remained in their clubs, but their community activism had subsided by the time Rotary, Kiwanis, and Lions clubs were attracting hundreds of thousands of small businessmen and professionals with the same type of community betterment activity that women's clubs had pioneered. None in the men's clubs acknowledged the influence of their feminine counterparts, and all three men's clubs were anxious to lay claim to being the first organization dedicated to service.

This failure to recognize women's clubs' achievements shows an unfortunate male blindness. But by the second decade of the twentieth century, service had become a general middle-class ideal, with connotations completely apart from the feminine sphere—ironically, partly because of the successful efforts of women's clubs in advancing a doctrine of community work and social activism.[59]

A Community Shaped by "Service"

Service now stood not just for selfless devotion, but for the assumption of community responsibility through cooperative voluntarism. It had become the subject of exhortations from college presidents and prominent ministers, who urged, as Harry Emerson Fosdick did, that "our helpfulness must be extended, not individually from one person to another, but through the medium of cooperative organizations. . . . Service cannot refuse to face the necessities, and to use the instruments which the new age has brought."[60]

It was as instruments of a new age that Rotary, Kiwanis, and Lions clubs entered local communities in the teens and twenties. Fraternalism still had enormous appeal, and many men responsible for founding clubs in their community remained proud of their lodge affiliation. Indeed, in expanding their clubs to different communities, club officials often sought as local organizers "live wires" who were "good joiners." But by the 1920s only a minority of club members also claimed lodge membership.[61] In his promotional brochures Harris stressed that he offered "fraternity without rituals, passwords and secrets" and that the club's "classification" system of membership guaranteed only the "top representatives from each business or profession." Harris's organization promised an informality and exclusivity that fraternalism could not match.

On the other hand, the scheme for classifications was provided by the national headquarters. Gone was the strictly local determination of membership characteristics of the lodges. Joining on the basis of occupation meant a new conception of one's place in the community, defined apart from local contacts and family ties.

In fact, with club membership almost disassociated from a traditional domesticity, there remained little rationale for a male-only association. Several Rotarians first proposed female membership in 1911, and it was periodically discussed up into the 1980s. Even those arguing against the admission of women in the 1920s were forced to admit "that in Great Britain and in North America women are occupying positions as Members of Parliament, Magistrates, Judges, Members of Congress, Governors of States and are more and more entering business and professional life." But no action was taken until the issue was forced by a U.S. Supreme Court decision in 1987. Members had moved away from the Victorian division of spheres that influenced fraternal lodges, but the majority still could not envision women as social and professional equals.[62]

Similarly, even though the clubs' occupationally determined membership provided no grounds for excluding African-Americans, they were barred for years because of claims that they would disrupt the camaraderie of white members. This exclusion was made even more unfortunate by the distinction made between "colored" businessmen from foreign countries and American "negroes." Starting in the twenties, Rotary and Lions club members tolerated foreign members with dark skin at international conventions but refused to associate on a weekly basis with black businessmen from their own town. Club officials were well aware of this contradiction, and Paul Harris hopefully answered "yes" to the question "Can We Absorb the Negro?," which he posed in the *Rotarian* in 1927. Unfortunately, even though they recognized the conflict between the ideal of service and club practice, most officials in the twenties and thirties felt with Will R. Manier that "though in theory Rotary would belie the principles which it professes, in particular its universality, if the negroes were proscribed. . . . The thing to do is to sidestep the issue and take care in the establishment of clubs to avoid the possibility of the issue being raised."[63]

Traditional prejudices remained potent, but, as officials were aware, nothing in the ethic of club service required members be of similar gender, race, or religion—nor even that members be sober and virtuous. What club service did require was business or professional standing and a sense of community stewardship. In principle, if not always in practice, service clubs had moved away from the criteria that had determined lodge membership. Occupational prestige and a faith in the necessity of community development became crucial components of service-club identity, sometimes overriding the social demarcations central to fraternalism.

In particular, the barriers of sectarian religion began to crumble as the majority of club members accepted the tenets of the new middle-class faith, which downplayed age-old Protestant prejudices in the name of social harmony. Within the more economically exclusive confines of club life was a relative tolerance of religious difference, and Jewish and Catholic members, though certainly not welcomed in every locality, were paid every courtesy at national conventions.[64]

Not all within the middle class accepted the more economically based consensus urged by the clubs. Another organization that was immensely popular in the early 1920s, the Ku Klux Klan, attracted a segment of the middle class all over the country by repudiating the effects of consumerism and corporate economic development. Not even the Klan was immune to the appeal of service—the organization boasted that it was "active in its ministry of helpfulness and service." In general the Klan's reaction to modernization was an obdurate defense of traditional values of home and family and a rejection of the bureaucratic intrusion into their community. An indication of their reactionary nature is their reliance on lodge traditions such as costume and ritual, perhaps a further attempt to preserve the Victorian values that the fraternal enclave once supported.[65]

Recent studies of the Klan have established that they were opposed on the local level by those in the business class most likely to join Rotary and Kiwanis clubs.[66] There could be several reasons for this opposition. Certainly the organization represented a controversy that was "bad for business." The Klan threatened the middle-class unity that service clubs hoped to promote. But clearly, also, the conflict was based on a different vision of community; service club members were far more willing than Klan members to welcome the transformations of the corporate economy and its associated bureaucracy and consumerism.[67]

Their own perpetuation of racial and gender restrictions shows that service organizations had hardly jettisoned the boundaries that defined Victorian middle-class life. Nevertheless, Rotary, Kiwanis, and Lions clubs reorganized the local business community in ways that accommodated the social and economic trends of the twentieth century. Klan membership declined dramatically after a brief heyday, but service clubs continued to find a hospitable environment in the later twenties and beyond—it was service clubs that were the associations of the new age.

The Fate of Old-Style Fraternalism

Even though the Moose and the Elks sustained a slow growth through the Depression all the way into the 1970s, remaining attractive with simple rituals, plenty of recreational activities, and the satisfaction of occasional charity, sociologists from the twenties on pointed to the gradually declining status of these fraternities. Another set of lodges, the Fraternal Order of Eagles, also experienced some growth through the twentieth century among the lower middle classes and working class, though there, too, by the thirties "the accent was no longer on secrecy but rather on service."[68]

For the largest nineteenth-century orders, especially those that had attracted a cross-class constituency, the Odd-Fellows most prominent among them, new conditions proved difficult. Struggles for the fraternal orders began during the twenties, though all experienced a dramatic surge in membership immediately after World War I. Aggressive recruiting drives on the part of the orders fit with a concern for social solidarity left by wartime sentiment. The lodges might also have benefited from a general desire to return to the stability of traditional institutions.[69]

Yet this growth could not be sustained, and both orders rapidly lost members in the later twenties. The Masons did make an effort to adapt; with the Shriners leading the way, Masons formed dozens of auxiliary organizations that focused on recreation and entertainment or sought a "practical fellowship" through community service. After 1925, however, even these changes did not stem the loss in membership; Masonry could not shake its association with stuffy and useless ritualism.[70]

For the Odd-Fellows, suspensions for nonpayment of dues outnumbered new members even before 1925. Despite some rewriting, the organization remained saddled with an archaic ritual, and, unlike the Masons, it had never commanded the status that might continue to appeal to sons of former members. Leaders blamed a loss of fraternal spirit and perceived a growing materialism that concerned itself only with insurance benefits. "We do not exemplify toward our brethren the spirit of our lessons," lamented the Odd-Fellows' grand sire Lucien J. Eastin, as he observed the quarreling of lodges over assessments in 1924. "Brotherhood, in all that the word implies, was once the supreme purpose of the organization," observed his successor, Herbert Thompson, in 1925, but now the "contractual relation" was all that was important to members. Though recognizing that "today the philosophy of America is pragmatic," he wondered if the Odd-Fellows lodge today "radiates friendship or shall it be activated by the cold steel of business relations?" To avoid the latter, he advocated abolishing insurance benefits.[71]

Although the I.O.O.F. did not immediately take up Thompson's suggestion, it did finally adopt adequate insurance policies in the late 1920s. That move, however, did not stem the loss of members, whose numbers by 1930 had dropped by half from their peak of over two million in 1920. The fraternity had made the transition to service too late and too halfheartedly. Writing in the 1930s, Grand Sire Thomas G. Andrews referred to the order's opportunity for service. Yet he still placed more emphasis on the refuge of the lodge, arguing that "a brightly lighted lodge room, which is warm in the winter and cool in summer; which is equipped with comfortable seats and an adequate floor covering; which is kept clean; which is used as a place where men may combine their efforts and aggregate their contributions for the relief of distress in the community . . . is attractive today. Such a place is able to compete with the automobile, the radio, and the picture show."[72]

Odd-Fellows Andrews and Thompson both missed the mark when they targeted materialism and technology as the main threat to old-style fraternalism. A new leisure ethic, which readily adopted the car, radio, and movies, had made lodges offering recreational opportunities more attractive. Nevertheless, the efforts of the women's clubs, the Elk, Eagles, and the Moose to move beyond self-fulfillment and fun demonstrated that the middle class was as willing as ever to organize around an ideal. What lodge members now knew as old-style fraternalism no longer supplied a satisfying form of sociability.

Well-adapted to Victorian society, old-style fraternalism observed all proprieties and celebrated nineteenth-century domestic and economic virtues. Most important, it provided a fellowship that, through ritual and paeans to brotherhood, transcended the humdrum rounds of daily life and softened harsher realities of social insecurity and inequality.

But a large part of the twentieth-century middle class needed something other than a refuge. It wanted a more clearly defined basis for social cohesion—as in organizations open only to the top men in each occupation, organizations working efficiently in practical affairs. It sought the satisfactions of a carefree intimacy, like that promoted by recreation, reinforced by first-name banter and hearty song. The businessman in the early twentieth century did not completely abandon the lodge. But its rituals had lost their meaning for him, and its brotherhood no longer seemed so rewarding. To achieve the community he valued—forward-looking, harmonious, and orderly—required his "service."

CHAPTER 2

Serving Business

At the same time that middle-class Americans turned to service as a rationale for sociable association, a new thinking emerged among businessmen about the practice and purpose of their pursuit of profit. One of the most eloquent of the new business spokesmen was Owen Young, chief executive at General Electric. On June 4, 1927, Young spoke at the dedication of the George F. Baker Foundation of the Harvard Graduate School of Business Administration, celebrating the first multimillion-dollar gift to business education. "Today and here business formally assumes the obligations of a profession," he declared. From now on, business should expect of its practitioners "responsible action as a group, devotion to its own ideals, the creation of its own code . . . and the responsibility for its own service."[1]

More symptomatic of the depth of ideological transformation was a speech given two years earlier, far from the cultural and business centers of the nation, in Clarksburg, West Virginia. George Dudderer, a member of the Parkersburg, West Virginia, Rotary Club, told the third annual conference of the twenty-fourth district that it was "possible for American business men in all lines of commerce and industry to develop high standards of conduct or Codes of Ethics, and eventually get together upon one platform of high ethical principles and conduct of service." He thought that Rotary businessmen "had it within their grasp to make us missionaries for all time, of a newer and purer conception of man's relation to his fellowman both socially and in business."[2]

Few scholars of American business culture would find the concurrence of views between these two men remarkable. Though their economic interests often conflicted, only rarely in twentieth-century American history have ideological splits between large and small business been vigorously expressed. In the Progressive era, sporadic cries of protest were heard from local entrepreneurs, but by the twenties, when the business of America was business, prosperity and public prestige encouraged the unity of the capitalist community.[3]

While big business's domination of the economy ensured that its leaders would play a large role in shaping American life, the triumph within business of an associational ideology of service, professionalism, cooperation, and efficiency was remarkably thorough by the end of the second decade of the twentieth century. In part, this triumph was aided by the larger social trends described in chapter 1. Nevertheless, the quick and relatively protest-free adoption of this ideology by small businessmen in both cities and peripheral towns has not received adequate attention; even today's historians tend to assume that small businessmen in the twentieth century reflexively clung to a version of nineteenth-century political economy. A recent discussion of small business thought, to take one example, stressed traditionalism, independence, and enterprise as recurring themes in small business culture throughout the twentieth century, despite the evidence to the contrary provided by the energetically conformist and always-up-to-date community boosting of small-town chambers of commerce.[4]

Prominent among those who have recognized the united front of small and big business was C. Wright Mills, who in 1951 in *White Collar: The American Middle Classes* contemptuously described the "diminished world" of the local entrepreneur. "Driven to the wall" by corporate economic power, small businessmen had allowed themselves to be hoodwinked by corporate leaders. Big business had convinced these small-fry that unions and government bureaucracy were the enemy. In their hunger for the prestige of corporate association, small businessmen "willingly tendered" to big business the ideology of free enterprise and civic responsibility, which corporations then used as a shield to protect themselves from public criticism. Thus big business, in Mills's striking metaphor, "toys with little business as a wilful courtesan treats an elderly adorer."[5]

This portrayal of the ineffectual small businessman clashes strongly with the innovative small entrepreneur celebrated in capitalist folklore, but in fact it is not distant from another stereotype of the small businessman, that of a blustering but easily cowed Babbitt. The organizations most closely associated with Babbittry—Rotary and other service clubs— might seem to confirm Mills's depiction. As they expanded in the United States and worldwide, the clubs appeared to be voluntary proselytizers of the American corporate order, carrying modern business thought into towns and small cities in the United States, organizing important members of each business community along similar lines, and ensuring that even the smallest retailers in the most provincial communities would extol the virtues of the new "code of service" governing business conduct. This connection between clubs and new business values was made by contemporary critics other than Sinclair Lewis, one of whom talked of the "mendicant friars of Fra Roger [the financier Babson] preaching the new gospel on the highways and by-ways among the Kiwanis and Rotarians."[6]

However, a close examination of the message of the service club "converts" reveals that their version of the new gospel was interpolated with old truths. The membership of clubs indicates that local businessmen sought productive alliances with big business representatives, and undoubtedly the words of corporate vice presidents carried more weight in club meetings than those of the local grocer. But while both the corporate agent and the local retailer might talk of efficiency, the clubs often also heard paeans to neighborliness; references to professionalism rarely neglected the necessity of loyalty to the community through membership in the chamber of commerce. In club life, new concerns about professionalism and corporate responsibility were easily transmuted into the familiar themes of community influence and town boosting. Club members accepted the outlines of big business ideology but made it relevant to their local economic and status concerns.

Thus the service club's rise to prominence illuminates the process by which the worldview of local capitalists accommodated itself to the corporate transformation. Responding vigorously to their "diminished world," small businessmen and independent professionals who joined service clubs sought to retain vestiges of familiar practices, acquire a place in the new order, and avoid, as Mills would have it, becoming cuckolds of the corporate doyenne.

Service above Self

Just as corporate leaders in the early twentieth century sought to escape the unpredictability of the market through mergers and price agreements, so did those businessmen with less economic influence search for the cooperative key to financial security. One of the many who offered to eliminate the guesswork from profitability—for a fee—was Arthur F. Sheldon, the founder and proprietor of the Sheldon School of Chicago and author of *The Science of Efficient Service, or, the Philosophy of Profit Making.* Sheldon had himself escaped the less-than-lucrative profession of public schoolteaching to set up his own correspondence business college in 1901. By 1911 he was enjoying a measure of success, claiming "60,000 students scattered throughout the country." To hopeful salesmen, retailers, and clerks, studying alone or in groups, he offered the results of "many years of patient investigation into the methods of successful men and successful institutions, with a view to discovering the natural laws of success in the world of business—the world of 'busy-ness,' the world of human effort. Hence the course we offer is designed for adoption by institutions of every nature but primarily by business houses, its object being so to harmonize and articulate all departments as to promote the general good of each individual engaged in the service of the institution."[7]

In fact what Sheldon delivered to his students was a confusing amalgam of ersatz scientific formulas ("E.V. = I − N.S. = W − E or Efficiency Value equals individual minus needed supervision equals work minus errors"), positive thinking exhortations ("Declare the fact silently to yourself, 'I *am* more sincere' "), and didactic examples ("his position was lost to a younger man who was willing to visit every customer in the territory and push the specialties as well as the staples"). Sheldon's "teachings" belong in the long line of empty-but-profitable self-help manuals that continue to boost their way up the best-seller list. But in 1908 Sheldon did something institutionally more lasting than founding Sheldon Schools: he joined the Chicago Rotary Club and in 1911 delivered the keynote speech at the national convention that helped inspire Rotary to service and gave Rotary its slogan: "He profits most who serves best."[8]

It was inevitable that Sheldon and Rotary would find each other, given Rotary's origins as a surefire cooperative business proposition in which members agreed to exchange business with each other. Like Sheldon's school, the club offered to provide an answer to the uncertain and anonymous urban market in which its members operated. Rotary's founder, Paul Harris, had grown up in Wallingford, Vermont, and had traveled extensively before arriving in Chicago, attracted, as he put it, to its reputation for "unrest" and excitement. Undoubtedly, as an aspiring lawyer, he was also attracted to the opportunities represented by its phenomenal business growth, which had made it the headquarters for some of the nation's first major corporate enterprises.

In founding Rotary, however, Harris did not model his club on the boardroom connections of corporate leaders. Instead he drew on another tradition, more readily available to a lawyer from a small town—that of the businessman as booster. Based on profits and "spirit" rather than professionalism and organization, boosterism spurred businessmen to unite for the benefit and growth of a community as a basis for greater individual gain.

Rotary's initial pitch turned this traditional booster strategy on its head: the common pursuit of individual gain served as the basis for a close-knit club community. As Harris argued in a promotional pamphlet, Rotary "sweeps away subterfuge and pretense from the solicitation of business." Instead of hiding behind a veneer of sociability or community interest, Rotarians asked directly for business from their fellow members, producing a mutual helpfulness, "a condition of friendship and fellowship upon a higher plane than the usual selfish and sordid relationship of commercial life."[9]

Harris had adapted a local business ethic to metropolitan life by creating a limited community of interest within which the "booster proposition" could operate. Further, membership was restricted through a "classification" system that enabled only one member in each line of business to join. Thus the club offered small businessmen in a big city the ready-made market and restricted competition they might enjoy in a town. "The idea of my making a lot of new friends who presumably would be working overtime to get people to come and have their clothes made at my place struck me as a pretty good proposition and I told them they could count me in on it," recalled one of the first Rotary members, the tailor Hiram Shorey.[10]

Undoubtedly this is what attracted Sheldon, as it did many entrepreneurs who served other businessmen: prominent among the early members were stationers, printers, and typewriter salesmen, who joined small-firm lawyers, doctors, and architects to form a membership dominated by locally interested businessmen. As Rotary expanded—first to the major cities of the West Coast (San Francisco, Seattle, Los Angeles), then to the East (Boston, Philadelphia, New York)—the small business character of its membership continued.[11]

Nevertheless, the fact that this gathering of local retailers and small businessmen was occurring in a corporate age was clear from its initial expansion, which was engineered in the West by the efforts of a salesman for the Sperry and Hutchinson Company, assisted by agents for the Travelers Life Insurance Company. Some of the names on Rotary's early membership lists also hinted that Rotary might play another role besides serving as a marketing outlet. Standing out in the largely mercantile rosters were locally interested representatives of corporate industry—railroad and utility agents.

When the local Bell Telephone representative, A. M. Ramsay, joined the Chicago club in 1909, a large segment of the membership was immediately suspicious. "Some of the members seemed to be a little bit skeptical of the wisdom of having a utility man in the organization, and made bold to ask me what I expected to get out of the club," he recalled.[12]

Ramsay eventually became club president, but this story of suspicion and skepticism, evidence of tension between local businessmen and the large outside-owned utilities upon which their businesses were dependent, was repeated in other communities. Because of this tension, as Rotary expanded to towns and cities of all sizes, local freight agents, Bell telephone managers, and gas and electric executives were invariably eager to join. Representatives of those lines saw the good business sense in demonstrating their community spirit and personally assuaging the hostility to their enterprises. Like the local chambers of commerce that the clubs often helped form, the clubs allowed local retailers and these corporate representatives—men who needed each other's business but whose interests might otherwise be at odds—to associate over lunch in friendly surroundings.

The need for such organizations in a corporate-dominated economy was partly what Harris was responding to when he stressed that Rotary could create a "mutual helpfulness" among businessmen. Chicago in 1900 was without a general chamber of commerce. The one organization of businessmen claiming to be representative was the Commercial Club, whose membership numbered a highly selective sixty men, including such dominant retailers as Marshall Field and such prominent industrialists as Cyrus McCormick. Harris was not the only Chicago businessman feeling a need for a citywide organization of broader scope. Just prior to Rotary's formation, an all-inclusive Association of Commerce was founded in 1904. It quickly became an overwhelming success, attracting twelve hundred business members in its first three years of operation, including both Commercial Club members and the majority of Rotarians.[13]

The stress on business unity that appears from the beginning in Rotary demonstrates that possible profits were not the club's only attraction. By promising to overcome the fragmentation of city life, the club offered a modern remedy for those small businessmen suffering from pangs of anomie. As the New York organizer Daniel Cady wrote a potential member, "This is an age of organization and cooperation, and the Rotary spirit is the idea of cooperation among gentlemen, bringing together those who would otherwise remain strangers, and turning the business of members and their friends into honest and brotherly channels."[14] Many of the early members were, like Harris, small-town natives who spoke of wanting to know again the "character" of their merchants, lawyers, and doctors.[15]

An objective observer may question Rotary's tactic in attempting to recapture small-town life. Members acted toward each other with an exaggerated informality. Hearty handshakes and loud wisecracks soon became standard ritual, and a backslapping, first-name familiarity became the trademark of Rotarians in Chicago and elsewhere. Should any member forget himself and address a counterpart with a formal "Mister," he was immediately fined. Further, as the early city clubs all grew rapidly to membership in the hundreds, members soon had to be identified to one another by name badges and photograph rosters. With its self-conscious informality disguising an essentially impersonal affiliation, Rotary's brand of small-town fellowship could not entirely avoid the patterns of urban sociability that characterized "the lonely crowd."

Yet it soon became apparent that members preferred even a shallow amiability to the blatant efficiency of open trading. Rotary's original emphasis on trade gradually gave way. Members who had initially found the club's marketing network appealing began to chafe at the pressure to trade only with other members. Early local clubs kept statistical summaries of business exchange, and promotional pitches for goods and services dominated club proceedings. "Every week we would wonder whose curtain rods, life insurance, or buggy robes we would be pressured into buying next. I wanted to sell my goods to anybody who liked them. It seemed out of line to promise all my purchases to just club members." This Oakland Rotarian resigned his membership, as did others dissatisfied with Rotary's benefits. Some businessmen in small cities, where character could still be widely known, declined to join, worried, as one businessman from Lancaster, Pennsylvania, put it, "that people on the outside of the membership would feel prejudiced against the members."[16]

Responding to these pressures, the Chicago Rotary Club decided to deemphasize the "backscratching proposition" and team up with the newly formed Chicago Association of Commerce to put public restrooms in the city's main business district. This type of public improvement, well within boosting traditions, soon became an important part of club activity.[17]

By 1910 Harris was arguing that Rotary members should deemphasize business dealings among members. Supported by the leaders of clubs in Minneapolis and Seattle, he swayed enough members at the national convention in 1911 so that the phrase "to advance the business interests of the individual members" was removed as an objective of the club.[18]

While business connections could still be made within club meetings, club pronouncements could now concentrate wholeheartedly on the "spirit of fellowship" the club helped promote. Members could devote themselves to the type of business-building advocated by the Chicago Rotarian Sheldon, who gave the banquet address at Rotary's first national convention. He declared that "the distinguishing mark of the commercialism of the twentieth century is to be cooperation. . . . man comes to see that the science of business is the science of human service. He comes to see that he profits most who serves his fellows best."[19] When Sheldon used that last phrase again at the 1911 convention, it was greeted with roars of acclaim; delegates voted unanimously to make "he profits most who serves best" the official Rotary slogan. Rotary's primary purpose was now "to develop the capability for service" with programs concentrating on business ethics and community improvement.

In explicitly adopting service as its rationale, Rotary joined corporate businessmen and middle-class progressives in an ideology that stressed co-operation, organization, efficiency, and social responsibility. Rotarians re-pudiated the rugged individualists of an earlier business generation. "The genius of Rotary exists more in cooperation than in competition," stated Rotary's code of ethics, adopted in 1915. An article in the *Rotarian* agreed that Rotary's "greatest contribution to the hour" was its "preachment that individualism finds its best and truest expression in social unity."[20]

In practical terms, this meant that business could no longer ignore pub-lic needs. As Rotary international president Glenn Mead put it at the 1913 convention, "The people of our time have firmly and definitely set their minds to consider business as their proper servant, whose primary purpose is service. This bloodless revolution in business has taught it the whole-some lesson of social service. . . . out of this epoch comes Rotary." Though Rotarians rarely criticized current business standards openly, their discus-sions of service implied that business ethics needed improving. A Rotarian minister perhaps went too far for most members when he declared at the 1917 convention, "Rotary is war to death with competition, with the evil effects of the competitive system." But most could agree with Seattle presi-dent E. J. Skeel that by stressing cooperation and business responsibility, the Rotary movement "fulfilled a definite and urgent need in our present industrial situation."[21]

The Business Sources of Service

The majority of Rotarians quoted in the last several pages were lawyers— Skeel, Mead, Cady, and, of course, Harris himself. Their words and club prominence point to the important role that lawyers played in shaping early twentieth-century business ideology. A non-Rotarian lawyer of somewhat greater prominence, Louis Brandeis, in 1912 spoke of business as a profes-sion, calling on businessmen to seek "achievements comparable with those of the artist or the scientist, of the inventor or the statesman." As Thomas L. Haskell has argued, Brandeis and other progressive social thinkers looked to professionalism primarily as a means of curbing the amoral excesses of an unrestrained market. Rotarian leaders were undoubtedly attracted to this ideology of professionalism, but they also looked to the personal rewards and status that came with community and national influence. Har-ris, for example, wrote proudly of his efforts to establish comfort stations as an attempt to "organize all of the civic organizations in Chicago into one concrete working organization." He talked of his hopes for Rotary as "a National movement of benefit to the whole country" standing "in the very foremost ranks of clubdom." [22]

If self-interest is apparent here, so too is a strain of progressive idealism. Harris himself claimed to have considered joining a settlement house, and in the twenties the Rotary Club funded several charitable projects sponsored by the University of Chicago social settlement. One of the early presidents of Rotary was Allen Albert, a journalist and "sociologist" specializing in "community improvement." In his inaugural address in 1915 he spoke of "the movements which have produced playgrounds, bathing beaches, vocational schools, good government clubs, nonpartisan municipal politics. . . . there has that spirit asserted itself which has produced the Rotary club." [23]

In fact, it is no accident that Rotary developed during the heyday of the progressive movement. The club attracted the same native, old-stock constituencies that were leading progressive reform in Chicago, Los Angeles, and Seattle—and perhaps benefited from the organizational awareness created by progressive reformers. [24] Chicago in 1905 was home to more than one hundred women's clubs, two-dozen charitable societies, eighteen social settlements, and a dozen civic betterment clubs, and Rotarians were well aware of these progressive agencies for social improvement; both the University of Chicago sociologist Graham Taylor and the independent progressive Charles Merriam spoke before the Chicago Rotarians. [25]

The progressive thrust of Rotary came from more than big-city and professional influences. Socially concerned businessmen drew on both new theories of urban reform and traditional ideas of community loyalty and local obligation. In the turbulent circumstances confronting the middle class at the the turn of the century, the boosterism of small businesses in small cities could easily take a reformist turn. In California, the first area of Rotary expansion, small entrepreneurs, who were battling railroad and real estate oligarchies, voiced their opposition in the 1890s through chambers of commerce. These organizations helped create what Kevin Starr calls a "pre-progressive reform sentiment" among the smaller businesses of California. [26] The future Rotarian and progressive journalist William Allen White led the business class of Emporia, Kansas, in a series of local reforms that his biographer calls a "booster progressivism." Similarly, a study of small cities in the Ohio Valley discovered an influential variant of progressive reform led by John Patterson of National Cash Register. Both Patterson and his son were active Rotarians. Out of such local responses, Americans all over the country shaped a new social order in response to corporate capitalism, and Rotary contributed to their efforts. [27]

There was yet another crucial ideological source of the clubs' rhetoric of service. Thousands of men schooled in the new principles of salesmanship plied their trade across the country. As they attempted to win customers through their personal attention, they also stressed the general social relevance of the service ethic; perhaps they did so as an article of genuine faith, perhaps because any words that might increase trust and convince the customer of sincerity would also increase business. Impressed by a salesman's efforts in selling him gauges, the future Rotarian John Crummey asked his secret and received his first Sheldon booklet. "By the time I finished the fifth lesson, I was a completely changed young man, I knew I could sell; I had come to realize in those four chapters that being in a small town like Los Gatos wasn't any handicap at all."[28]

In cases like those of John Crummey, the conversion to this new philosophy of service via a corporate evangelist could prove a revelation—one all the more powerful because much of it was familiar. Sheldon's lessons "awakened" Crummey to commonsense business-building principles such as treating customers and employees fairly, organizing supplies and deliveries efficiently, and advertising effectively. Other provincial businessmen found the ethic of service could energize their business practices and help strengthen their prospects. But not all experienced similar benefits. The service preached by the veritable army of salesmen marching through towns all across the nation most directly served the corporations that employed them. At the mercy of big-city suppliers and unable to match the low prices offered by direct order, local businesses lost out to the larger interests despite their own cooperative efforts.[29]

Rotary, which benefited directly from its salesmanship and service connection, could itself become an agent of corporate America. In the Midwest, the western sales manager of the Pittsburgh Water Heater Company, Lee Mettler, organized the club in Kansas City and encouraged the founding of clubs in Sioux City, Des Moines, Davenport, and Cedar Rapids. When visiting cities, he would first contact the most prominent architect, the gas company representative, and the busiest plumber, and explain to them the principles of Rotary—also, undoubtedly, the virtues of the Pittsburgh water heater. Although an associate attested to the boost in business that occurred with Mr. Mettler's club work, Mettler himself noted that "in many of the towns, merchants and others were boycotting anyone who belonged to any type of club such as Rotary, and you can imagine the care and judgment necessary to see that the friction was kept down to a minimum." Not everyone initially welcomed Rotary because it could be seen as yet another attempt by outsiders to corner the local market.[30]

Nevertheless, Rotary combined the suggestion of greater profits (though mentioned less and less as expansion continued), a voguish philosophy of business-building, and a progressive idealism suitable to the contemporary middle-class milieu yet still familiar to every small-town retailer and set it all within an atmosphere of male camaraderie redolent of lodge brotherhood. Little wonder the number of clubs had reached 356 by 1917 and that they were rapidly moving into smaller communities.

The appeal of this kind of activity was so broad, it could not be accommodated by Rotary, and imitations began to appear. Some of these clubs drew on the commercial organizations already in existence, while others were begun by promoters hoping to profit through initiation fees. Among the latter was the Kiwanis Club, founded in 1914 by a failed lodge promoter named Allen Browne. Unhappy in the territory given him by his employers, the Loyal Order of Moose, Browne instead organized a Detroit club similar to the early Rotary, based on the exchange of business among members. Searching for a suitably exotic name, similar to lodge appellations, he hit upon an Indian word, "Kiwanis," meaning, he thought, "we trade." Browne was single-handedly responsible for the early expansion of Kiwanis, traveling to Cleveland, Pittsburgh, and Rochester, starting clubs and collecting initiation fees.

Unfortunately for Browne, the popularity of Kiwanis clubs soon exceeded his organizational range. Club members, especially those not recruited by Browne, resented his control over the treasury. At the national meeting in 1917 Browne and Kiwanis leaders quarreled over a series of contractual disputes, and in 1919 leaders gathered enough capital to buy out Browne's control of the franchising of new clubs. By that time the club had followed Rotary's example and switched to service as its main goal.[31] What was to be the third major service club, the Lions, formed in Chicago when club member and insurance man Melvin Jones called a number of unaffiliated city commercial clubs to convene in Chicago in 1917. With the examples of Rotary and Kiwanis before them, they were able to establish themselves immediately as a service organization.[32]

The Benefits of Wartime

All three organizations benefited from America's participation in World War I, which sharpened concerns about cooperation and social cohesion while making a national duty precisely the kind of voluntary activity the clubs could best provide.[33] All of the businessmen's luncheon clubs jumped at the chance to prove their ability to serve. They provided inspirational speakers (the so-called "four-minute men"), spearheaded war bond drives, supported the Red Cross, and built recreation facilities and equipment for soldiers' camps. Rotary in particular took great pride in its official recognition as an organization "essential to the war effort" and devoted much of its 1918 international convention to "how Rotarians can best cooperate in War activities."[34]

The war's end left Rotary exulting that "no set of men has been more responsive to the war calls than Rotarians, and in all great undertakings none have been more faithful and efficient." They acknowledged "the influence of war . . . that causes to be born in people the spirit of comradeship, which is the true basis of community feeling."[35] Both Rotary and Kiwanis supported postwar efforts to maintain this spirit with "universal citizenship service." Sharing in the fears that swept the country in 1919, clubs stressed the importance of "cooperative right thinking." All of the service clubs backed the 100-percent American movement, though none more fervently than the Lions, who adopted the anagrammatic—though otherwise nonsensical—slogan "Liberty, Intelligence, Our Nation's Safety" and conducted community campaigns to register aliens.

With the armistice came an era of explosive growth in club membership and the number of local clubs. In the two years following the war, Rotary grew by 17,000 members, with the number of clubs nearly doubling from 415 to 758; Kiwanis membership increased by 12,000, with the number of clubs more than doubling, from 74 to 156; and the Lions attracted 5,000 new members, more than tripling the number of clubs, from 28 to 113. By the end of the twenties, the combined membership of these three organizations totalled nearly 400,000 business and professional men in 7,000 clubs.[36] To club leaders these numbers represented nothing less than a dramatic awakening. "Men had been waiting for this very thing. It became a 'living force' in the lives of many men who had been obsessed with the one idea of making money, transforming them into men who chose for their motto 'he profits most who serves best' instead of the old standard of 'he profits most who accumulates most in material things.' "[37] But as the characteristics of the new membership indicate, the clubs' dramatic growth represented less a transformation of human nature than the changing circumstances of both the local businessman and the American town during the twenties.

Rosters of newly formed clubs show the type of businessmen who joined remained the same—retailers, small manufacturers, and independent professionals, with a sprinkling of corporate officials and, especially in college towns, school administrators and teachers (see table 1). However, the clubs had shifted geographic ground. Though the original big-city clubs retained an important place in their respective organizations, the majority of clubs now functioned in towns and small cities. As Rotary, Kiwanis, and Lions

Table 1. The Occupational Composition of Thirty-five Men's Service Clubs, ca. 1925

	No. of Members	Percent of Total
Retailers/wholesalers	957	37
Services (contractors, plumbers, undertakers, photographers, etc.)	431	16
Manufacturers	281	11
Agriculture-extractive (milling, canning, packing)	150	6
Medicine	150	6
Transportation/utilities	120	5
Insurance	108	4
Educators	107	4
Journalists/editors	54	2
Government officials	48	2
Lawyers	45	2
Engineers	39	1
Real estate	36	1
Organizations (Chamber of Commerce, YMCA, Boy Scouts)	34	1
Clergymen	24	1
Farmers	21	1
Architects	12	1

Source: These numbers were drawn from the following published rosters: the Rotary clubs of Allentown, Pa., Baltimore, Md., Berlin, N.H., Cairo, Ill., Chicago, Ill., Evanston, Ill., Fergus Falls, Minn., Fitchburg, Mass., Gadson, Ala., Greenville, N.C., Indianola, Iowa, Irvington, N.J., Jasper, Ala., Kingman, Ariz., Lakeland, Fla., Lancaster, Pa., Laredo, Tex., Lincoln, Nebr., Marquette, Ill., Los Angeles, Calif., Modesto, Calif., Palo Alto, Calif., Philadelphia, Pa., Richmond, Va., Sacramento, Calif., and San Jose, Calif.; the Kiwanis clubs of De Kalb, Ill., Dixon, Ill. Rockford, Ill., Trenton, N.J., Schenectady, N.Y., and Washington, D.C.; and the Lions clubs of Muskogee, Okla., Reading, Pa., and Toledo, Ohio.

continued to grow, their small-town membership became even more predominant. Throughout the twenties more than 80 percent of new clubs were founded in towns with a population under ten thousand; by the end of the twenties, 70 percent of service club membership resided in towns of this size.[38]

For businessmen in these towns, World War I had left a legacy of voluntary service. More important, it had accelerated the expanding influence of urban and corporate culture and had heightened community awareness. The clubs, already prominent in cities and eager to expand beyond them, stood ready to supply a social outlet. Overflowing with confidence engendered by their organizations' success and the decade's general prosperity, Rotary, Kiwanis, and Lions officials, working in international headquarters all located in Chicago, felt they now occupied an advanced place in the nation's business community. They joined the nation's corporate leaders in celebrating the new role of business as society's servant, and they eagerly pushed individual clubs to educate members in the new ideology.

On the other hand, the clubs' cooperative ethic differed in ways that showed members pursuing goals separate from those of corporate leaders. Although they welcomed the prestige that came from belonging to a large organization dedicated to service and took their program cues from a secretariat, the discourse of individual members indicates an orientation more to local economic circumstances than to a professional business class. The distinction suggests the local uses of a philosophy of associationalism that was also influencing national and corporate leaders.

Club Volunteerism: The "Middle Way"

Partly as a legacy of war rhetoric, business activities in the name of service were commonplace in the 1920s. Advertising men latched on to the word; a survey reprinted in the *Rotarian* found that 25 percent of all advertisements by 1920 included the word "service." Corporate businessmen, meanwhile, attempted to convince the public that it "had wholeheartedly accepted the conception that industry is not primarily for profit but rather for service," in the words of leading industrialist Gerald Swope.[39]

In the early twenties service had acquired the mystical force accorded a well-established platitude: its invocation signaled support of all things good. Here is honorary Rotarian Warren G. Harding before the 1923 Rotary convention: "I tell you, fellow Rotarians, service is the greatest thing in the world and you are doing something—I don't know how consciously—but you're saving America from a sordid existence and putting a little more soul in the life of this Republic. . . . if we can all get down to service—honest service, humble service, help service . . . then there will come out of the great despondency and discouragement and distress of the world a new order."[40] Talk of service grew so pervasive in the twenties that the secretary of Rotary, Chesley Perry, advised moderation. "It may be about time for Rotarians, as well as others, to put the soft pedal on the word service," he wrote in his newsletter to local club secretaries. Perry thought that the popularity of the word was a good sign of Rotary's influence but called for "more discriminating use" by club members."[41]

As service became a universal theme in the business discourse of the 1920s, phrases describing an age of cooperation, heralding how business was assuming public responsibility, and urging the mutual helpfulness of unforced association rolled off the tongues of corporate spokesmen and club luncheon speakers alike. Yet among those who took it seriously, a clearly defined social philosophy lay behind use of the word. Leading those who subscribed to this philosophy was Herbert Hoover, who in 1922 wrote of "a glorious spiritual force . . . the ideal of service" abroad in the land. He found it exemplified in "the vast multiplication of voluntary organizations for altruistic purposes," displaying "the widespread aspiration for mutual advancement, self-expression, and neighborly helpfulness." They expressed the essence of a "progressive individualism," based on equality of opportunity, economic cooperation, and social responsibility.[42]

Ellis Hawley calls the philosophy behind this kind of rhetoric an "associational ideology." Fueling this ideology, he argues, was a vision of an open economy comprised of independent enterprises operating a just marketplace regulated by Christian ethics. Drawing on traditional values, yet influenced by modern organizations, it regarded voluntary association as the ideal "middle way" between stifling government regulation and unrestrained individualism.[43]

Although club members drew on the more conservative aspects of this vision, associational ideology also meshed well with the progressive organizational ethic, which envisioned the efficient cooperation of separately organized private institutions run in the public interest. Many corporate businessmen found this philosophy attractive because it allowed them to institute market controls in the name of cooperation, avoid government interference, yet still claim allegiance to traditional American values. In fact, a type of associational ideology appeared as a prominent facet of a developing corporate liberalism. In the twenties, corporate and government leaders presided over an emerging set of institutions that mingled the public interest and private interest—an "organizational sector" made up of trade associations, organized interest groups, and state agencies and regulatory boards staffed by businessmen. Technical and managerial expertise, rather than class or locality, shaped the interests of these organizations, which sought to control the state, balance the needs of competing social groups, and develop a corporative commonwealth. When these business and government leaders talked of service, they hoped to convince the public of the morality and disinterestedness of their corporate institutions.[44]

Few club members belonged to the national business elites shaping a corporative commonwealth.[45] Nevertheless, characteristics of the national club platform fit neatly with trends producing an "organizational sector."

Though they no longer claimed practical business benefits, all three service clubs continued to insist that local membership be limited—one member from each line of business, in the case of Rotary, and two, in the case of Kiwanis and Lions. This classification system made membership selective, presumably admitting only the most successful in each category of business. A rigid adherence to the classification system, a Kiwanis officer argued, encourages members who are "men of quality, of inspiration, and men of leadership and influence, who will be vigorous and powerful, not only in their own clubs but in their communities." [46]

Some club officials appeared to feel that the membership limitation was the main attraction to successful or powerful businessmen in a community. Classification thus became the basis of a club's success and permanence. Prestigious members increased the status of the club within the community and made for successful club projects, which in turn attracted additional community leaders to membership. Or as an editorial in the *Lion* put it, "The Lions Clubs will soon be the finest in the world. Men of Affairs want to belong to the Best Club or Best Anything and because they are Men of Affairs they'll get what they want. They'll WANT to be members and they WILL BE." Rotarians also spoke of classification as "enhancing the value of membership in the judgement of all both within and without the movement." In fact all clubs claimed, like Kiwanis, that classification preserved " 'the prestige of selection' a direct result of which is the distinctiveness of Kiwanis." [47]

Classification thus played a dual role. On the local level, it enhanced the prestige of the club. But it was also the mainspring of a business betterment program that club leaders hoped would result in further recognition of their organization's business leadership. Of all the service clubs, Rotary gave the most serious consideration to this "vocational service," which took the form in the twenties of industry-wide codes of business behavior. This work, begun in 1921, was given impetus by Guy Gundaker, a Philadelphia restaurant owner active from the early years in Rotary organization. Inspired by his observations of wartime industrial cooperation, Gundaker recommended that Rotary work for codes as a logical extension of the Second Object of Rotary, "to encourage and foster high ethical standards in business and profession." When Gundaker rose to the international presidency in 1923, Rotary's campaign for codes of correct practice became the major activity for the year.

Gundaker later claimed that hundreds of codes of business were written as the result of Rotary's efforts, including those of the Implement Dealers Association, the National Shoe Retailers, the National Association of Real Estate Boards, and the National Restaurant Association—the last drafted by Gundaker himself. He regarded code-writing as a panacea for business ills. Given a written statement of their employers' ethical business practices, labor would become less suspicious. The public would be re-assured, and continued observance of standards of correct practice would "render proposed restrictive governmental legislation unnecessary." But most important, when all businessmen had written codes, "businessmen will compete on a common ground of high business standards, sales will be made on the basis of service, and then that paradox of the imagination—cooperative competition—will be a reality."[48]

Codes, classification, and other aspects of vocational service reflect the influence of nationally oriented professionals within the movement. A Kiwanian paid tribute to the doctors, lawyers, educators, and clergymen who "by their Kiwanis contact with merchants, bankers, manufacturers, and other businessmen have materially aided the movement."[49] In fact, an examination of the club directories shows that throughout the twenties lawyers held 35 percent of the clubs' elective national leadership posi-tions, far out of proportion to their number in overall club membership. Furthermore, 60 percent of available club offices in the twenties were held by four occupational groups—lawyers, bankers, doctors, and educators—that together made up less than 20 percent of the aggregate membership.[50]

These representatives of the traditional professions, with education and prestige beyond that of the typical small businessman, traditionally held community leadership positions as well as various offices in voluntary asso-ciations. However, election to these offices did not merely indicate prestige. It required a significant amount of financially unreimbursed time spent on administrative matters and in visiting local clubs. Professionals could perhaps spare the time more easily than the average small businessman, but, even more, they showed a greater commitment to the national club agenda.[51]

Still, most of these men did not occupy themselves promoting manage-rial expertise. Their associationalism, as with other members, had as its locus the small-town community rather than efficient organization.

Typical of club-member associational rhetoric was the 1925 convention speech of Rotarian Ed Silberstein. While actually advocating membership in a trade association, he suggested that the vast expansion of business had "completely cut the personal touch which had always been a deter-mining ethical factor. It ended the reign of neighborliness." This Rotarian believed that business needed to become "re-personalized." Others advo-cating membership in trade organizations made frequent references to the businessman's "craft" or his "vocation," again demonstrating the combi-nation of backward-looking, nostalgic aspects with elements of the new business ideology.[52]

For club spokesmen, the themes of cooperation, responsibility, and ethical business practice assumed a nearly religious intensity. This spirituality points to a further difference between club service and the corporate ideology of efficiency and organization. All clubs had a code of ethics laying down rules for proper business behavior. Rotary's code required of members that their "business dealings, ambitions and relations shall always cause [them] to take into consideration [their] highest duties as a member of society." The Lions' code of ethics demanded a "decision against self" in all questionable business situations, and Kiwanis called for "the living of the Golden Rule."[53]

References to the golden rule frequently occurred in club speeches and added a vague religiosity to calls for cooperation. Members appropriated the language of the social gospel to support their activities—even suggesting that, through service, the clubs acquired the high calling of a religious institution. As one Kiwanian described the "religion of business and the business of religion": "No longer can we separate business and religion and education and government. . . . it therefore has become the religion of business to interest itself in the particular advancement of those characteristics that make up fine citizenship, intellectual integrity, and spiritual personality."[54] A priest opened a national Rotarian convention session by praying, "While it is not a religious service that we open with this prayer, O God, Rotary is, in no exaggerated sense, the fruit of Christianity . . . inspired by the spirit of brotherhood, of sacrifice, of self-denial, or service."[55]

Service carried the responsibilities of moral stewardship; club members often referred to themselves as missionaries. As successful and ethical businessmen in an age celebrating business, club members thought themselves well suited to carry the meaning of service to the public. The "great message of life was first committed to the church, but the church had so many concerns in mind that it has made poor progress," said one Rotarian. Finally "this message to the world has been committed to the hands of men with the real problems of life. The men who are doing the work of the world are the men best capable to lead in spiritual as well as in material things."[56]

There is some rhetorical excess in these business-as-religion pronouncements. A thorough reading of local club minutes gives little indication that Rotarians, Kiwanians, and Lions when away from the convention lectern saw their club in the sacred terms that earlier businessmen had viewed their lodge. Nevertheless, the clubs' "practical spirituality" infused an element of sentimental idealism into members' talk of modern business practices. Club religiosity—along with hearty fellowship and charitable projects—showed that members found limited personal satisfaction in an ideology of business-building phrased only in terms of organization and efficiency. Although they were doomed to disappointment, those in the clubs who sanctified business sought some spiritual meaning in the emerging corporate-dominated consumer economy.[57]

Local and Organizational Conflict

Other evidence of tension with a big business–defined organizational sector appears at the level of local club activity. Virtually all club members expressed their support of classification rules and vocational service in theory. But in practice they proved themselves quite willing to put aside the promise of professional prestige in order to meet the realities of community life. Especially in small towns, compliance with classification was often difficult. Some towns simply did not have enough members to fill a roster by strict adherence to the classification procedure. In many small clubs, too, members would not risk offending friends or influential men in the community just because a classification was filled. Rosters indicate that clubs disguised their failure to observe the rule of one member per occupation group by classifying members under obscure occupations; for example, a second dentist in the Sacramento Rotary Club was admitted under the classification "pyorrhea."[58]

Club officials were well aware of this bending of club rules. Committee chairmen spent a great portion of Rotary and Kiwanis convention time in the twenties rebuking clubs for "laxity in the standards of classification" or "apathy toward the business standards program." Inspirational addresses and articles continually reminded club members that their work as "missionaries of service" began in their own occupations. "We cannot preach ideals and unselfishness in Rotary one day a week and then for six days go out and practice selfishness in our business. If we do, good-bye to this organization."[59] Yet having made that assertion, clubs did not feel they needed measures to enforce it. A Kiwanis committee on raising business standards suggested "the quiet investigation of the business and professional standards of individual members," but it realized the implementation of this idea was unlikely since "the average business or professional man does not like advice on how his business should or should not be conducted." At Kiwanis conventions it appeared to be common knowledge that the business ethics committee was the least active committee in each club.[60]

In general, judging from local rosters, conference proceedings, and local club reports, club members not in national leadership showed little interest in any of the practical implications of vocational service. The failure of their national business standards program to generate concrete action does not mean local members were unethical, nor does it imply that they repudiated the concept of universal business standards—although undoubtedly few businessmen joined service clubs because they thought their business ethics needed improvement.

Instead, conflict over this program gives evidence of what members found more important. At conventions and in letters to headquarters, local clubs in discussions of classification requirements and program guides expressed resentment over the "outside interference" from international headquarters. While members who were small businessmen welcomed the national objectives of prestige through vocational service and listened to a large number of speeches promoting better business practice, local members resented attempts to enforce these objectives from the national headquarters. Far more club effort was expended boosting the local community than promoting business professionalization. Most members, it appeared, joined more as an expression of loyalty to local communities than to a nationwide professional class.

As the chapters that follow will show, club presence in the twenties would intensify local awareness and contribute a good deal to the continued vitality of town life. The formation of a service club could stimulate community activity in the business class and "bring a dead town to life." By placing community consciousness on more formal terms ("crystallizing" it, as a Kiwanian put it), the club could awaken local businessmen (in the words of a California Rotarian) to "the great need of acting in terms of community interest and community unity."[61]

International headquarters, which attempted to standardize local clubs through unwanted "vocational service," could also shame or inspire clubs into community activism by requiring a monthly report of activities and awarding trophies for club accomplishment. Clubs thus pursued hundreds of activities on behalf of their towns—community improvements from park building to safety signs; charity that ranged from Christmas baskets of food for the needy to expensive equipment for the local health clinic; and youth work that included both boy scout programs designed to instill enough community loyalty that young men remain, and scholarship programs that sent worthy students away to the university to bring credit to their town.

"By our association here at weekly meetings," hardware store owner Elmer Embree told the De Kalb Illinois Kiwanis Club in 1924, "Kiwanis is giving to De Kalb a body of men of broader vision, who are ready to actively cooperate and support any worthy cause for the betterment of our community."[62]

Thus organizational conflicts such as those over classification and vocational service assumed a local-national character as members defended their autonomy from infringement by international headquarters. They chafed at most organizational regulations that required local clubs, no matter how remote and small their location, to answer to a central head-quarters located in cosmopolitan Chicago. The international secretariat of each of the three major clubs set club policies, edited the general club magazine (to which all members were required to subscribe), and mailed a steady stream of educational pamphlets to the local clubs. District offices were run by elected governors who visited local clubs, reporting on problems and accomplishments to the international headquarters. Other sources of conflict were the rules requiring clubs to meet weekly, to expel any member who missed several meetings in a row, and to send delegates to the annual international convention.[63]

This hierarchical system of big conventions and centralized publications along with local chapters conformed to a formula for organizing voluntary associations that had been developed as early as the 1820s, when evan-gelical benevolent societies used it to pursue moral reform.[64] Centralized administration was efficient, and it often supplied direction and needed reinforcement for local branches. But as generally applied in the early twentieth century, and certainly in the case of the service clubs, national organization also enforced standardization.[65] It gave rise to administra-tors who stressed the integrity of the central organization above all local concerns.

Melvin Jones, the first general secretary of the Lions, who controlled association policy for more than twenty years, worked from the early twen-ties to "cultivate local club secretaries as vital communicative links."[66] The first general secretary of Rotary, Chesley Perry, also played a major role in the tightening of the Rotary association.[67] Writing as early as 1914 to a Philadelphia member who warned against "dictation from the Associa-tion," Perry defended standardized local club constitutions prescribed by the central administration. While it was true that "the early feeling of the Association was that it had no jurisdiction over the local affairs of the constituent clubs," "can this condition continue in view of the increasing importance of the clubs as a body in the association?" Perry was convinced that it could not, and he worked for thirty years to centralize Rotary ad-ministration. By 1922 a member of Perry's staff would write to a member of the club in Lincoln, Nebraska, explaining that the club members must meet every week of the year, even though Lincoln's summers were unbear-ably hot. "You know that throughout Rotary, its a common expression that 'our club and town are different.' If we look at it from a broad viewpoint we realize immediately that there is nothing to that expression."[68]

While most of the service clubs eventually fell into line with this standardization, there were enough signs of resistance to indicate their strong orientation to the local community. The president of Rotary's board of directors noted in 1922 what he termed "a harmful tendency toward provincial individuality and lines of division local in character."[69] The editor of the *Kiwanis Magazine* was alarmed in 1924 that members were inclined "to use 'you' speaking of Kiwanis International and 'we' speaking of his own club" and warned against it. Still, the practice must have continued, for at the 1927 Kiwanis convention another official spoke against "the error of the lay Kiwanis's mind to think and speak of the International as something apart from the cycle of its understanding, activity, and participation—as some sinister superstructure imposed upon a hapless unwilling constituency."[70] It was clear that the service club organizations could generate these local-national tensions even though they claimed small-town community as their touchstone.

Club, Community, and Corporate Culture

Local members' expressions of distaste for club bureaucracy shows their attempt to wend their own middle way. Through their clubs they tried to satisfy the traditional obligations of local loyalty and neighborly association, and preserve the rewards and prestige of their occupational and community lives while at the same time accommodating the business clout and cultural influence of large-scale, nationally based institutions. They often capitulated to more powerful outside business interests, and they brought further bureaucracy into their communities even as they complained about its effects. Nevertheless, the appeal of the service clubs lay in the way they personalized service and gave it a communal significance.[71]

The nature of the club members' ambiguous relationship with the bureaucratic culture of corporate America bears comparison with the response of a group of people well removed from the club milieu, urban workers in Chicago. Of course, these workers had little in common with the business-class members of a provincial small city. But drawing on the depiction of these workers by Lizabeth Cohen, several similarities emerge that suggest a common response to twentieth-century economic development. Workers who confronted mass culture did not give up their ethnic loyalties, as defined by their membership in mutual benefit societies and churches, and their patronage of locally controlled banks and grocery stores. If anything, they were even more supportive of these ethnic institutions. But the institutions themselves changed in response to corporate pressure and competition from outside agencies. The ethnic support network became, as Cohen describes it, "more commercial and bureaucratic."[72]

Local businessmen had a much greater financial and emotional investment in the developing economy than ethnic workers did, and they had slightly more influence over its direction. Still, when confronted with unprecedented corporate intrusion into their business lives, they also sought greater community solidarity—in a locally based associationalism. At the same time, however, the institutions they chose to express their loyalties— clubs and other organizations such as chambers of commerce—meant a further bureaucratic intrusion into their lives and a certain standardization of local business practices. Both workers and small businessmen in the 1920s refused to sacrifice their community spirit to encroaching corporate culture; but for both, their sense of what constituted a "community" was itself changing, under the pressure of bureaucratic development.

By the end of the twenties small-town businessmen pursued business and community interests within a maze of local voluntary bureaucracies, seeking to serve not only in luncheon clubs but also in chambers of commerce, merchants' associations, and manufacturing and retailing organizations. Their world had not been diminished so much as more formally delineated, with the local entrepreneur's responsibilities as a "representative member of his trade" and a "citizen of his community" clearly laid out. The Rotary, Kiwanis, and Lions headquarters continued to prod businessmen into cooperative effort, while individual clubs took their place among other organizations clarifying how local bankers, insurance salesmen, haberdashers, newspaper men, florists, school superintendents, grocers, and car dealers could play a meaningful role in a corporate economy.

CHAPTER 3

Serving the Community

With a parade, band concerts, and meetings held all over town, the 1920 convention of the twelfth district of Rotary International hit Bloomington, Illinois. The *Daily Pantagraph* could not restrain its prose. "Yesterday's convention was one of the most extraordinary that ever came to Bloomington."

> On the surface it looked like Bloomington had been invaded by troupes of troubadours, gangs of comedians and whole lodge halls full of hail fellow well met lounge lizards strong with the big mit and the patent grip but weak on action. The colored hats and jiggling strains of jazz helped that effect. But down in the Chatterton theater, the heart of Rotary was discovered. Men launched hot shots of pious gospel, camouflaged in slang, across the footlights to other men, deeply affected and boisterous in their approval.

The gospel's keynote was sounded by delegate "Dad" Rompel of Waukegan, Illinois. "One thing I like about Rotary is that it keeps men kids," he said, making a "masterly" appeal for constructive boys' work. The convention ended with the delegates singing "Till We Meet Again." "They swung slowly back and forth in their chairs, each man's arm about his partner's neck, crooning the song, choked with emotion, overcome by the intensity of the moment, each man glad that the lights were out so his neighbors could not see his eyes."[1]

Ebullient gatherings such as these, propelled by pep and saturated with sentimentality, swept into small cities and towns all across America in the 1920s. Beyond the singing and mawkish platitudes, service clubs offered community businessmen an up-to-date, "progressive" way to pursue the traditional goals of town boosterism. With a minimum of social disruption, service clubs could bring unity to the town business community while bolstering the economy through new outside contacts. For local participants the service club meetings represented part of the new order of business, an order that included membership drives for the chamber of commerce, scientific surveys of local conditions, and community-building campaigns run by outside agencies.

Yet within these innovations appears the ambiguity of local business life in the twentieth century. Businessmen proud of their community and their businesses thought that survival required growth and development. But forces of economic integration—corporate-controlled industrial plants, mass marketing, chain stores, the automobile—meant that growth often came at the cost of local autonomy. More than ever before, local business leaders faced a difficult dilemma—how to assure community prosperity without completely undermining their own influence, or, at worst, utterly destroying locally based enterprise. Service clubs appeared to offer a partial answer. By reaffirming civic loyalty among local businessmen, clubs could strengthen community cohesion and help establish the continued prestige of their members.

Unfortunately, the club solution brought its own costs to community distinctiveness. The clubs were themselves products of outside influences, and many of their activities—such as building new roads or founding a local chapter of a national youth organization—tended to weaken local autonomy. Thus a businessman who attempted to reaffirm his local responsibilities through club membership might undertake new activities in defense of his community only to find that they encouraged the further subversion of local loyalties and the greater standardization of patterns of community life.

In the teens and the twenties, however, the standardizing influence was less significant to club direction than the members' enthusiastic infusion of boosterism into club service. From the moment the clubs were organized, they intensified the members' local concern. The organizational imperative of club activity—to justify through service—pushed members into pursuing new conceptions of community welfare. Members moved from appeals for good roads to sponsoring an active boy scout troop to building a tree-filled park with a pool. As these local activities multiplied in communities across the country, they shaped the thrust of the national organizations and equated service with community.

Local Economies Enter the Twentieth Century: Illinois's Example

The Midwest—particularly the state of Illinois—offers a good example of towns and small cities responding to large-scale changes in economic and social life. With a major metropolis and an array of small cities and towns, from the heavily industrial city to the one-crop agricultural town, the state's communities covered the full range of urban economic development in the early twentieth century. Illinois was also a center of service club activity. All three major clubs were based in Chicago. Except for California and (later in the 1920s) Texas, Illinois had the highest number of local club chapters—over four hundred by the end of the 1920s. The state's numerous small cities and towns, with their tradition of competitive boosterism, provided fertile ground for the service clubs' promise of community rejuvenation.[2]

These towns had long been part of a regional urban network that was first based on rivers, roads, and canals and then, after the Civil War, on the railroad. This network was dominated by the largest midwestern communities—Chicago, St. Louis, Cincinnati, Cleveland, Detroit, and Milwaukee. By the late nineteenth century the business classes in other communities had been consigned to a provincial status.[3]

Still, even though no economic decision in these outlying locales could succeed without the imprimatur of big-city business leaders, town businessmen deluded themselves with visions of regional grandeur. These illusions often led to misguided enterprises. For example, the Ottawa Farm Bureau sponsored the state fair in 1872, as a "confirmation of the pretensions of Ottawa as a leading central point," even though the enterprise bankrupted the bureau and left the town unable to hold even a county fair until the twentieth century.[4]

If they did not overreach, local businessmen in the late nineteenth century could always comfort themselves by their centrality within the town's local catchbasin of trade. Their communities did not necessarily suffer economic damage from increased regional integration. Small cities and towns had always served an important mercantile function, and they also provided an entrepôt for the products of the rich midwestern soil. Improved transportation and a looming big-city economic presence did not immediately undermine those roles. As the railroad brought the products of an urban-industrial order to the countryside, town businessmen faced the competition of brand names and mail-order merchandise. But they also reaped the benefits of additional business provided by the increasing population, agricultural productivity, and prosperity of the surrounding area.

Even beyond their function in a rural economy, by the late nineteenth century outlying communities in the Midwest, particularly in Illinois and Ohio, were populated with innumerable small industries such as metalworking foundries, clothing factories, oil refineries, and watchmaking shops. These small firms contributed to the economic vitality of the Midwest and provided an extensive foundation for fast-growing centers of major industry like Chicago and Cleveland. Many of these hinterland factories emerged in response to the railroad; others were funded by big-city capital. This small-scale industrialization, often locally controlled, provided the benefits of economic development to residents without a sense of the vulnerability that continuing development would soon entail. Thoroughly integrated into a regional economy, towns in the late nineteenth century could still sustain the illusion of autonomy.[5]

New Pressures on Town Life

Any apparent equilibrium between outside influences and local control over a town's economic fate was soon upset by turn-of-the-century developments. The arrival of energy, communication, and transportation utilities involved the towns more intimately with major corporate enterprise. The material result was to improve the quality of local life; by the 1890s Illinois communities could enjoy the benefits of gas, electricity, telephones, and interurban railways. Each one of these services became essential for boosters' claims of community progress. But each necessitated, at the very least, importing outside capital and further relinquishing local autonomy. Especially in the early years of these utilities, supplying consistent service at a price low enough to satisfy customers yet high enough to ensure an adequate profit was difficult, even for an outside firm with experience in the field. Small cities and towns thus experienced periodic changes in ownership, with corresponding variations in service, all the while battling through franchising agreements to keep rates as low as possible.[6]

Largely beyond local control was the interurban railway, which had an enormous impact on Illinois small cities and towns during its short heyday in the first two decades of the twentieth century. Because of the local scale of its service, the interurban almost played a larger role than the railroad in increasing contact with immediately neighboring communities, and effectively enlarging the sphere of local business. "It has been the means of cementing a strong bond of business and social relations between the cities of Joliet on the east, Princeton and Ladd on the west, and Streator to the south," proclaimed an Ottawa resident in 1914. "With its hourly passenger service it has made possible the quick interchange of social and business visits, and has been the making of such educational projects as Chautauquas, fairs and public gatherings of all kinds."[7]

But in Illinois most of the interurbans were run either by a syndicate owned by William McKinley or by a Chicago corporation controlled by Samuel Insull. McKinley's Illinois Traction Company operated a railroad between Peoria and St. Louis, ran the Chicago, Ottawa and Peoria Railroad, and controlled the Western Railways and Light Company, a conglomerate of short interurban lines and electric and gas plants in Illinois, Kansas, and Iowa. McKinley was able to demand inducements of well over one hundred thousand dollars from towns for the initial construction of his interurban; those business communities without the resources or will to come up with the money, like Jacksonville, Illinois, never received its services. For those communities that were united by the railway, there were predictable quarrels over the number of stops and the frequency of service. The interurban in Illinois therefore gave even small-town residents experience in dealing with a "trust" of the sort big-city progressives were battling in the early twentieth century.[8]

In the first three decades of the twentieth century local businessmen experienced both the good and the bad side of urbanization and economic consolidation. Undoubtedly there were considerable benefits. In Illinois, except for coal towns in the south, which suffered an early depression with the coal industry in the late twenties, the first three decades of the twentieth century were prosperous. Migration from the countryside slowed, but urban growth continued, and few towns suffered unduly from the vicissitudes of the agricultural market. On the other hand, the steady increase of outside pressure meant that competition for markets and challenges to retailing, banking, and manufacturing practices intensified. Energized by prosperity but threatened by centralization, successful business communities sought to reinforce town prospects and to increase their degree of cooperation.

The Progressive Organization of Local Community

As local businessmen responded to new economic pressures, they undertook community-wide efforts to improve the business prospects of their towns, from sponsoring street fairs to pooling capital to attract new industry. Efforts like these had always been made informally. The small city of Aurora, Illinois, for example, fueled a late-nineteenth-century industrial boom through the private cooperation of local businessmen, who provided financial incentives and donated land sites to encourage new companies to locate in Aurora.[9] Increasingly, however, businessmen found such informal arrangements inadequate; the complexity of ensuring economic growth without overburdening local resources seemed in the twentieth century to require a more sophisticated organized response.

In particular, business firms from outside the community—often actually referred to by local business as "foreign" companies—worked in complex interaction with local economic interests to galvanize more highly organized cooperative efforts. The case of Sterling, Illinois, shows how hostility and collaboration combined to change business boosterism. Like the merchants of many towns, Sterling retailers at first united against the threat of outside merchandisers and foreign interests in a merchants' improvement association. A battle with the railroad took a group of them to Chicago in 1912 to "see about getting better service on the Chicago, Burlington, and Quincy." While there they accepted an invitation from the Chicago Association of Commerce to attend the associations's luncheon, and they returned to town with promises of assistance in organizing a chamber of commerce for Sterling. These businessmen saw this new entity as an additional tool for local economic betterment. The Chicago association, meanwhile, saw it as a chance to build local ties. "New industries want to move into a city which has a live, active, powerful and influential commercial club, which acts as a rudder in the development of the city," an official of the Chicago Association of Commerce told the Sterling businessmen. He was perhaps aware that such a rudder would also give Chicago more navigational influence over Sterling's course.[10]

The articles of incorporation for Sterling's commercial association differed little from the traditional booster goals of growth, unity, and economic loyalty: "to create and maintain civic spirit, to promote community ethics, to discover and correct abuses such as outside patronage; to establish and maintain uniformity in commercial usages; to prevent or adjudicate controversies or misunderstandings of a commercial character; to encourage immigration; to secure the location of all kinds of industrials." Yet not long after its founding, the Sterling Chamber of Commerce employed a Mr. Elkus of the City Service Company of Indianapolis, Indiana, to build membership. Soon Sterling had also recruited a secretary from outside the town, who talked of the association as "a modern business organization, to be managed along the same lines as a modern corporation. . . . Scientific distribution of service follows the lines of modern cities." From then on the activities of the business community were shaped by the chamber's efforts at scientific service—a round of surveys, celebratory sale days, and intercity cooperative meetings.[11]

Seeking to improve their towns' prospects amid a centralizing economy, the businessmen of Sterling and other towns had turned to what they called "progressive" measures borrowed from their big-city counterparts. Although they might have used "progressive" only to mean "forward-looking," these measures reflect the influence of the progressive reform movement as well. The progressives' concern for cooperation and the middle-class thrust of their social reforms meshed well with the goals of traditional boosterism. Reinforced by the objective expertise provided by community development agencies and public relations advisors, boosters' calls for economic growth and social harmony acquired a new authority. At the same time, they pushed their town to integrate more thoroughly with an urban- and corporate-dominated economy.[12]

Even in towns without close Chicago connections, World War I (which for some Americans was the last great progressive crusade) ensured the triumph of organization. To whip up wartime enthusiasm the Council of National Defense had attempted to organize local councils of defense in every school district across the country. The national success of these voluntary local councils in generating intense patriotism and huge volumes of war bond sales spawned imitations in the twenties, which witnessed an unprecedented number of chamber-of-commerce drives, community-chest campaigns, and town-center constructions.[13]

Unfortunately, however, the triumph of this business ideology of organization, efficiency, and service did little to shore up the economic autonomy of towns like Sterling. As loosely configured merchants' associations and ad hoc delegations gave way to formal chambers of commerce, organized in committee form and headed by professional secretaries, big-city firms such as the American City Bureau and Pace Incorporated were employed to raise membership. By the early 1920s the Illinois Chamber of Commerce had been formed, and town chambers were urged to affiliate with both the state chamber and the National Chamber of Commerce. The local goals of business and community betterment, long shaped by regional integration, now were defined within a national framework.

The Service Club and a New Vision

Businessmen in these Illinois cities and towns began to join service clubs in the second decade of the twentieth century. By then, most of these men must have been familiar with the rhetoric of service and efficiency; still, the clubs were definitely the product of "foreign" influences. In these early years, both Rotary and Kiwanis expanded haphazardly, dependent on local contacts for club formation. But in almost every case, the impetus for a new branch came from either traveling salesmen, who combined business interests with club commitments, or else newcomers to the community who had been members of branches in their old communities. Men with these outside contacts—insurance salesmen, lawyers, educators, and utility executives—were most frequently credited with establishing Illinois clubs.

Early Rotary expansion in northern Illinois, for example, occurred through a group of Joliet businessmen who had formed a club to study "Sheldon's Principles of Salesmanship" and then converted it into a Rotary affiliate upon contact with Chicago members in 1913. One of the Joliet

Rotarians, Edwin Lord, who advertised himself as a "Sales and Advertising Councillor and Efficiency Engineer" (his slogan was "Ask Lord—He Knows"), then traveled down the interurban to Morris, Ottawa, and La Salle, interesting businessmen in these small towns in the "Rotary idea."[14]

Rotary headquarters, however, represented by Chesley Perry in Chicago, refused at first to charter clubs in these towns, partly because Perry thought the towns were so small the clubs would fail for economic reasons, partly because he could not understand why the limited business sphere in these small communities would require Rotary, which, with its "representatives" of hundreds of business "classifications" was really better suited to the economic life of the big city.[15]

Later, in the twenties, looking back at a decade of incredible growth in towns with a population under ten thousand, club officials claimed now to understand why there existed such an enormous demand for what one *Rotarian* article condescendingly called "Rotary for Rubens." Small-town problems, this article and others argued, particularly needed the "spirit of cooperative study such as Rotary suggests and fosters." An article in the *Lion* agreed: "Petty differences and jealousies are more rampant in small communities." By "collecting representative citizens around the luncheon board once a week," Lionism provided "a splendid cure for these ills."[16]

There is some irony in these 1920s prescriptions for small-town squabbles. After all, Rotary and the other clubs had been founded in the metropolis, inspired in part by small-town neighborliness. But club references to small-town factionalism did not refer to a lack of community feeling or to a disappearance of gemeinschaft. Instead, it is apparent from the stories of dead towns brought to life by clubs that much of the factionalism that the clubs helped overcome referred to fissures in business consensus, perhaps caused by the increasing pressures on small-town business life. Prospective club members were most often part of that faction pushing for more rapid growth and economic development. The club could either help move the town toward a more dynamic expansion or else reestablish a pro-growth consensus, and thus serve as an agent of business community modernization.

This role of the clubs helps to explain the persistence of businessmen in Ottawa and Morris, who went so far as to form facsimiles of Rotary until Perry relented and allowed them to join the national organization. In Ottawa club organizing efforts gave evidence of the tensions within a changing small town. One Ottawa resident, himself a former member of Chicago Rotary, wrote to Perry in opposition to Rotary in Ottawa. As a "member of one of the settling families of Ottawa," he felt that "a bunch of young fellows new to the community" were wanting "to start something new to appear to become a factor in the welfare of the community with the hopes that they can break in" to local society. While snobbishly dismissing their efforts, clearly the Ottawan was annoyed at the pretensions of the newcomers and the change that they represented. Another local citizen, also a former member of Chicago Rotary, described the would-be Rotarians more charitably as "young fellows who are very energetic, with a great deal of push, and fellows who would at all times be ready to lend assistance in any way possible." This latter letter carried more influence, and the young outsiders won their entree into Rotary, and perhaps into Ottawa society, when the Ottawa club affiliated in 1915.[17]

The town of Morris, meanwhile, called its unaffiliated club the "Grundy Efficiency Club" (named after the county) and discussed efforts to build a deep waterway near town and bring a canning factory to Morris (both eventually came to fruition). Rotary also offered Morris a new angle on these chamber of commerce–type initiatives, however. "We hope to try out the idea of linking the town and country interests a little closer," a member wrote Perry. They planned on "including the leading farmers in our club." Once it had won affiliation, in 1915, the Morris Rotary Club helped overcome one of the deep factions in the community. During a stunt intended to build fellowship, the representatives of two warring grain mills were able to exchange wisecracks. Like the chamber of commerce, Rotary in Morris meant an energized pursuit of economic growth, while the club's sociability promised a new level of unity among the businessmen in the community.[18]

An equally vivid illustration of how clubs could figure in community development appeared a few years later in Jacksonville, Illinois, a town whose story was featured in the pamphlet *Making Service Pay,* written by "community development advisor" Fred High. In 1919, according to High, "a general state of demoralization" prevailed in Jacksonville. City services were inadequate and finances were at a low ebb. But at that point a Rotary club was formed, and its members invested one hundred dollars apiece for a community survey. According to High, "This was the beginning of Jacksonville's era of cooperation." Subscriptions were solicited, a bond measure was passed, and the city built a new water plant. Inspired by this example, a member of the Rotary club, the banker E. E. Crabtree, purportedly asked, "Why can't businessmen, from a nonpartisan standpoint, interest themselves unselfishly in municipal government?" Running on a "no pay, no politics, everything for the good of the city platform," he won election as mayor and presided over several years of business growth. High ended his inspirational story with classic booster rhetoric: "Their city has a vision, and the vision of the businessmen is that if they can hold it together that nothing is impossible for Jacksonville."[19]

In fact, its location off main transportation routes but close to the larger city of Springfield, the state capital, made it difficult for Jacksonville to sustain any vigorous growth, and despite Crabtree's best efforts, by the end of the decade the town had once again lapsed into provincial somnolence. Even the Rotary club lost its momentum, as the Kiwanis club attracted the "young blood."[20] Nevertheless, the story of the club's initial boost to Jacksonville's era of cooperation indicates the way a club's modern vision of efficient service could rouse a small city's business class, and it provides another reason why service clubs proved so attractive to local businessmen, uneasy about their towns' economic future.

The Club in the Community

As Rotary, and then its imitators, Kiwanis and Lions, became more familiar—and as their means of expansion became more formal, with officially designated sponsors and then later a recruitment staff—club expansion proceeded rapidly through Illinois. The outlines of the Illinois urban network and the levels of its urban hierarchy are clearly visible in this expansion. Rotary growth in Illinois moved from Chicago by 1915 to the medium-sized cities of Rockford, Joliet, and Springfield via Chicago contacts, and then from those cities into surrounding towns, often along the interurban lines. Starting several years later, Kiwanis staked out medium-sized northern Illinois cities first, beating Rotary to Aurora, Elgin, and De Kalb, and following Rotary into towns such as Galesburg, Rockford, and Kankakee by 1920. Beginning the latest of all, the Lions utilized paid organizers in the twenties to move from Chicago directly into the suburbs and small towns that their brother clubs had earlier disdained. The Lions found fertile organizing ground in towns such as Chatsworth, Gibson City, Mahomet, and Momence, all with populations under five thousand in the 1920s.

Distinctions in status emerged as the separate service organizations expanded into the same territory. Rotary, because of its early start, often was able to claim the best available "timber" (as organizers referred to prospective members), with the Kiwanis and then the Lions attracting prospects with somewhat lower local prestige. An adage soon making the meeting rounds expressed the relative status of the clubs: "Rotary owns the town, Kiwanis runs the town, and the Lions have fun in the town." In fact, although this relationship generally held true, in some communities organizational prestige varied. In De Kalb, Elgin, and Jacksonville, for example, even Rotary officials acknowledged that Kiwanis attracted the younger and more active men. The Lions, early into the smallest communities, could shut out the other clubs' later organizing efforts. In any case, it is difficult for the outsider to tell simply from club rosters which club carried the most prestige, since all three clubs attracted the same mix of professions and occupations.

Occasionally friction developed between the clubs. One Rotarian complained that the Aurora Kiwanis Club "was taking every Tom, Dick, and Harry, more eager to keep Rotary out than in tending to its own business." But on the whole, relations were cordial and conflict was muted in the shared interest of community building. "The Lions club will be a valuable addition to the civic organizations of Aurora," wrote Kiwanian D. S. Wentworth to a Rotarian official. "We can't have too many organized forces pulling for the public betterment." [21]

The early rosters of these Illinois clubs included the male representatives of local middle-class society, with membership reflecting the totality of the local economy. The clubs of the economically diversified small city of Bloomington in the late teens and early twenties, for example, attracted new members who not only included prominent local department store owners like Rotarian C. A. Klemm but also the secretary of the Farmer's Grain Dealers Association of Illinois, Lion Lawrence Farlow, and a professor of mathematics and the registrar at Illinois Wesleyan University, Kiwanian Cliff Guild. Even the most powerful businessmen in Bloomington, men with extensive outside interests, were club members. The candymaker Paul Beich, the president of Meadows Manufacturing Company, John Rocke, and the seed magnate and soybean pioneer Eugene Funk were Rotarians.[22] These prominent businessmen, it appears, were first attracted to Rotary by the extensive regional and national connections it promised. Although they are not today household names, Illinois businessmen like Funk, the Rockford oil refiner E. E. Smith, and the Springfield electric meter manufacturer Charles G. Lanphier were in the process of building businesses with worldwide interests, and they were early and enthusiastic Rotarians. Funk, in fact, was on his way to the 1917 International Rotary convention when he was summoned by Herbert Hoover to advise the Food Administration.[23]

Ultimately, however, the interests of these men diverged from those the club pursued, and they later resigned or played a much less prominent role in club affairs. Local men building national businesses in the later twenties, like Bloomington resident, John Mecherle, the president of State Farm Insurance Company, did not join the local clubs. Instead, Bloomington club rosters from the 1940s and 1950s show a number of State Farm vice presidents and other second-level managers.

As the twenties proceeded, the service clubs thus lost or never acquired the membership of some of the most prominent businessmen living in these small Illinois cities. Within many of these cities and some of the towns, population growth and economic complexity made it far more difficult to maintain a cohesive and locally committed business elite that would automatically involve itself in every community enterprise. Emerging in small cities like Bloomington, Peoria, Decatur, Rockford, and Springfield by the 1920s was what sociologists would describe as a bifurcated power structure, with outside "economic dominants" wielding great influence but concerning themselves with the community only on issues that affected their own interests.[24]

Rotary's expansion into outlying communities had been driven in part by the organization's big-city connections and the promise of outside business ties. By the twenties, however, a host of other trade and specialty associations now provided more valuable, strictly business connections for nationally concerned entrepreneurs. The clubs, with their stringent attendance and service requirements, required more time and promised less certain rewards.

The clubs continued to attract members from both the old middle class, men who built independent businesses from the local ground up and who joined clubs because of their vital concern with the community, and the new middle class, made up of corporate managers and professionals, whose first loyalties were to a corporate organization and who joined clubs for quick access to the community. But by the mid-1920s the clubs in the hinterland had become firmly affiliated with localism, and the early prewar connotations of an innovative business progressivism were deemphasized.

This change in focus took place particularly as Rotary, Kiwanis, and Lions clubs expanded into even smaller communities, where the club's booster function acquired primary importance. In towns like Villa Grove the business community saw Rotary as a fortification of local interests and experienced "a spontaneous desire on the part of a few business and professional men to have a service club before any outside organization activities were undertaken." Even more typical of the small-town club focus was Herrin, where prospective Rotarians accepted the sponsorship of the Harrisburg club but "whooped it up for Herrin; we knew Herrin, not Harrisburg, was the BEST TOWN in Illinois and knowing it, shook hands and became friends in common cause." When undertaken by clubs like those in Herrin, service projects that carried the aura of efficient charity in Chicago, such as a "survey of local conditions," acquired the eager air of unabashed boosterism.[25]

By the end of the twenties the clubs had settled into a locally oriented routine. The record of meetings for the Springfield Lions Club shows a typical range of club concerns (see table 2). Advocates of local economic interests and community development were a significant presence—

Table 2. Springfield Lions Club Record of Meetings, 1929–30

July 2	Installation of new officers (90%)[a]
July 9	Club debate on the year ahead (82%)
July 16	W. B. Walraven, Sanitary District Engineer, on the new city sewage disposal plan (83%)
July 23	Hon. Homer T. Tice on the Illinois State Fair (80%)
July 30	Visit to, dinner at, and program at Boy Scout Camp (85%)
Aug. 6	Lion John W. Scott travelog on Quebec (80%)
Aug. 13	American Legion program (70%)
Aug. 20	Entertained 30 members of North Side St. Louis Business Club (75%)
Aug. 27	Annual Vacation Story Contest (77%)
Sept. 3	Business session
Sept. 10	Mr. C. S. McDonald, Consulting Engineer, on proposed Lake Springfield (83%)
Sept. 17	Harold Plumber on his experiences as salesman in Orient (83%)
Sept. 24	Entertained Board of Directors, Chamber of Commerce (88%)
Oct. 1	Probate Judge Roger S. Chapin on the Constitution (87%)
Oct. 8	State Fire Marshall Marshal S. Leigred on fire prevention (81%)
Oct. 15	Mr C. L. Quaintaince, of Central Illinois Public Service Co., on Thomas Edison's life (95%)
Oct. 22	Walter A. Townsend speaking on Lionism (78%)
Oct. 29	Ladies' Night Halloween Party, Walter Townsend speaking (90%)
Nov. 5	Guy Bingham, Father and Son Week (89%)
Nov. 12	Armistice Day Stage Party (90%)
Nov. 18	Competitors' Day, Rotarian W. S. Lodge on competition (95%)
Nov. 25	Thanksgiving Day, Gifford Players, entertainment (80%)
Dec. 3	Frank Sheets, Chief Engineer, Illinois Division of Highways, on South America Good Roads Congress (89%)
Dec. 10	Entertainment of high school football team (90%)
Dec. 17	National Safety Week Program play (94%)
Dec. 24	Christmas program, talk by Lion Rev. Ed Young (86%)
Dec. 31	President's business meeting (90%)
Jan. 7	National Health Week talk by Dr. Nelson of State Dept. of Public Health (78.8%)
Jan. 14	Day of Entertainment, special stunts (78.3%)
Jan. 21	National Thrift Week, talk on national saving by Carl Weber, State Dept. on Building and Loans (81.5%)
Jan. 28	Park Board president John C. Lamphier on the present and future of Springfield parks (89.2%)
Feb. 4	Harry W. Offer, Business Manager, Springfield Board of Education, on business of Board of Education (91.8%)
Feb. 11	Washington Birthday talk by Phillip Hutchinson, State Division Insurance (92.6%)

Source: Yearbook, Springfield Illinois Lions Club, 1929–30.
[a] Percentage of membership in attendance.

speakers appeared boosting the state fair, a new sewage plant, trade with St. Louis, the chamber of commerce, and local parks. The young also were subjects of club activity—the Lions visited the Boy Scout camp, celebrated "Father and Son Week," and entertained the high school football team. The rest of the meetings were devoted to club business, entertainment, and inspirational or educational lectures given by local businessmen and officials.

These types of activities received the most attention and created the greatest impact in towns and small cities. Thus Rotary, Lions, and Kiwanis clubs quickly became familiar and influential institutions in communities like Springfield, Urbana, De Kalb, and Villa Grove. Their very success in these smaller communities began to affect the clubs' national image and the organizational priorities of club life.

At their big-city headquarters, club officials presided over international organizations expanding in both scope and ambition throughout the twenties. Yet if the club had helped widen urban influences on hinterland communities, now local concerns had to be acknowledged by national officials. Club service during the twenties was thoroughly local in character. By 1930 the president of Rotary echoed Kiwanis and Lions officials in recognizing that "one of the reasons that [the clubs] have been favorably known to hundreds of thousands of non-Rotarians throughout the entire world, is that Rotarians and Rotary clubs have devoted their energies to the service of their communities."[26]

The Scale of Service

In 1925 the nation's Lions clubs reported 904 different activities directed to children's welfare, 1,141 projects of civic improvement, and 498 actions on behalf of the blind, the poor, and the handicapped. During the same year Kiwanis claimed 3,003 instances of aid to youth, 1,918 community improvement efforts, and 889 miscellaneous acts for the public welfare. While Rotary did not publish an annual compilation of local club servic projects in 1925, each month the *Rotarian* detailed hundreds of examples of clubs' youth work, town beautification projects, and other charitable activities.[27] The clubs often inflated reports of their activities, offering resolutions as accomplishments and counting small-scale acts of charity that individuals could easily have performed without club sanction. Nevertheless, throughout the twenties the service clubs were vehicles for a remarkable degree of civic activism (see table 3).

Behind this list of projects lay a variety of preoccupations and apprehensions. Shaping club service were broad concerns about middle-class

Table 3. Kiwanis Activities, 1922–29

Type of Activity	No. of Projects	Percent of Category	Percent of Total
Youth work	19,880		44
Underprivileged child	5,083	26	
Educational work	3,296	17	
Boy Scouts	2,828	14	
Athletics	1,919	10	
Boy's work	1,876	9	
Playgrounds and recreation	1,800	9	
Music	1,186	6	
YMCA	560	3	
Vocational guidance	493	2	
Girl's work	253	1	
Camp Fire Girls	241	1	
Girl Scouts	236	1	
YWCA	109	1	
Community service	14,808		33
Better town and country relations	3,725	25	
Improvement of civic conditions	3,704	25	
Aid to business and industry	2,843	19	
Good roads	1,473	10	
Assistance to chamber of commerce	980	7	
Street and road signs	949	6	
Libraries	359	2	
Tourist camps	304	2	
Memorials	284	2	
Street lighting	140	1	
Commission form of government	47	—	
Charitable work	6,526		14
Assistance to needy	1,715	26	
Charity organizations	1,009	15	
Health and sanitation	834	13	
Community Chest	821	13	
Hospitals	793	12	
Red Cross	531	8	
Salvation Army	394	6	
Comfort of patients in hospitals	328	5	
Near East relief	101	2	
Citizenship activities	2,423		5
Citizenship	928	38	
Patriotic activities	911	38	

Table 3. (*continued*)

Type of Activity	No. of Projects	Percent of Category	Percent of Total
American Legion	440	18	
Preparedness	77	3	
Soldiers' comfort	67	3	
Miscellaneous	1,616		4
Safety First	657	41	
Miscellaneous	638	39	
Conservation	275	17	
National and state parks	46	3	
TOTAL	45,253		

Source: Compiled from *Kiwanis Activities,* vols. 2–8, 1922–29.

influence and anxieties about the precarious situation of the nation's youth, which was growing up amid twentieth-century temptations. But local interests predominated. Virtually all the clubs' service activities reveal the changed circumstances of towns and cities in the 1920s, as members sought to improve community economic prospects, reinforce business morale, and reassert local authority.

Boosting Service

Fueled by both the organizational impetus of chambers of commerce and service clubs and the fears of local businessmen about survival amid economic consolidation, boosterism took on a new urgency. Service clubs either shouldered the burden of encouraging economic growth themselves or cooperated with—or even founded—chambers of commerce to work for similar goals. A great many of the myriad service projects were attempts to improve local business conditions through growth and modernization, such as attracting industry, appealing to customers with special promotions, and putting in street lights (creating, as the clubs put it, a "great white way").

As service clubs worked with chambers of commerce to "sell" their town, they sought to incorporate new techniques into their local business-building. Many embarked on scientific surveys of their communities, enlisting the help of state universities as well as community development corporations. A business professor at Western Illinois University surveyed Moline, arguing that the "unexamined community is a community not worth inhabiting." The dean of the business school at the University of Illinois at Urbana-Champaign, Charles M. Thompson, who served as president of the Urbana Rotary Club, helped put together a comprehensive survey of labor conditions in Champaign.[28]

Their surveys completed, clubs and chambers turned to other organizational innovations to make their business communities more efficient. Members sponsored building and loan campaigns to provide an additional source of development capital. They replaced informal credit reporting and records with credit agencies and systematized credit ratings. They affiliated with better business bureaus for protection against fraudulent business propositions from outsiders. And, like any modern business enterprise, they advertised—not only in local and regional papers but also in the growing numbers of national trade journals.

In using new techniques to build business, some clubs even welcomed as fellow members the bane of many small-town retailers, the representatives of chain stores such as Woolworth, A&P, and Kroger's. An Urbana Rotarian, and the secretary of the local chamber of commerce, George Chapin was one club member who encouraged club cooperation with chain stores. Chapin felt, contrary to many other small-town businessmen, that the chain store "could be a magnet that benefits other retailers." For their part, executives at these stores recognized that to cultivate Rotarians like Chapin helped establish local goodwill. Occasionally Chapin himself found it useful to remind the chain stores of their outsider status in order to extract local benefits—for example, in Urbana Kroger's increased its deposits in a local bank in response to a letter of complaint from Chapin, while A&P was a major source of promotional funds for Urbana's "Dollar Day." By encouraging organized cooperative efforts, Chapin sought to accommodate big business and yet still retain some local control.[29]

Prominent in every business community was an attempt to accommodate the impact of the automobile. The promise of the new mobility it afforded to expand local markets was immediately appealing. A town's future appeared to depend on what *Kiwanis Activities* called "the progressive good roads movement." But while every club supported road building as a means of extending a town's economic community, they also realized progressive roads could give customers the mobility to travel elsewhere. In many midwestern towns that meant local businessmen evinced sudden interest in town-farmer relations. These relations had often been less than amicable because of the town's exploitation of the farmer's limited choices for supplies, prompting Thorstein Veblen to label the town as the "perfect flower of self-help and cupidity standardized on the American plan."[30] In the twenties, however, along with the increase in farmer-consumer mobility came hard agricultural times and a threat from chain stores, which meant country-town retailers had to scramble to retain their share of the market.[31]

The clubs provided outlets for this merchant concern, conducting good-will tours "to see crops and build good-fellowship," sponsoring product fairs and giving prizes to the boy or girl who grew the best crops, and holding "Buy Our Town" days, with special discounts to farmers. They encouraged the state universities in agricultural extension work; for example, the Kiwanis clubs of Decatur and Peoria worked to spread information about the proper use of fertilizer and lime and how to combat pests like the corn borer. Clubs also sponsored "Farmer's Institutes" in town, encouraged the hiring of county agents, and tried to work closely with local farm bureaus, inviting their representatives to join their clubs. All these efforts attempted to overcome potential conflicts of economic interest by bringing the club ideology of cooperation, organization, and expertise to bear on the local farm population. Kiwanis made the "development of better town and country relations" one of its "international objectives" in 1922. All three clubs worked throughout the twenties to show what this Kiwanian from Iowa professed: "My Kiwanis community is not confined to the city limits of my hometown. My Kiwanis community is bounded by a county line and consists of thirty-five townships." [32]

Unfortunately, while service clubs helped counteract some of the narrow and calculating conceptions of local business, they did little to alter businessmen's perception that what was best for business was automatically best for everyone else. Downplayed in local club programs, for example, were presentations concerning labor relations. At national club meetings members expressed agreement with the attitudes of those industrialists who advocated a form of "welfare capitalism"—the payment of adequate wages, the provision of some benefits, and the tolerance of a small degree of employee representation—and hoped for "the harmonious relationship between labor and capital." [33] At local formal meetings club members preferred to avoid publicly considering the subject of labor, which was always fraught with controversy and seemed to involve areas of irreconcilable conflict. When they did focus on what spokesmen called "vocational service," they preferred to discuss their relationship to the consumer or to their competitors, giving some indication that members considered harmony in these areas more crucial to their business and community success than rapport with workers.[34]

Many workers in small cities and towns saw the clubs not as broad-minded catalysts of community but rather as hardheaded representatives of selfish business interests. The president of Urbana Local 363, the Brotherhood of Painters and Carpenters, wrote to the city's Rotary club president in 1925 protesting the employment of out-of-town labor. "Our local is a unit in the business life of this locality," he reminded the president. "Our employees operate on the principle . . . spend their money where they earn it." In Dixon, Sterling, and Rockford, local businessmen fielded similar protests over their recruitment of out-of-town labor to procure lower wages.[35]

Still, local labor's appeal to community loyalty carried some weight for businesses. Retailers whose livelihood depended on workers' trade were far more sensitive to the needs of labor than the large corporations that operated branch plants within the community. Members of the Dixon Kiwanis Club joined with the Dixon Chamber of Commerce, for example, to urge the St. Louis–based Brown Shoe Company to raise its wages at its Dixon plant in 1928. Six months later the plant had apparently responded to the satisfaction of the local business community.[36]

Social Service

In their boosterism, members in towns and small cities sought to extend and consolidate the economic influence of local business interests. Yet the clubs' cooperationist ethic also made them aware of workers' concerns. At their best, the clubs carried members to a larger conception of community welfare and defined civic responsibility in other than purely economic terms. As members worked to create a community identity that extended beyond the sphere of business, they hoped to deepen a sense of responsibility to those "less fortunate." A Lion described the "ideal community" as "the community where the needs of every individual as to health, food, shelter, and clothing are recognized as essential community demands, and if there be those who because of mental or physical infirmity or misfortune in any other particular are not able to provide these particular means, then it becomes the duty of the community to make provision therefore."[37]

In practice, this aspect of the clubs' service—their work for social welfare—was piecemeal and individualized. When clubs set out to perform acts of charity, they were first of all attracted to the dramatic cases of human suffering. The widow who lost her home in the fire, the poor worker who needed an operation, the family without coal for the winter—these cases were typical of the immediate beneficiaries of club relief. The atmosphere of meetings, with their constant exhortations to service, could encourage these spontaneous acts of charity—a moving story would be told, the hat passed, and the money given directly to the victim. Without discrediting the genuine altruism involved in these good works, it is clear that the emotional rewards of this kind of charity were high—the results were clear and the response was immediate and gratifying.

Beyond individual cases of relief work, members pursued projects establishing or benefiting a local institution. Buying and donating equipment to a hospital, funding a new recreation room at the county poor farm, and raising funds for a workshop for the handicapped were typical club projects. In the least personal aspect of their public welfare work, clubs held fund-raisers for established charities such as the Salvation Army and the Red Cross, and they helped organize and run community chest and associated charity drives.

Among this long list of projects involving, in the aggregate, millions of charitable dollars a year, were some impressive accomplishments. One might expect that the resources of large clubs in cities like Chicago would allow a considerable impact on local charity, and, indeed, the Rotary, Kiwanis, and Lions clubs combined were able to contribute tens of thousands of dollars a year to poor relief, hospital service, and crippled children. In Los Angeles, the Rotary club established and took an active interest in a settlement house in a neighborhood of Mexican immigrants for ten years—though by the mid-twenties they found the annual budget of thirty thousand dollars too burdensome and sold the property. And in 1925 after Helen Keller challenged the Lions to become "knights of the blind" at their annual convention, the club did some important work in this area. It was a Lion in Toledo, Ohio, who conceived of the white cane as an aid and identification in 1928, and Lions were responsible for the cane's free distribution and wide dissemination, which led to its universal acceptance.[38]

Clubs in small cities and towns were also able to make a considerable charitable contribution. In 1925 the Cairo, Illinois, Kiwanis club established a community health clinic, to which the clubs' doctors and dentists donated several weekends a month. That same year the Pittsfield, Illinois, Lions provided clothing for thirty-five children and gave eight needy families each a ton of coal. A perhaps more typical record of small-city giving appears in the financial statement of the Urbana Rotary Club. In 1927 it gave about $464 to charity, including a $115 donation to the Red Cross, a $167 gift to the local sanitarium, and a number of smaller assistances to the poor.[39]

Critics might have pointed out that the Urbana Rotary's expenditure for charity was far less than the almost $710 spent on "entertainment and conventions." In general, little of the clubs' charity work was systematic or sustained, and once a community welfare project was complete, the members moved on to other interests. For many clubs, baskets of food and clothes at Christmastime made up the extent of their work for the less fortunate. Observing the intermittent nature of the clubs' charity interests,

Charles F. Marden likened the service club as a welfare agency to "the boy who rakes up the scattering hay left in the path of his father's hay wagon. And like the boy, it gets tired and stops to play frequently."[40]

If Marden's judgment was harsh, he was responding to the overweening pride in charitable service to be found in club magazines. No matter how grating the self-congratulatory tone of club reports, however, the clubs never claimed to function as welfare agencies. In fact, national leaders, worried that local clubs might assume financial and time obligations that would drive away members, repeatedly reminded clubs they were not to take the place of the local "church, board of trade, or charity agency." Instead they urged a more inspirational approach, one that involved the club leadership but required fewer personal commitments.[41]

To reaffirm their claim to charitable leadership, members once again borrowed progressive techniques and sociological expertise. Despite the personal and spontaneous nature of their own charitable work, clubs welcomed the authority of experts in social work in the community. They provided strong fiscal support for the YMCA, Salvation Army, and local relief and aid societies, even, in at least one case, "urging the County Commissioners to retain the County Welfare Officer, Red Cross Worker and County Agent."[42] Social science provided sanction for their own service projects; before several of the larger Rotary clubs undertook major youth work, they conducted a "survey of community needs" led by social work researchers. The Chicago Rotary Club initiated this practice in 1919, working closely with the University of Chicago sociology department. Subsequently, a general community survey by professionals was recommended by all three service clubs in order that each club could understand and meet community needs efficiently.[43]

Social workers themselves were in the process of building up bureaucratic agencies in a drive for authority and professional prestige. Since club members were also admirers of the "power of organization," they readily accepted the associated charity agencies and community chests that promised to coordinate charity activities and reduce the number of fund-raising requests. Clubs did not, perhaps, defer to social workers as often as these emerging professionals might have wished. As Roy Lubove points out, the social workers' goals of bureaucratic rationality and administrative efficiency soon submerged the concern for public welfare that clubs liked to display. As Lubove puts it, with the community chest "an anonymous public supported an anonymous machinery to serve anonymous clients." Given the rise of such impersonality, it is little wonder that club members preferred to develop their own projects and witness the tears of gratitude on the faces of the recipients.[44]

Clubs like the Aurora Kiwanis Club and Champaign and Urbana Rotary clubs had another way to overcome the impersonal efficiency of a community chest drive: they sold it as a booster proposition. Forming teams that competed to get the most subscriptions, soliciting contributions with slogans such as "Be a real neighbor—Your Community Loyalty will show in your contribution to the Community Chest" and "The Community Chest is your Protection Against out of Town Charity Solicitors," club members linked national agencies such as the Salvation Army, the YMCA, and the Family Welfare Society with the good of the community.[45]

This pattern was repeated in all local club service projects, in which members ignored the concerns of some of the national officials and followed their own path of service. Local clubs were never reticent about taking their full share of credit, nor did they confine their welfare activities to the quiet efforts of individual club members. Pride of place, anxieties about social status, and a genuine social concern existed in sometimes uneasy juxtaposition with more bureaucratic forces. The nature of club charitable activities—sporadic, unsystematic, locally oriented, and always well publicized—fits David Macleod's characterization of service as "the affordable gospel of wealth," pursued by a middle class uncertain of its standing and worried about the changing characteristics of its communities.[46]

Boy's Work

Perhaps no activity better integrated class and altruistic motives with a community motive than a third category of service—what the clubs called "boy's work." In thousands of projects involving youth education, the Boy Scouts, and recreation centers, club members clearly revealed their preoccupation with the nation's youth—and with civic unity as well. For clubs in the twenties, boy's work provided the least controversial and most fulfilling outlet for members' class and community anxieties.

Rotary was the first of the service clubs to recognize the potential of boy's work as a service activity when the 1916 convention appointed a standing committee on "Work Among Boys." In doing so, it joined an organizational movement focused on youth that had been developing since the late nineteenth century.[47] Boy's work was not at first emphasized above other activities. But it quickly rose to prominence, given impetus by the war, which focused attention on young men as representative Americans, and boys as "men in the making." As the twenties proceeded, Rotarians devoted more and more of their time to what they termed "the boy problem." "A neglected boyhood means a neglected America in the days of the future," warned Rotary director Raymond J. Kneoppel in an interclub publication, "The Boy." Citing crime statistics—"there is more than one chance in fifty that the boy will be arrested this year"—he urged clubs to "help give the boy the right environment."[48] Boy's work advocate and Rotarian William Butcher also felt it was necessary "to do some work in spending a dollar for the boy in the 'teen' age, when it will do some good, rather than spending a hundred dollars on damaged goods when it is too late."[49]

To bring attention to the boy problem, Butcher advocated a "boy's week," a project first started in 1920 by the New York City Rotary Club in cooperation with other civic bodies. For a week the club showcased boys with ceremonies, newspaper articles, sermons, and speeches. Boys were given tours of business and industry, and a "boy mayor" was designated. The week culminated in a "boy's loyalty parade" down Fifth Avenue.[50] This much-publicized event did a great deal to stimulate interest in boy's work throughout the organization. Boy's week became the centerpiece for a boy's work program that included the building of recreational facilities, vocational guidance, and support for the YMCA and the Boy Scouts. Rotary developed its boy's work program so thoroughly along these lines that the 1922 Kiwanis Executive Committee on Public Affairs was left feeling "preempted." The committee, still anxious to do youth work, opted for "underprivileged children's work" under the slogan "A Square Deal for the Child." Despite this attempt at a different emphasis in its youth activities, Kiwanis Club members on the local level eventually directed many of their efforts toward the boy.[51] The Lions Club, meanwhile, did not think it necessary to differentiate its program from Rotary's, and it even followed the plan of a "boy's week." All three service clubs conceived their role in boy's work as that defined by the 1921 Rotarian "Manual of Procedure"— "to furnish leadership in awakening the community to a realization of that community's duty and obligation to boys."[52]

Given their emphasis on the boy problem, one would expect a series of activities designed to reform the "problem boy." Several clubs did work with the local juvenile court, counseling and advising its wards. The Lancaster, Pennsylvania, Rotary Club funded a detention home to prevent underage boys from being sent to jail, a venture they called a "house of affection and not of correction."[53] But work with the delinquent was rare. In 1928 the Kiwanis Committee on Public Service recommended that care be taken in which children were selected for personal service work. "Religious affiliations, racial and national characteristics should be taken into consideration. The bad boy . . . should usually be avoided—special knowledge is required."[54]

Even when working with boys within their own social class, club members felt expertise was necessary. "Many parents, employees, and teachers still misunderstand boys and fail to plan for their development along the lines which have been approved by men who have given their lives to studying and working with boys."[55] They therefore turned to boy's work theorists whose views had begun circulating prior to the war, men such as J. Adams Puffer, Joseph Lee, and William Forbush. These men spoke before service clubs in the twenties, and their ideas provided the controlling assumptions for most club endeavors. These men were influenced by the "recapitulationist" psychology of G. Stanley Hall, which saw the development of youth as a progressive reliving of human evolutionary history. To ensure proper maturation, the boy had to be allowed to live through each phase before finally becoming "socialized."

Boy's workers, attempting to establish their specialty on a scientific basis, found this theory particularly suitable. It placed the boy's development in a universal psychological framework rather than stressing class or ethnic peculiarities. Boy's workers therefore could avoid the sociological analysis of problems such as poverty and discrimination and could escape dealing with complex family dysfunctions. They could focus instead on easy remedies such as supervised recreation, for in recapitulationist psychology play was a crucial area of development, where the boy gave outlet to his "social instincts."[56]

Club members were similarly attracted to this psychology; it allowed them to speak of the boy problem as a community-wide difficulty, affecting even the apparently well-adjusted middle-class boys with whom they preferred to work. Club rhetoric also reveals members' concerns about their own children, and, judging from speeches and club activities, they felt that theirs was, as the title of an article in the *Rotarian* put it, "A Dangerous Age for Fathers." This article advised the Rotarian father to "put aside the austerity and remoteness of fatherhood." He had to become a "pal" to his son and reach "the free meeting ground of mutual interests and understanding." Otherwise, "rebuffed too many times, the boy will never seek friendship there again."[57] While the father had to "chum with the boys," an article in the *Lion* argued for the corollary of such closeness: a father had to be frank with his son, speak to him "man to man," for a man without an understanding with his son "will never have the right attitude toward boys of his community."[58] In advocating fatherhood through friendship, and in the general thrust of their boy's work activities, club members sought to breach the distance between child and adult.

This attempt reveals the complex of anxieties disturbing the club members as fathers. As discussed in chapter 1, gender roles were changing, and with them association rhetoric: the remote patriarch of lodge ritual had been replaced by a backslapping pal. Masculine uncertainties over this change perhaps help account for the clubs' particular emphasis on boys and for the thrust of club activities toward vigorous recreational activity. Club activities also reflect broader changes in middle-class child rearing. Daniel T. Rodgers notes that the Victorian emphasis on discipline and work gave way in the late nineteenth century to an encouragement of spontaneity and play, as fears of oversystemization partially overcame older concerns for character development. On the other hand, by the early twentieth century still another set of worries concerning the breakdown of social unity influenced parents' attempts to make boys models of co-operation and "team spirit."[59] A Kiwanian, speaking at the end of the twenties, summarized the clubs' boy's work psychology in a way that expresses all of these concerns: "Boys need help before their personality reaches a crisis. . . . Where our young manhood finds no adequate outlet for their strongest native capacities and the outlet for their special abilities blocked they are thwarted. They become neurotic, apathetic or savagely rebellious." To combat this damaging frustration in a boy, club members had to "function" in a "positive" way, "allowing each new generation to acquire the full heritage of our social experience. . . . by this service, security and solidarity will be part of their social consciousness."[60]

Central to the transfer of this social consciousness was, of course, formal education. Club members hoped to encourage academic endeavor by offering a range of prizes and scholarships and by holding essay and oratory contests. Vocational guidance, provided by club members visiting schools and speaking on their professions, was one part of this service. Enlightening boys with their business and professional experience, club members could provide a corrective to an aimless schooling. "We have played grab-box with our children's futures long enough," thundered an Oklahoma Rotarian. "It is time for the schools to face the problem squarely. The aim of education should be to assist a child to discover that business or profession for which he is best fitted."[61]

Boy's Work and Community Loyalty

While vocational guidance became a common part of the clubs' educational activities, more often than not members in small cities and towns sought to link their educational activities with the school as a community institution. In the early twentieth century educators and community leaders in rural areas had enthusiastically supported school consolidation, with the school buildings located in local population centers. Advocates of consolidation praised its educational virtues and increased efficiency, but they were also aware that it was a way of linking outlying students and their families more closely with the town and its businesses. By the 1920s club members in hinterland communities had thoroughly identified the local schools with the community, and they were solidly behind the school system, eager to support bond issues for new schools. Some even "hooted out of town anyone who resisted school taxes," as did the Harrisburg, Illinois, Rotary club.[62]

Nowhere is the support of a school as a community institution more evident than when the residents of a small city or town root for their high school athletic teams. In the twenties the town spirit seemed to be expressed in high school athletics. As *Kiwanis Activities* described it, athletics "is not only doing much to develop the health and strength of contestants, but it is helping considerably to develop community and intercommunity spirit, and is doing much to bring favorable publicity to those cities in which such activity is engaged." Holding a club lunch meeting with the team and coach present was an obligatory part of the club's booster function, particularly when the team was victorious. Even with a losing team, the club might score triumphs like that of the Elgin Rotary Club in 1922. It invited the losing high school football team to lunch, explained to the team members the principles of Rotary, compared "unselfish service, loyalty, and cooperation" with "team-work so vital on the football field," and then cheered them on to victory in a big intersectional game, a win "due to the hearty cooperation of the whole city."[63]

Beyond athletics, club members felt the way the president of the Charlotte, North Carolina, Rotary club did: "The boy's play, far more than his eating or sleeping, concerns the neighborhood and becomes a community responsibility."[64] Clubs could help fulfill this responsibility by providing proper facilities such as a well-designed camp, playground, or school athletic field. They did so in abundance: in 1925 the three clubs reported building, funding, or sponsoring over a thousand camps, playgrounds, swimming pools, and ice-skating rinks. The Rockford, Illinois, Rotary club provides a striking, but by no means atypical, example of devotion to this type of service. In 1921 the club bought land and began developing a Camp Rotary for the city's youth. In ten years, it added buildings, drilled wells, and put in a sewage system, installed electric lighting, built a large pool, and developed a regulation athletic field—total expenditures ran over one hundred thousand dollars. The camp was Rockford Rotary's "greatest achievement," one into which they put so much effort that a district governor grumbled that "Camp Rotary was running the club, not the other way."[65]

Besides creating new community institutions, club members also de-

voted much time and financial support to those adult-organized agencies—
in particular the YMCA and Boy Scouts—which lent themselves to community identification. In the smaller cities and towns, club support went
almost entirely to the Boy Scouts, for which they provided both administrative and financial support. By the mid-twenties Rotary had organized
more than half the supervisory scouting councils in the United States and
was an indispensable aid in fund-raising.[66] Kiwanis prefaced its report on
club service to the Boy Scouts by saying, "Kiwanis clubs have concentrated
their services on behalf of those boys which could properly be classified as
under-privileged, rather on those boys who enjoy normal advantages. . . .
since it is the latter type which makes up Boy Scout troops, the list of activities is not as comprehensive." It then proceeded to list nearly four hundred
examples of organization and support, only slightly less comprehensive
than the approximately seven hundred activities for the underprivileged.[67]
This level of adult sponsorship supports David Macleod's argument that
the Boy Scouts and YMCA prospered because of their administrators'
success in appealing to the organizational, class, and community sympathies of local businessmen, not their success in meeting the desires of boys
themselves.

Of particular appeal to these businessmen was the scout troops' representation of the community. For example, a Lion in Bordentown, New
Jersey, complained that in their Boy Scout efforts the Lions "did not receive value for funds raised locally." He warned against allowing a church
to sponsor a troop, since "the community, not a particular church, should
get the benefit of the capable leaders that will serve as scoutmasters." A
community organization "such as the Lions" should sponsor the troop.[68]
Macleod argues that community defensiveness, based on fears of urban
corruption reaching town boys, partly accounts for the predominance of
scout troops in small towns—while only 25 percent of the population lived
in towns of under twenty-five thousand in population, 40 percent of scout
troops were in towns of that size.[69]

Service Clubs and Local Community

This intensive commitment to boys' activities—viewing the success of a
scout troop as protection against urban corruption and victory over a rival
football team as representative of Rotary principles—suggests how potent
the amalgamation of community, class, and fatherly concerns could be.
Of course, the larger goals of local service could not succeed. Young men
continued to migrate to cities, the expanding metropolis and corporate
economy continued to swallow up small towns, and the Depression would

soon overwhelm club welfare efforts. Club members exercised less and less influence over their businesses, their communities, and their families.

Obviously such matters were beyond the power of the clubs to remedy. But their attempts did result in a rapid formal organization of varied aspects of their community life, from sociability to child rearing. The various organizations they sponsored—YMCAs, community chests, chambers of commerce, automobile clubs, scout troops—had mixed results. To most club members they indicated progress. To residents less concerned with economic development the achievements of organization seemed limited; already, in the late twenties, the Lynds and other sociologists were hearing complaints of overorganization and mutterings of the divisiveness of club membership.[70]

For the Lynds and other observers, the organization that the clubs brought to their towns meant a waning of communal spirit—a "group cohesion" empty of deep-felt loyalty, a town boosterism more coercive than cooperative. *Middletown* presented the clubs as among the institutions most responsible for forcing Muncie, Indiana, into a nationally standardized mold.[71]

Despite the Lynds' considerable insight into the workings of a small city, however, their perspective undervalues and oversimplifies the club members' response to the new centralizing pressures on local life. Certainly the clubs drew diverse communities into a nationwide round of organizational activity. In welcoming service clubs and chambers of commerce, businessmen created local institutions that served national business interests, introduced further bureaucratic constraints on town society, and gilded their boosting with slogans bought from advertising agents. But club membership also encouraged individual businessmen to enter a new sphere of community interest, and it incorporated newcomers and new business methods within the community. Club activities promised members a chance of continuing the privileges and influence of a close-knit business leadership, even as the surrounding community was changing.

In general, the story of twentieth-century economic development has been one of nationally organized business interests overriding traditional attachments to community. But the clubs' role in local life illustrates that this development could also generate new patterns of community loyalty and reaffirm, albeit in changed form, a sense of local belonging. The building of parks, the sponsorship of seasonal festivals, and the occasional significant contributions to health and education helped awaken native pride and create a sense of civic responsibility among a broader citizenry, and some activities extended beyond the business class to enrich the entire community.

Even as the clubs suffered the brickbats of an articulate group of social critics for their philistinism, conformity, and "hypocritical" talk of service, and although they experienced disappointments in their efforts to strengthen their communities, there appeared to be no flagging in the number of service projects they eagerly adopted. Their civic morale reinforced by organization, they would weather the impending collapse of economic fortunes and continue to work through the twenties and early thirties at smoothing over impediments to civic spirit and community development.

4

The Clubs and the Critics

Of all the mythic figures of the twenties—the flapper, the flagpole sitter, the gangster, and the silent picture star—none remains more vivid than a far-from-exotic literary creation, the businessman George F. Babbitt. In part because Sinclair Lewis's caricature was so comprehensive and authentic, in part because Babbittry still seems endemic to American culture, the portly businessman's characteristics are well known—materialism, hypocrisy, and conformity. In the novel one aspect of his life seems to encapsulate all these traits. To the great chagrin of Rotarians, Kiwanians, and Lions, Babbitt is a service club member.

The publication of *Babbitt* in 1922 was just the beginning of a stream of ridicule and criticism directed toward the clubs by an array of those whom members called "intellectuals." To the smart set of the twenties the terms "Rotarian" and "Kiwanian" became synonymous with Babbitt, representatives of Mencken's "typical Americano"—"well-fed, well-dressed, complacent, and cocksure, he yet remains almost destitute of ideas." [1]

The general impression has been that service clubs, if not oblivious to the ridicule, were defenseless against it. [2] Actually, club members were keenly aware of the critics and sought to vindicate themselves in ways that belied the Babbitt stereotype. Alternately defensive, indignant, or forgiving, club spokesmen countered attacks upon their character with vigorous prose and logical argument, although in the war of words club spokesmen were clearly outclassed by a formidable lineup that included, in addition to Lewis and Mencken, Dorothy Parker, Bruce Bliven, Clarence Darrow, Gilbert Seldes, and G. K. Chesterton, to name a few. To club member and critic alike, the battle lines seemed clearly drawn—one side consisted of "literary radicals," the other of the "booboisie."

Even during the twenties, culturally aware Americans saw the rebellion of the intellectual as one of the central events of the period. [3] The critics' disillusionment reflected a distaste for the old and a distrust of the new—their modernism rejected Victorianism and its restrictive sentimental pieties, while at the same time lamenting the standardization and materialism of the emergent business society dominated by corporations and consumerism.

The clubs offended on all counts. They retained enough local allegiances and traditional sentimentality to be considered barriers to cultural liberation. At the same time, their rhetoric and style of sociability rang with the brassy informality of the new commercialism. To the club members, on the other hand, the critics represented flippant disrupters of an increasingly fragile consensus; they were uncooperative obstacles to progress who could "only tear down, and not build up."

Yet despite the vehemence that characterized this cultural argument, on at least one level the essential concerns of the two groups were quite similar. Both the clubs and their critics were cognizant of powerful new forces arising from a corporate capitalism. The critics of American culture, who generally shared the social origins of their adversaries, were alienated more from the social products of this new capitalism than from the society as a whole. Despite their defiance of genteel standards, they saw individual initiative and organic community present in other parts of America's past. When they directed their satiric invective at an increased middle-class conformity and materialism, they were decrying departures from an American tradition.

Naturally, club members, who were mostly businessmen, expressed fewer reservations about the by-products of American commercialism. But their rhetoric and service activities frequently displayed the same concerns about the direction of corporate transformation. The local retailers, independent professionals, and small manufacturers who joined the clubs expressed an ambivalence about the developing system that threatened their autonomy and prestige. Convinced that their clubs compensated for ebbing community spirit and expanded possibilities for individual achievement, members at times appeared baffled by the critics' attacks.

The story of this particular cultural schism, then, is not really one of intellectuals' alienation from an unappreciative American culture. Nor do club members appear as an anti-intellectual and materialistic business class. Instead, the basis of the conflict between the clubs and their critics lies in the different ways they chose to confront the same twentieth-century problem—how to preserve a sense of individual significance in mass society.

The Debunkers

Criticism of business before the war had been deadly serious in tone as it attacked corruption and price-fixing, shoddy consumer goods, and employee exploitation. Although the small businessmen who joined Rotary clubs had not been the direct target of these attacks, still they saw their cooperative effort in service clubs as one answer to public concerns about the irresponsibility of unrestrained competitive enterprise. During the war, when a government supervised by progressive intellectuals directed business activity and encouraged local voluntarism, the clubs felt increasingly confident of their value to American society. This confidence increased as new members flooded into the clubs immediately following the armistice. American business, the clubs felt, showed new concerns for ethics, for social improvement, for service.

At the same time, however, the war brought disillusionment to those hoping for fundamental social and economic reforms. To one group of the discontented—a middle-class and well-educated group—America's business system seemed beyond reform. As America grew increasingly prosperous and politically conservative, it appeared to this group that the country had developed an entire culture centered on the practice of business. These disenchanted men and women gave vent to their dissatisfaction in cynical debunking critiques that differed vastly in tone from those of the earnest prewar reformers, not condemning the practice of business so much as ridiculing the manifestations of the new business culture. The burgeoning numbers of complacent club members presented a prime target.

Both to foreign observers and native social critics, the service clubs became representative of the injustice and philistinism of a prosperous business society. The Englishman Harold J. Laski wrote in the *New Republic* that "the American businessman has no real sense of impalpable values. He contents himself with material well-being." Lacking impalpable values, the club member's ideology of service was, in the words of French observer Andre Siegfried, the "doctrine of an optimistic pharisee trying to reconcile success with justice."[4] The hypocrisy was too much for Clarence Darrow, who "lashed" club businessmen in a 1924 speech cited in the *Rotarian:* "They know life is worthwhile, and the reason they know it is because they can get money. You will find optimists in the Rotary club . . . you will find them in the Lions club: here they roar about money. You will find them in the Kiwanis club, and wherever there are gathered together a body of 100 percent Americans, you will find them boasting and lying and stealing."[5]

But just as disturbing to the detractors of American business culture as its immorality was the conformity that it promoted and enforced among its supporters. Gilbert Seldes was one of many who downplayed the dastardly behavior suggested by Darrow's accusation. "These boy scouts of business do a dirty trick a day if they can get away with it, but it is a small trick. . . . in the aggregate they provide an army of contented cows." At the same time that they slavishly worshiped the god of mammon, the clubs discouraged dissent in their communities. Writing in *Harper's* in 1925, Duncan Aikman went so far as to suggest that the clubs were harbingers of an American fascism, displaying a "home-town mind" that allowed no deviance from the chamber-of-commerce line. Less alarmed but still harshly critical, Bruce Bliven blasted the clubs in a *Scribner's* article for "standing in the way of genuine municipal progress" by "enforcing a single attitude of mind." So commonplace was the notion that clubs were engines of conformity that Ruth Sapin could predict for her son, "Babbitt, Jr.," who "cares not a whoop for being an individual," a future Rotary presidency.[6]

The clubs were singled out not just because of Lewis's devastating caricature, but also because of the general "revolt from the village" that he represented and explored. Because of their heavy concentration in small midwestern towns, the clubs were easily associated with these towns as symbols of monotony and provincialism and as crushers of individual aspiration.[7] Along with their geographic associations, the clubs embodied several characteristics in the new business society that critics found antithetical to cultural achievement. The clubs, they felt, represented the extension of business values into everyday life and a concomitant loss of spiritual awareness. The club members stressed moral uplift and emotional solidarity, and they were easy dupes for the latest fad. All these activities devalued individual creativity and serious thought, preventing any appreciation for the truly good and beautiful. With his aesthetics determined by cash value and his opinions handed him by the crowd, the club member in caricature would not know an original work of art if it came up to him, slapped him on the back, and called him by his first name.

The Clubs' Response

As the clubs began to encounter the ridicule they were to experience throughout the twenties, they could fortify themselves with expressions of gratitude from recipients of service. Local papers, as concerned with boosting their town as much as the clubs were, gave club members a generally favorable press. Even the *New York Times* placed its stamp of editorial approval on a group of men who were "longheaded and yet sometimes a little naive, eager, bustling, gregarious, hopeful and free-handed . . . a characteristic expression of the composite, migratory, trustful, and boyish nation of their origin."[8]

Later, as the debunking tide rose, club members could find plenty of editorial support, among both newspapers and middlebrow magazines such as *Liberty,* the *Saturday Evening Post,* and the *World's Work.* A *World's*

Work article, written by the novelist Booth Tarkington near the end of the decade, was characteristic of the defenders. Businessmen, argued Tarkington, supply the material basis of civilization, but they also endow our great cultural institutions. Rotarians and their service were the exemplars of business's "incalculable" aid to progress, and Tarkington ended the article by recalling a Christmas day on which he witnessed Rotarians delivering packages to the needy in horrible weather.[9]

Club spokesmen were quick to cite this article, as they did all other published praise. Yet club members were equally sensitive to their attackers and returned time and again to the critics. Club magazines carried articles analyzing the critics' motives; convention speeches frequently referred to them; the Muncie, Indiana, Rotary club even devoted a meeting to a discussion of *Babbitt* and other "sharp criticisms" of service clubs to see "what could be done if caustic comment was deserved, and what might be done to correct wrong impressions."[10] Club members attempted to respond to charges of conformity by arguing that they promoted a responsible individualism. "It is not the group activity of which Rotary is most proud," said the club's director, Raymond Kneoppel, in *Scribner's*. "Rotary stands for the development of the individual."

In a thoughtful *Rotarian* article discussing the critics' charges, Arthur Hobbes echoed these sentiments, calling for the individual Rotarian to "conduct himself by the rule of reason—liberal and untrammeled—rather than by the rule of the crowd. . . . Rotary Clubs can well see to it that their influences encourage the development of real merit, skill, genius, and educational ambition." Hobbes's article was illustrated by a cartoon showing an adult "average member" looking out a window puzzled at a hive of angry bees labeled "critics," while a shamefaced boy holding a stick with the tag "irresponsible member" hid behind the door. "I wonder what stirred them up?" reads the caption. Responses such as these, reasonable and aware, granted to a surprising degree the validity of the critics' charges, while attempting to disprove by counterexample the image of unthinking conformity.[11]

Particularly disturbing to club members, however, were those caricatures which could not be combatted by reason and led to the discouraging sensation that educated men held them in contempt. "We all have been disturbed and chagrined at a spreading attitude of derision," wrote Will Garrity in the *Rotarian* in 1926. "Men who like to pose as leaders and educators of public opinion, men who assume a liberal and forward-looking attitude, men who preach the gospel of culture for culture's sake, have been extremely critical of Rotarians."[12]

Tarkington had written partly because he felt that the service club members had become a "satirist's joke." "The debunking writers have ridden their joke so hard it has become popular. . . . until now it has almost the prevalence once possessed by the stock plumber joke and the stock mother-in-law joke." Since clubs included in their ranks educators, professionals, and businessmen who liked to think of themselves as liberal and forward-looking, many club members found it galling to be, in Tarkington's words, "the chief figure of fun for the critical 'intelligentzia' [*sic*]."

None of the purveyors of what the *Rotarian* called "literary bunk" bothered to take the clubs' service achievements seriously. Instead, as an editorial complained, they focused on "the weekly luncheon meeting with its friendly camaraderie."[13] William Feather was one of those who lampooned the foolishness of the weekly meetings—"some hold beauty contests among their members, requiring the candidates to do aesthetic dances and pose as the 'dying bootlegger'. . . . a favorite form of recreation is for each member to lie on his back and kick a basketball with his feet. At Thanksgiving and Christmas each member brings a newsboy or an orphan to the meeting for a big feed."[14]

What made satire like this so frustrating to club members was that they could not absolutely refute it. Local clubs did hold beauty contests, kick basketballs, and sponsor newsboy feeds. Obviously these occurrences did not constitute the whole of club life. "One might as well try to give a true picture of the national congress and its position in American affairs by reporting the amusement of senators over a story in the lobby before they take part in an important session," wrote the infuriated editor of the *Kiwanis Magazine*.[15] In response, the clubs made a conscious effort to limit publicity of their meetings and instead promote their service activities. Even that effort brought Bruce Bliven's satiric sketch of "the heart-rending picture," of "this cowed band leaving the luncheon room, peeking around apprehensively to see whether Red Lewis be not lurking behind each onyx pillar, as they scuttle back to their offices, to sink back blissfully under the soporific "Do it Now" mottoes."[16]

Short of changing their mode of expression, clubs could do little to combat the caricatures. Satirists delighted in the clubs because of the contrast between the self-conscious informality and boyish stunts that dominated club conclaves and the lofty rhetoric members used proclaiming their noble purposes. As articles such as Hobbes's in the *Rotarian* showed, even some of the staunchest defenders conceded that the absurdities of club behavior were fair game.[17] The *Handbook of Entertainment for Rotary Clubs,* for example, suggests such "rich stunts" as dressing initiates in diapers, having a member pretend to be a "woman speaker from Washington," and serving "fake fritters—pieces of cork camouflaged with a little dough and sauce." Juxtapose this with the pomposity of Rotary's founder, Harris, in describing the movement's origins: "If one standing on a promontory of time could have donned his metaphysical spectacles revealing thoughts and deeds standing out in the affairs of men, he would have observed a memorable struggle for existence—the persistent and irresistible "Will to be" of an ideal, which eventually found expression in Rotary, Kiwanis, Lions clubs and a dozen kindred organizations." Contrasts such as these created ready-made caricature.[18]

Double-barreled Ridicule

For the two critics who set the intellectual tone of the decade, Sinclair Lewis and H. L. Mencken, service clubs became a favorite target. Ranging over the same debunking ground, Mencken and Lewis fired an overwhelming barrage of ridicule and satire at even trivial club lapses in taste and expression. Both were particularly sensitive to language and were able to capture precisely those utterances which made club members appear most ridiculous.

Lewis had an extraordinary talent for mimicry, and the monologue of Lowell Schmaltz, in his post-*Babbitt* caricature, "The Man Who Knew Coolidge," bears a remarkable resemblance to the convention discourse of a certain kind of club member. "Why say, just this past year our Zenith Kiwanians have put up no less than two hundred and sixty-three highway markers within forty miles of Zenith and we gave the kids at an orphan asylum a dandy auto ride and free feed. And believe me, it was one fine ad for the Kiwanians, because we took the kids out in trucks, and each had on it a great big red sign 'Free outing for the unfortunate kiddies, provided free by the Zenith Kiwanis Club.'" And here is William Winkler, a real-life Kiwanian from Hobart, Oklahoma: "See, we are going to build a lake for the community, and we are going to name it Kiwanis Lake; right in the cement we are going to put Kiwanis. But we haven't got enough money to pay for it. But you see, the thing to do is just put a little good business sense into a Kiwanis club, get a little bit of credit, and let the whole town or community pay for it."[19]

For his part, Mencken dispensed with imitation and reproduced actual club material. Club members made up a significant portion of his monthly catalogue of public folly, the section of quotes and excerpts Mencken entitled "Americana." Newspaper headlines provided him with "George H. Shaw lauds Christ in Rotary speech," and a record of "red-blooded he-men Kiwanians" seeking "recreation from the burdens of service" by holding balloon-busting contests. The club members themselves gave him the chance to quote verbatim such statements as "Tolstoy was an unconscious Kiwanian"; "The first president of Lions International was Jesus Christ. I quote you from the Bible: He was the Lion of the tribe of Judah"; and "Had there been a Kiwanis club in Civil War days that great conflict would have been avoided." [20]

Behind these quotes and vignettes was the image of an uncultivated, self-satisfied businessman, a member of "the booboisie" straining for profound expression—a "go-getter," in the words of Zenith Booster Club member Chum Frink, hustling to "Capitalize Culture." Simply by drawing attention to members' fatuous statements, Mencken and Lewis exposed to ridicule not only the clubs but all the pomposity, sentimentality, and materialism that blighted middle-class American culture. "All organizations, in America, seem to draw rhetoricians," Mencken wrote to a Rotarian who had asked him what was wrong with the club and how to improve it. "What is to be done about it, I don't know." [21] In "Americana" Mencken cited politicians as often as club members, using their platitudes to limn their true character—blowhards spouting pretentious nonsense. An important part of his brief against the clubs (and politicians) was that they dishonestly misused language to conceal from themselves and others their true purposes: "Whenever a group of real estaters get together and sob for service, somebody's going to be done."

Both Mencken and Lewis took a contrary joy in what Mencken called the "commonwealth of morons" and relished confronting the philistines with their ignorance. Speaking in front of the Rotary Club of Kansas City, Lewis first imitated the types of post-luncheon speakers that Rotarians invited—"the effeminate highbrow," the "rambling journalist," and the "he-man talking he-language." Then he launched his attack in earnest, contrasting boosterism with a genuine appreciation for culture. "Should you be surprised if the man from Stratford-on-Avon came to Kansas City not because of your beautiful parks and boulevards, but because one Theodore Dreiser thought Kansas City important enough to lay a book there? When you go through London, do you think much about its exporting or importing business or about the characters of Dickens walking through the streets?" [22]

The Kansas City Rotarians were rightfully annoyed at such condescension, and to suggest that Lewis was more sympathetic toward the values of service clubs than Mencken would have brought no consolation. There seemed no distinction between the contempt both men shared for service clubs and boosterism.[23] Yet a close reading of the two critics reveals Mencken's rejection of service club culture to be far more complete. Lewis attacked the commercial capitalism that he took the clubs to represent, but he was attracted to the unaffected egalitarian fellowship that club members themselves hoped to foster. Mencken, however, saw the clubs as a symptom of chronic ailments afflicting American democratic life. He revealed no ambivalence in his contempt for democratic society.

In a thoughtful analysis of Mencken's social criticism, George Douglas has argued that Mencken harkened to a nineteenth-century individualism that stressed independence, work, and responsibility. Mencken criticized democracy in a way that recalls the nineteenth-century thinkers James Fenimore Cooper, Charles Dana, and Henry Adams. Even had the clubs not made public statements Mencken regarded as "utterly idiotic," they would still have experienced his bombastic derision because of the way they illustrated the foolishness of democratic man.[24]

In his essays on the clubs and elsewhere, Mencken follows a train of thought reminiscent of Tocqueville's observation on "the restlessness of Americans in a democracy." Believing in equality, Americans at the same time attempt to subvert it, by elevating their own position and pulling others down. This envy and ambition creates dissatisfaction with the commonplace and a turning away from down-to-earth realities to grandiose illusions, among them that "soaring humorless Vision that is the essence of Rotary." Why did a businessman join a service club? To Mencken the answer was clear: the clubs were misguided attempts to achieve dignity, to convince members they were really "citizens of mark." The American businessman

> needs something more than is to be got out of blowing spitballs and playing golf. So he searches for that something in the realms of fancy. . . . He reads the dithyrambs of Edgar Albert Guest, Arthur Brisbane and Dr. Frank Crane. He listens to the exhortations of itinerant rhetoricians, gifted and eloquent men, specialists in what it is all about. He intones "Sweet Adeline," and is not ashamed of the tear that babbles down his nose. Man cannot live by bread alone. He must hope also. He must dream. He must yearn.

And so he also joins a service club, which, with its supposedly selective membership, convinces "used car dealers, insurance agents, newspaper editors, trucking contractors and butter and egg brokers" that "they are somebody."[25]

Mencken's criticism of American democratic society focused on its moral, aesthetic, and psychological inadequacies. Only rarely did Mencken concern himself with political or economic injustice. In fact, had club members been able to look beyond the ridicule of this literary radical, they would have seen a conservative whose views had something in common with the most reactionary among them. Mencken wrote of his respect for work as a moral ideal, his dislike of the revolution in morals, and his regret over the decline of civility. In an essay, "Das Kapital," from *Prejudices, Third Series,* Mencken displayed his economic conservatism. Capitalists, according to Mencken, deserve our praise, because it is only in their occupation that some pride of workmanship survives. Among the workers it is dead, having been killed by a unionism that "devotes its power to safeguarding bad work." [26]

In his economic conservatism, Mencken perhaps revealed his background as the son of an independent small businessman. In fact, many of his values appear consistent with those of a respectable nineteenth-century burgher. The conservatism of the club members, on the other hand, was imbued with a twentieth-century cooperative ethic. Their philosophy of action was therefore far removed from Mencken's conception of individual initiative. Clubs predicated their service on goodwill and egalitarian participation, something Mencken was sure would produce only folly. Members placed their faith in the power of harmonious community, an ideal Mencken dismissed as foolish illusion. The clubs' outlook was framed by twentieth-century organizational life, Mencken's by nineteenth-century individualism. Even though neither felt entirely comfortable in modern America, their reactions remained utterly incompatible.

A less iconoclastic frame of reference lies behind Lewis's fiction. His work does not attempt to expose the ultimate foolishness of democratic community but rather to detail how materialism and capitalist greed convert community into an engine of conformity. His three novels of the early twenties, *Main Street, Babbitt,* and *Arrowsmith,* direct their ire at an institutionalized commercialism that beats down individuals and molds them to quiescent consumerism. The character Carol Kennicott joins other small-town failures whose souls have been flattened by "the beautiful big balloon tires that roll over the new pavement on Main Street"; Arrowsmith successfully escapes the McGurk Institute and its standardizing of "the erstwhile chaotic spiritual activities of America" to make them "as practical and supreme as the manufacturer of cash registers"; Babbitt struggles with, and then succumbs to, the materialist community organizations "fixing what he believed to be his individuality." Although these characterizations are more complex than the stereotypes they came to represent, in all three a well-organized commercialism corrupts general men and women and augments the oppressiveness of natural community.

Of Lewis's books, *Babbitt* best catalogues the twisted relationships that occur in a corporate commercial society. The book begins with a Babbitt already seduced by soul-sapping consumerism. "These standard advertised wares—tooth pastes, socks, tires, cameras . . . were at first the signs, and then the substitutes, for joy and passion and wisdom." Briefly awakened by his experiences with his friend Paul Riesling, with whom he enjoys a genuinely sympathetic relationship, Babbitt is finally forced back into the commercial order. He acknowledges his defeat by rejoining the false camaraderie of the Boosters' Club, where relationships depend on the potential for profit.

Lewis's caricature of the club members in *Babbitt* is at once harsher than Mencken's (he holds them responsible for ruthless economic exploitation) and less damning (their companionship has moments of redeeming value). Even while Lewis reveals Babbitt to be shabbily corrupt in his real estate dealings, he shows him capable of genuine affection and loyalty. Here and in his other writings Lewis reveals ambivalence in his feelings toward democratic community. He revolted not against the small town in which he grew up—he remembered it as a "good time, a good place, and a good preparation for life"—but instead against the Main Street of Gopher Prairie, "a force seeking to dominate the earth, to drain the hills and sea of color, to set Dante at boosting Gopher Prairie, and to dress the high gods in Klassy Kollege Klothes."[27] Lewis enjoyed the hunting companionship of Minnesota Rotarians, and his portrayal evidences an affection that Mencken and many other reviewers missed on first reading. In Lewis's later novels the hero is a solid middle-class citizen, the apotheosis of the Babbitt type. Lewis, in other later pronouncements, declared that men like Babbitt were those "he really enjoyed," and that he wrote the book out of love for Babbitt.[28]

In his later years Mencken also claimed to have softened his judgment of the clubs. But a notebook entry published in the 1956 *Minority Report* demonstrates once again the differences between his sardonic perspective and the ambivalence of Lewis. The "Rotarians and their imitators, almost forgotten," Mencken wrote, were simply stupid fellows seeking a moral system to substitute for Christianity. To their credit, unlike theologians, they did not attempt to force anyone to believe in service. They avoided pressure politics, "paid cash out of their own pockets for all their crusades," and were not a public nuisance. Of course, they were comic, "but only in the benign sense that a dog chasing its tail is a comic character." Mencken, as "one who spent a good deal of time and energy crying them down," was happy to proclaim publicly their innocence.[29]

Babbitt as Social Analysis

Few club members in the twenties found Lewis's critique more palatable than Mencken's. Yet most Americans, while they would never reject democratic culture, shared at least some of Lewis's distaste for standardization and increasing commercialism. Johan Huizinga noted in 1926 that "the Americans can no longer get rid of Babbitt as a warning example. He is more than a literary figure, he has been a force. Nobody wants to be a Babbitt, and most people in fact detect in themselves traces of 'babbittry.' "[30] Even club members admitted to Babbitts in their midst, though one member who saw in each club "a certain number of babbitts" proposed "shearing them of any Babbitical tendencies and class consciousness by impartial assessment of fines," a solution that by its very foolishness would have delighted both Lewis and Mencken had they encountered it.[31]

Criticism that singled out the commercialization of middle-class life was in fact also congenial to the thrust of service, which sought to add moral considerations to cold cash in business transactions. Lewis and other detractors took the club members' moralizing as evidence of blatant hypocrisy, when instead it too revealed an ambiguity toward the new commercial order. Hoping the public would grant them the high status of "professional"—one who operated from motives other than profit—club members also looked back to what seemed a simpler business age, when character counted as much as cash.

Club members and most other Americans who were able to enjoy the prosperity of the decade celebrated the technological advances and organizational development widening the scope of corporate consumer society. Nevertheless, some thoughtful citizens were concerned about the direction of social development, and about the indulgences of consumerism and the anonymity of mass production and bureaucratic structure. It was these apprehensions, rather than Mencken's general skepticism of egalitarianism, that prevailed in two respected contemporary interpretations of the period.

The first, the Lynds' study of Middletown, described in nearly *Babbitt*-like terms the impact of the car, the radio, and advertising in standardizing community behavior. Nowhere was this standardization more to be seen than in leisure, which had once been spontaneous and carefree and now was "over-organized": "Men and women dance, play cards, and motor as the crowd does; businessmen play golf with their business associates. . . . for those who look wistfully beyond the horizon a hobby tends to be like an heretical opinion, something to be kept concealed from the eyes of the world." Leading the way in the overorganization of leisure were the service clubs, "challenging the member and his world at no point, often proving of actual cash value in his business." Where once a club of leading Middletown business and professional men were "stirred to fierce indignation over philosophic and social questions," now the "leveling effect of credit" had produced these "quietistic" clubs.[32]

As Richard Wightman Fox has argued, the enemy in the Lynds' portrayal is consumer capitalism, turning Middletowners away from community-centered self-reliance. Although Fox discounts the influence of Babbitt, he believes that the tone of *Middletown* reveals a hopeful Robert Lynd calling for democratic resistance against the enforced conformity of corporate consumer culture.[33]

While the Lynds gave Lewis's critique the backing of sociological research, Frederick Lewis Allen lent it the sanctions of a historian in his popular review of the decade, *Only Yesterday*. David M. Kennedy, in a recent revisit to the book, notes that Allen identified the emergence of a media-induced consumerism and faddishness. Allen blamed the "disillusionment" produced by war for undermining traditional verities—simple honesty, self-dedication, and genuine religion. The American people lay open to the blandishments of "ballyhoo" and the attractions of false religion such as that offered by the service clubs, whose "mysticism" expressed "the national faith . . . in the redemptive and regenerative influence of business." Since business after the crash proved itself to be a tin god, Allen, too, was hopeful the American people would return to the solid ground of democratic values.[34]

Allen, like all critics of business society, saw the new commercial order as one destructive of individual integrity. The American people, seduced and emptied of conviction by the siren call of advertisers, fell into lockstep consumption of the newest fad. The clubs' booster idealism was a false spiritualism. Devoid of all but material values, it only reinforced the conformity and commercialism of the new age.

With such unfortunate developments so thoroughly identified with the clubs, it remained only for the Englishman G. K. Chesterton, speaking in 1931, to label the twenties a "Rotarian Age." "Filled with the wind of self-advertisement," the clubs had done their part to undermine individual dignity. Characteristic of the shabby level of human discourse was the hearty backslapping and first-name-calling that "debased human friendship." The clubs enforced a comradeship that, like the age, was "gross, common, vainglorious, blatant, sentimental, and in a word, caddish."[35]

Stunts and Sentimentality

To charges of boosterism, sentimentality, and adolescent informality the clubs could only plead guilty. But in their animus against the service clubs, the critics often confused club manners, which they disdained, with club intentions, which they underestimated. If club men made strained attempts at moving eloquence and engaged in foolish practical jokes, they did so not to commercialize social relations but to restore a human element they felt ebbing away.

Of the many dramatic contrasts between the critics' taste and that of the clubs, one in particular explains their mutual disdain. Where critics responded to the confusions of modern life by stressing critical thought and individual responsibility, club members employed both sentimentality and stunts to build unity and a sense of common purpose. Undoubtedly the clubs' kind of thinking put little value on aesthetic judgment or critical analysis, although it did encourage the type of culture that could be justified in terms of community betterment—supporting institutions such as museums, libraries, and schools.

The work of the versifier and Rotarian Edgar "Eddie" Guest provides a good example of club cultural sensibility. His nationally syndicated rhymes were frequently used by club members to add an "inspirational note" to their speeches. Guest is perhaps best remembered for the line "takes a heap o'livin' in a house t' make it home." The rest of his literary efforts are of similar quality. But Guest's work was extremely popular among club members, in part because his themes were those of club activity. Guest's work rang the changes on fellowship ("there's nothing like the comradeship which warms the lives of those / who make the glorious circle of the Jacks and Bills and Joes"—"First-Name Friends"); community boosting ("it doesn't matter much be its buildings great or small / the home town, the home town is the best town after all"—"Home Town"); and close father-child relations ("Be more than a dad / be a chum to the lad"— "Father and Son").[36]

But beyond these congenial themes, the operating aesthetic of Guest's work attempted to bring to mind what all men supposedly had in common. Who among the club members had not experienced the warmth of friendship, smiled at a cavorting child, or felt a twinge of nostalgia thinking of the old home town? Highbrow modern art intended to challenge common perceptions, stimulate rethinking, or reward a discriminating intellect. Guest's verses sought to reaffirm accepted truths, and they were successful if his audience responded with a nod of agreement or a chuckle of recognition. Undoubtedly, even some club members must have found Guest's lame and mawkish verse unpalatable, but few would have disagreed with its unifying spirit.[37]

Similarly, occasional protest appeared at conventions over the sometimes forced use of first names, but this practice, too, had its clear justification. Club members hoped that by removing, as a Rotarian put it, "the barrier of polite formality," they could "speed the evolution of acquaintance into friendship." Through such friendship, a Lion claimed, isolated men could be made "part of the warp and woof of their community life." Gradations in status, so obvious and significant in small cities and towns, would be undermined, as club members could "mit [sic] the biggest man in town and call him by his first name, or better still his nickname." Critics saw only the artificial quality of such relations. Aware of its illusory nature, many club members felt that their hearty backslapping might, in a small way, remedy the impersonal fragmentation of modern life. "No assaults by literary anarchists with misguided ideas of community life can breach the fortification of idealism and relations between humanity which build a more happy and harmonious world," declared a Kiwanian defending club sociability.[38]

Critics could point out that club idealism was often fortified by unison versions of "Old McDonald's Farm." Yet even the group singing and foolish stunts had their communal rationale. By "checking their dignity at the door," members acted on terms of true equality. Assuming an atmosphere of boyish innocence and good-natured fun, club members (so their reasoning went) escaped the workaday world with its artificial distinctions between men, and, as the *Lions Stunt Book and Toastmaster's Guide* phrased it, they were inspired to "work harder in the spirit of play than they would feel like doing if it were merely work."[39]

Many club stunts were games designed to encourage familiarity with names, occupations, or personal peculiarities, while much of the clubs' "play" involved practical jokes. Members recalling the early fellowship of the Chicago Rotary Club, for example, remembered such affairs as switching suitcases, employing an actress to interrupt a meeting to accuse a club bachelor of fathering her child, and staging a fake fistfight over an issue that was of vital concern to particular members. Undoubtedly members saw these gags as attempts to deflate pretensions, defuse conflicts, and preserve the harmony of club life. Although it might be tempting to place a deeper psychological or anthropological interpretation on such foolish behavior as inducting new members in diapers or dressing club officers in skirts, here too the object seems to have been an equality enforced by indignity. Members might have found such stunts amusing because of the contrast between the members' serious business lives and the playful fellowship of the clubs. Searching for metaphors to describe their unencumbered egalitarianism and explain their playfulness, they often reminded themselves of their common origins: "The staid old businessman is after all but a boy on stilts."[40]

Such thinking and behavior are easy objects for ridicule. More serious criticism saw in this sociability the triumph of what C. Wright Mills called the managerial demiurge, the artifical and manipulative intimacy of a society exploiting human relations for material ends. Nevertheless, the clubs' vision could be defended as a response to this type of spiritual emptiness. Speaking at the 1927 convention, Rotarian Bill Elliot described the dilemma of the age as one of "destructive specialization." He then addressed himself to "Mr. Mencken and Mr. Lewis," saying he found entertainment in their work, but "where is the constructive integrating idea which you are trying to present to the world?" Elliot admitted "there are what you are pleased to say Robots in Rotary" but found that the movement's limitations paled "compared with the great fact that Rotary is a movement which is trying to present to the world a constructive and integrating idea."[41]

The integrating power of sociability had become for members a dominant concern, and one with which they hoped to combat the same technological change, the same institutional encroachment, the same changing communities decried by Lewis, the Lynds, and Allen. Of course, the critics and clubs responded to these social problems in vastly different ways. Lewis and other analysts valued free intellectual inquiry, and they felt it could dissolve the falsities of consumer capitalism and restore individual autonomy and a vital democracy. More concerned about the impersonality and fragmentation of modern society, club members stressed consensus and harmony of sentiment. But both were eager to return to an organic and constructive community.

The Decline of Stunts

By the thirties club fellowship in general had lost some of its early exuberance. In 1930 the *New York Times* headlined an article, "Rotarian Pep Called a Myth—Survey Shows Growing Dignity." The *Chicago American* in 1932 carried a story of yet another battle between Mencken and the clubs, but this time the stakes were less consequential. In a cruise to Panama, Mencken triumphed over a group of Rotarians, Kiwanians, and Elks in a beer-drinking bout by downing a liter of beer without pausing to draw his breath. Making joking reference to Prohibition, which was soon to be repealed, Mencken assured an interviewer that "not one passenger has lost his sobriety on the trip."[42] The decade of the twenties was itself passing into caricature.

When the Minneapolis Rotary Club published its twenty-fifth-year anniversary history in 1935, it recalled, along with its notable service achievements, the "rough and tumble of badinage" that flourished at meetings a mere ten years before. In what reads like a wiseacre's digest, it recounts the horseplay of the twenties: "underwear worn to the installation ceremony of the president; straw hats torn to shreds; electric seat pads; electrically charged rings; water glasses with holes in their sides; Burma Shave served as frosting for chocolate eclairs; fake telegrams; snake dance parades 'a la Shrine.' " These were "gorgeously hilarious affairs" in "striking contrast" with the "serious roundtables and governor's breakfasts of today."[43]

The highbrows had made their impact. A decade of derision had taken its toll and, combined with the Depression, had sobered the gaiety of club meetings—not only for Minneapolis Rotarians but for club members across the country. Clubs had become self-conscious about looking ridiculous; their past hilarity now represented bad public relations. Rollicking club behavior became less acceptable and less appealing. In the thirties, though all clubs required group singing and members still called each other by their first names, only with caution did members "check their dignity at the door." One would not want to exaggerate the extent of this new decorum in club behavior. Thirty years after the Minneapolis Rotary historian lamented the decline in hilarity, the Rockford Rotary Club ushered in its new president, a former FBI executive, by dressing him in prison attire and handcuffing him to the local police chief.[44] Such antics undoubtedly continue today. Nevertheless, the boyish zest that characterized club expression in the twenties had faded.[45]

What some members called the maturing of club life involved further integration into a culture dominated by the mass media and consumerism—and an organization behaving with public-relations prudence. As radio and movies presented models of cosmopolitan sophistication, perhaps their juvenile frolicking was now seen as uncouth and provincial even by the club members. Perhaps also, in the easy intimacy of a society that had rejected Victorian restraints, that was now dominated by consumerism and acutely aware of "personality," club members had become so accustomed to relaxed first-name friendliness that stunts to encourage such familiarity seemed redundant.[46] As clubs enlarged their scope of influence and acquired worldwide interests, and as local businessmen suffered economic hardship, boyish hijinks appeared inappropriate. The joy buzzer, the whoopee cushion, and the shaving cream pies fell by the wayside.

Given this aftermath, it would be easy to consider the controversy between the intellectuals and the clubs another bit of cultural trivia, a quaint relic from the age of bombast and ballyhoo. But the issues that the clubs and critics raised remain central to middle-class culture, issues of community, responsibility, autonomy, and authenticity. While today it is easy to laugh with the critics and at the clubs, the rationale that members presented for their behavior deserves serious consideration. Asserting that through service they acted in the community's interest, and that by first-name camaraderie they increased the sum of cheerfulness in the world, they appear convinced that they were meeting—glad-hands extended— the challenges of modern society. As some members themselves realized, their convictions did not negate the observations of the contemporary critics. One can still regret the derogation of human dignity when, to quote Mencken, "the first Rotarian called John the Baptist 'Jack.'" Nevertheless, as events in the thirties were soon to make clear, the club members' ethic of cooperation would allow a successful adaptation to the inhospitable conditions of economic depression.

CHAPTER 5

Adjusting to Hard Times

If the service clubs had failed to survive the Depression, few of their critics in the twenties would have been surprised. Even some of their dedicated members confessed later to doubt the clubs' ability to prevail apart from a general prosperity. Yet after a sharp drop in membership during the early years of the Depression, club membership figures again climbed steadily and reached new highs by the end of the thirties. Considering the time and expense the clubs exacted of their members, this growth was a significant achievement.

For the most part, clubs attracted these members without undertaking special Depression service activities. This continuity is not entirely to the clubs' credit. Club service projects appeared to disregard the severity of the economic crisis; the clubs' sporadic Depression relief efforts lacked the enthusiasm with which members continued to approach boy's work or traffic safety projects.

Nevertheless, the Depression did change the thrust of club life. The helplessness of local business communities in the face of the crisis, and their dependence on intrusive New Deal agencies, forced club members to confront more directly the implications of integration into a national economic order, an order that they had inadvertently helped promote in the twenties. Members responded not by rejecting wholesale the patterns of modern organizational life but by complaining about its public manifestations—the restrictions and red tape of government bureaucracy.

At the same time, however, the process of assimilation into urban corporate America did not abate. The advance of the metropolitan periphery, and the clubs' continuing expansion into new communities, meant that an increasing number of club members lived in suburban areas. As would become clear from their local activities, these new members sought slightly different satisfactions from their clubs. They were less inclined to express their community concern through the vigorous boosterism characteristic of small-city and town clubs in the twenties.

Of course, local growth and development remained the primary goals of many individual clubs, but leaders at club headquarters sought new methods of building consensus and generating goodwill that would extend beyond the town or city to the nation and the world. As the thirties proceeded, these members talked less and less of service to the community, and promoted a subtle shift in the community spirit of local club service, stressing activities that encouraged larger loyalties. By the end of the decade Depression fears of economic collapse and social upheaval had combined with the suburban residential setting of new clubs to change the emphasis of club rhetoric. Speeches at club conventions and articles in club magazines less frequently extolled local cooperation. More often they called for social conformity and "adjustment."

Thus the clubs' response to events continued to reflect the ambivalence of small businessmen and professionals about creeping bureaucracy and declining local influence. But even as they railed at federal government interference, club members declined to express their resentment in forceful political action. Calling for increased consensus, they continued to adapt to national integration.[1]

Communities in Depression

As stunned by the sudden collapse of prosperity as the rest of the nation, club members soon after the Crash attempted to draw on traditional booster methods for attracting business and building community confidence. Towns in the hard-hit coal-mining region of southern Illinois, for example, began a vigorous campaign in 1929 to "land a factory." But they were whipsawed by outside firms that used the competition to demand outrageous bonuses, free land and buildings, and large tax concessions, and that then chose to pursue even better deals elsewhere. Even factories that had been attracted earlier in the twenties soon closed their doors, leaving communities in bonded indebtedness for the buildings they had previously donated to attract the industry. Many other towns in other parts of the country found themselves in similar straits, unable to counter locally the national trends draining their economic resources.[2]

With their attempts at economic development halted by hard times, many clubs tried, through exhortation and publicity, to overcome what they termed a "crisis in consumer confidence." In these early years of economic difficulty, club members still found convincing the theory that the Depression existed largely in the minds of the people, and they worked hard to renew optimism, boost spending, and thus increase prosperity. This interpretation of the downturn provided the core of the conservative critique of the New Deal. If government would act positively to boost consumer confidence and would quit meddling in the economy, then the natural recovery power of the business cycle would reassert itself.[3] For club members, the appeal of the confidence thesis was as much methodological as it was ideological. Arousing public sentiment was a central technique of the service ethic in the twenties, and the clubs sought to meet the crisis with familiar methods.

Thus clubs attempted to "bust the buyer's strike" and encourage spending through slogans and campaigns. Clubs initiated the spending of "hot dollars," checks purposely circulated quickly through club businesses to set an example for the "hoarding consumer." The Lions sponsored "Business Confidence Week"—"a campaign of optimism . . . to assist in relieving the minds of people." Kiwanis clubs put up billboards proclaiming "The Buy Way is the high-way to prosperity" and "Purchases are the minutemen of business." At least twenty clubs ritualistically killed off "Mr. D. Pression" and replaced him with "young man Prosperity." These solidarity campaigns might have temporarily raised morale, but they were of course pathetically ineffective as Depression remedies. Their failure left the clubs floundering, just like President Hoover—the most visible champion of local voluntarism—both proclaiming "prosperity around the corner."[4]

Nevertheless, club businessmen still possessed significant local clout, and they could act to salvage some local business institutions. In a response to a panicked run on all town banks at the beginning of 1932, the mayor of Urbana, Illinois, declared the banks closed. Urbana Rotarians called together all the town's businessmen, an event which the Urbana *Daily Courier* called "the greatest of all gatherings that ever assembled under an Urbana roof." "Today is the end of doubt in Urbana; the New and Better Day begins tommorrow; our banks shall live," the assembly declared. In addition to this vote of confidence, all business organizations except grocery stores and drugstores, transportation and utility agencies, and newspaper offices closed for a week in order to allow banks time to reorder their finances. This hiatus was apparently successful in restoring confidence, and most of Urbana's banks were saved.[5]

Town leaders who had been more concerned in the twenties with the development of the business community than with the circumstances of local labor now found themselves pleading for workers' support. The president of the Jacksonville, Illinois, Rotary club successfully appealed to striking workers at a local textile mill to return to work and thus helped reopen the plant. Similar persuasion was used by the business leaders of Aurora. After a run on the Bank of Aurora, a five-day holiday was declared by the mayor. The combined service clubs and other civic organizations then "organized the workers of the community in a confidence campaign." Workers were urged to sign cards pledging that they would not withdraw their money from the bank "except where it was needed" and that under no circumstances would they withdraw more than 10 percent of their savings. This action "saved the banking institutions of the city."[6]

Such appeals for cooperation could not, in the long term, preserve the economic health of the community, nor could they satisfy the demands of the suffering. Aurora was just one of many industrial towns that experienced a series of crippling strikes during the thirties. Club members' attitudes toward labor, which had been sweetened by the prosperity of the twenties and by club leaders urging the "stewardship of business" became less tolerant as workers demanded a fairer share of limited resources.

Organizational Responses

Before club businessmen could concern themselves with labor, however, they had to first save their own organizations. As the Depression deepened, club leaders expressed alarm as their membership rapidly dropped— Rotary, from 124,000 in 1930 to 102,948 in 1934; Kiwanis, from 102,150 to 74,577 in the same period; and Lions, from 80,456 to 75,725. In these early years of the Depression, with members reeling from the continuing economic slide, club dues seemed an extravagance. Hardship also brought business tensions out into the open. The Dixon, Illinois, Kiwanis club suspended membership in 1933 when a group of members quarreled with four representatives of utilities companies. Although the immediate cause was a feeling among the local businessmen that the utility representatives were flaunting their continued prosperity, traditional hostility between business and public service companies undoubtedly shaped the conflict.[7]

Declining membership rolls as a result of financial hardship and the collapse of clubs because of personal conflicts could be dismissed as unavoidable difficulties, beyond club control. But club leaders in the twenties had witnessed nothing but continuous expansion, and they now wondered if their clubs were on the right course. Articles that asserted "Lions club an essential institution, a tower of strength," or "Kiwanis exists for times such as this" sounded a cheery note that rang false even for the ever-optimistic club journals. More applicable to the situation at hand were sober articles and speeches discussing the "maturity" of the service club movement. Like the decade of the twenties (which club members, just two years after its close, spoke of as a "wild" and "youthful" time), the early Rotary, wrote Rotarian Edgar G. Dondria in 1931, "developed much that was trivial and childish." The next quarter-of-a-century "will determine whether it is to survive or go the way of transient and empty fads." And the attendees at the 1932 Kiwanis convention heard Wallace Austin's ironic reminder: "Surely we all realize that a long waiting list of desirable Kiwanis material as well as groups of men clamoring for Kiwanis charters are as remote as banks that insist on loaning you money to invest in the stock market." Membership had to be actively recruited.[8]

Although widespread concern over actual survival decreased soon after 1932, club leaders no longer put so much emphasis on classification as a limit on membership recruiting. Almost as soon as losses became apparent, in 1930, Rotary followed the Kiwanis and Lions clubs in loosening membership restrictions, allowing, in effect, more than one member in each line of business. In large part, this rules change and other subsequent liberalizations simply gave official sanction to what local clubs commonly practiced. But it also meant that the importance of classification to the community status of the club would no longer be the theme of convention speeches. Membership expansion, always an important concern, became an overriding theme of club policy, and it provided one of the dynamics for suburbanization and the foreign involvement of the clubs, which were important during the thirties and after.[9]

These new efforts, along with the nation's slow emergence from the depths of the Depression, brought a gradual upturn in membership by 1935, and the number of members would rise even beyond their peak 1920s levels by 1940. This growth, and the fact that even members in desperate straits continued to meet, attest to the groups' appeal. If they could afford the dues (and even if they could not—a number of clubs suspended dues collections for several years), businessmen found solace in an ever-optimistic club camaraderie. Herrin, Illinois, "has suffered extremely, but they are undaunted," a Rotary district governor reported of the coal-mining town's Rotary club. The town businessmen "seemed impervious in the face of difficulty and as if refusing to recognize the existence of such a thing. They take a deep interest in Rotary, sing lustily and go on their way as though they enjoyed the most prosperous time in their life."[10] Clubs lost resources through bank failures, plant closings, and, in at least one case, a treasurer absconding with funds, yet they refused to cease operation. The Kingman, Arizona, Lions club, for example, lost its deposits three times in three different banks and still "did not say die."

Judging from Rotary field secretary reports, the clubs that did well before the Depression continued to do so, while the weaker small-town clubs, in mining or poor agricultural districts, suffered the most.[11] On the whole, remarkably few clubs gave up their charters—within Rotary, fewer than fifty collapsed completely during the entire decade—and by the late thirties, club growth had resumed its previously rapid pace.

As new imperatives for growth began to assert themselves at club head-quarters, complaints from already established smaller clubs increased. Much of the local concern was, understandably in these lean years, di-rected at the percentage of dues going to the national organization. The Macomb, Illinois, Rotary club expressed a common concern when it wrote that the headquarters was providing "little help to clubs in smaller com-munities with little money to spend on programs." The Macomb secretary felt efforts should be made to "maintain what we have and in education of present membership rather than drive for more clubs and more member-ship."[12]

In its new form, expansion required further organization and additional bureaucratic procedures. For Rotary, increases in the number of clubs brought the redistricting of clubs into new administrative units. Chartering new clubs required a variety of signatures and paperwork from existing clubs nearby. The process became too much for one California district gov-ernor. "Rotarians in this neck of the woods are strong for the advancement of Rotary, not the hindrance of it thru a lot of red tape and useless legal folderol," he wrote the club secretariat.[13] Flashes of irritation such as these signified not a deep discontent with Rotary but a continuing distaste for centralized organization, which became clearly evident in club attitudes to the New Deal.

The Failure of Local Relief

The tenacity of local clubs demonstrated that members continued to feel the necessity of civic spirit: club participation in ceremonial observances, community improvement, and assistance to the local chamber of commerce did not falter. On the other hand, although *Kiwanis Activities* did report a tripling of "aid to the needy," clubs generally found themselves over-whelmed by the extraordinary demands of the Depression. Some clubs did make efforts to relieve Depression hardship. As reported in club maga-zines, the Easton, Pennsylvania, and Maywood, Illinois, Rotary clubs donated land and seed for "community gardens"; the South Bend, Indiana, Rotary club and the Portland, Oregon, Lions clubs harvested vegetables rotting in the fields and turned them into soup for the hungry; the Newton, Kansas, Rotary club gathered old shoes and gave them to the unemployed; the service clubs of Dallas, Texas, united in placing "penny jars" in local retail businesses and were able to divert "hundreds of dollars" in pennies to relief.[14] But these were exceptions. More characteristic were clubs like those of Muncie, Indiana, harshly described by the Lynds in their follow-up study published in 1937, *Middletown in Transition*. During the Depres-sion, the Lynds observed, the service clubs "continued to meet and to listen to speeches, but they have not as organizations shared in any concerted way in the solution of the city's urgent civic problems."[15]

Like many local service organizations during the twenties, the clubs hesitated to institute programs that interfered with business practices. Only a few clubs actually attempted to ease unemployment. For example, representatives of the Washington, D.C., Kiwanis, Lions, Optimists, and Rotary clubs formed a joint committee on unemployment to "furnish employment to one or more persons for work outside the ordinary routine." While it is doubtful that club members as small businessmen could have made a dent in local unemployment even if they had been so inclined, old shoes and pennies hardly constituted a significant response to the Depression. With their community and vocational service proving so inadequate, it seems that the clubs contributed to Depression relief the same way they contributed to the pressures of prosperity—by satisfying the small businessman's need for fellowship and his impulse to express civic spirit.

Of course, the inadequate relief response of service clubs illustrates only a small part of the total failure of local resources in the early years of the Depression. Historical studies of even the more prosperous and better organized cities point to the woeful limitations of voluntary relief efforts.[16] Even though a local community could hardly be expected to solve the Depression problem, the magnitude of suffering makes inexcusable the absence in many communities of any public mechanisms for relief. Part of the trouble, then, lay in patterns established in earlier decades. Throughout the twenties methods of unsystematic charity similar to service club activities prevailed in most communities. Emergencies brought quick response and volunteers eager to serve, but like that "drowsy giant," the Red Cross, the altruistic public could only be roused by "fire, sword, storm and flood."[17] Newly professionalized social workers discouraged volunteer participation but lacked the resources to conduct their work without government aid. As a result, government spending for relief, as meager as it was, exceeded private charity by a ratio of three to one—despite the broad claims of local charitable agencies. With no tradition of systematic charitable relief other than the community chest—a vehicle existing as much for businessmen's convenience as for its philanthropic effectiveness—little wonder that emergency local relief efforts collapsed so quickly.[18]

Aware of the responsibilities of service, club members could not be insensitive to the troubles around them. In the twenties, when confronted with a temporary emergency, clubs gave generously to social agencies equipped to deal with the crisis such as flood relief committees, the Red Cross, the Salvation Army. Unfortunately, when faced with sustained hardship, the clubs found it easier to pursue more routine activities. By 1937, when the Lions listed their cumulative club activities for the past year, 4,600 of the 28,000 projects listed were classified under "health and welfare" as opposed to 14,000 for community work such as road repair, parades, sports leagues, and city beautification. The difference in proportion is roughly comparable to that for the projects listed ten years earlier, when approximately 800 of the 3,600 projects listed involved social welfare. Only a very small percentage of these activities, in the thirties as well as the twenties, involved sustained relief. A comparison of Kiwanis activities in 1925 and in 1936 reveals the same result.[19] Clubs, as sociable organizations, did not normally function as social welfare committees. Instead, they talked of their responsibility to the local chapters of social service agencies. In the thirties, however, these agencies failed to meet the challenge, government took over many of those emergency duties, and the clubs bowed out.

Clubs and the New Deal: Resistance

Since club activities, from the outset, displayed a desire to protect the integrity of local community, the government's adoption of goals the clubs might have unanimously supported had they been privately sponsored created a deep ambivalence in the clubs' approach to the New Deal. Many club members shared with other Americans a distrust of government encroachment, as representative of a general trend toward centralization and consolidation.[20] After an initial welcome spurred by desperation, these businessmen soon turned against most New Deal programs.

This pattern prevailed in members' reaction to the centerpiece of the early New Deal, the National Recovery Administration (NRA). Clubs approved of President Roosevelt's appeals for spirit and unity, and they played a vigorous role in the "Blue Eagle" parades and sticker campaigns. Inspired to "do their part," members sent in songs to the *Rotarian*, such as this one, sung to the tune of "R-O-T-A-R-Y, that Spells Rotary": "NRA, that's the way, Roosevelt cleared the track / NRA, that's the way, Good times are coming back. / Each firm will sign, and then live true, the things set out in code to do / NRA, that's the way, Good times are coming back."[21] Rotarians in particular were well disposed toward the NRA in its early stages; since the twenties, leaders of Rotary's vocational service program had advocated business cooperation and the writing of ethical business codes, and club spokesmen saw the NRA as a legislative endorsement of their program. Favorable editorials and articles about the NRA ran monthly in the *Rotarian* from late 1933 and early 1934. "It stamps with approval the policy of industries that operate on the principle that business was made to serve men," noted one. "It constitutes the greatest single effort ever undertaken to bring spiritual values into effective daily use," argued another.[22]

Despite this interpretation of the NRA as reinforcing the principles of service, disenchantment occurred rapidly when the act failed to bring quick recovery. The *Rotarian* soon began receiving letters complaining that the magazine was "not truly representing the feeling of many Rotarians in its attitude" toward the NRA. The Rotarian president of Holgate Brothers, manufacturers of brush handles, argued that the bill "penalized severely the small town and small industry" with its regulations designed for big industries. Other letter writers agreed that the act was "forcing small business to the wall" by requiring it to meet codes designed for and by large businesses. Perhaps due to this negative response, articles favorable to the NRA and the New Deal appeared less and less frequently in the *Rotarian* as the year 1934 wore on. In September 1934 Rotary International discharged the NRA advisory committee it had set up in an early flush of enthusiasm for the act. In the same year, Lion founder and secretary Melvin Jones, who had never set up such a committee, blamed the increased staff and higher wages required by the NRA for his organization's budget deficit.[23]

William E. Leuchtenburg argues that contemporary commentators exaggerated the extent to which the NRA hurt small business. The small businessman's main grievance, he believes, was that government ended his exploitation of labor.[24] Club members' discussion of the topic, however, reveals more was involved than resentment of labor's wage demands. Above all, the New Deal heightened members' sense of encroaching bureaucracy. Past Rotary director Raymond Knoeppel lamented before the 1934 Rotary convention "the standardization, the regimentation, which we find today—bringing about standardized opportunity." The editor of the Rockford *Kiwanis News* jokingly wrote in the newsletter that "the statements made herein have been filed with the Federal Trade Commission and the Securities and Exchange Commission." He went on to say, "I immediately deny, disclaim and disavow any regulation by Commissions, Boards, Bureaus or any Alphabetical Agencies under the shining sun—so help me huey."[25]

Officials in the same northern Illinois Kiwanis district as Rockford vainly attempted to argue that federal programs provided opportunities for increased club influence. A newsletter told club secretaries in 1935 that "the government is preparing to spend millions of dollars in local P.W.A. projects and it is apparent to your district officers that Kiwanis should in a big way regulate the expenditures of these local funds." These official urgings apparently carried little weight, however, as the "Illinois Emergency Relief Commission has set up a department of community cooperation and no community in Kiwanis is taking active part in this program." Despite the New Deal's potential for generating local benefits, the majority of club members in northern Illinois and elsewhere were reluctant to be a party to intervention in their communities.

Clubs and the New Deal: Accommodation

Whether the clubs liked it or not, they could not reject the New Deal entirely, because federal intrusions into local life brought necessary funds into their economically strapped cities and towns. One agency, the Civilian Conservation Corps (CCC), received universal approbation among the clubs, partly because of its local benefits and partly because of its affinities with the clubs' own boy's work. CCC camps, placed away from morally enervating urban influences, provided an outlet for youthful energies similar to recreational summer campgrounds, a popular club project. And camp discipline, suggestive of the civilian military training often advocated by the service clubs, seemed just the character builder needed to protect troubled youth from dangerous propaganda. Finally, unlike the NRA (or, later, the WPA), the CCC did not attempt to interfere with business practices or stir the adult labor pool. Since the camps brought new revenue, jobs, and facilities into the community, service clubs and local chambers of commerce fought to obtain them, and they strenuously protested when they were removed. The CCC was the one New Deal agency that appeared with relative frequency in local club service activity reports.[26]

In general, the mix of big-city and small-town professionals and educators with varieties of small businessmen precluded a uniform national opinion on all New Deal measures. Rotary, for example, contributed members to the Liberty League as well as administrators to the New Deal. Among the latter were Rotary International's president in 1934 and a future U.S. senator, Clinton P. Anderson, who remained an active force in Rotary affairs at the same time he helped run several New Deal agencies in New Mexico.[27]

Kiwanian E. E. Embree of De Kalb, Illinois, was also one who saw federal programs not as a threat but as an opportunity for community progress. Placed in charge of the local Civil Works Administration (CWA), Embree made no distinction between his agency work and his other civic service. He defended with a booster's pride the local accomplishments of the CWA and accused complaining conservatives of being "knockers." "Every community has at least one person who takes an attitude contrary to prevailing programs and policies," he wrote of a fellow businessman's standard criticism of the laziness and inefficiency of workers employed by the government. Community development was community development, whether spawned by federal benefits or private enterprise.[28]

For Embree, federal aid boosted the community; for other club members, New Deal programs represented a loss of business independence and local control. Even those in the clubs who opposed federal interference, however, could not reject all of the major premises of government assistance, since New Deal relief programs paid homage to the traditional values of work and responsibility. Furthermore, the values of expertise and efficiency that governed New Deal operations appeared prominently in club proposals.[29]

Overall, club members' most strident objections to many New Deal programs dissolved into griping about "swollen taxes" and "inefficiency of government at the local level." When club spokesmen complained about government interference in business, an element of self-blame surfaced. "Even if this is socialistic, we had it coming to us," said Rotarian Cornelius Garretson, summing up a 1933 convention discussion of the New Deal. John McDowall told the 1936 Kiwanis convention that "if every businessman in his country lived up to the high precepts and principles of Kiwanis, there never would have been any occasion for the NRA." Clubs should not be too quick to complain of "government interference," another speaker reminded the convention, when their "municipalities were the first to call upon the U.S. government in time of need."[30]

No matter how they felt about Roosevelt and his policies, then, clubs shied away from vigorous political protest. In this tendency, the clubs reflected perfectly the apolitical climate of middle-class culture during the decade, which, in the face of apparent institutional breakdown, sought security, order, and consensus. Even the New Deal itself, as Alan Lawson has noted, took on the character of a cultural movement, stressing the collective strength of the "American Way," rather than divisive political partisanship. With government encouraging communitarian values, and with a feeling that security lay in the collective instead of the individual, service clubs, stressing cooperation, could thrive. Ironically, then, it appears service clubs, which attracted businessmen rallying against government intrusion into local affairs, also prospered because of an associative climate fostered by government influence. Thus the New Deal, the bane of many club members, helped boost club growth.[31]

Clubs and Consensus

Despite their complaining, the accommodation of small businessmen and service clubs to the New Deal reveals the role clubs played in reinforcing political and cultural consensus. In the strain of the Depression, a call for consensus was not a foregone conclusion, even in club life. With a triumvirate of oppressive bureaucracies—big government, big business, and, late in the decade, big labor—abetting a continuing economic crisis, club members might have instead formulated a cohesive oppositional ideology based on their position as "forgotten men." But while club members occasionally expressed their grievances in such a fashion—with government and labor bearing the brunt of their criticism—the club atmosphere of cooperation discouraged politicization.

Club members became more conscious than ever during the Depression that their membership represented what a Kiwanian called "middle-class business and professional life, the very grass roots of the capitalist system." A 1934 article in the *Rotarian* spoke of the independent middle class "melting away before our very eyes." The New Deal, Kiwanian district governor Clark Clement felt in 1934, was only hastening "the replacement of small business and professional men by the extension of great industrial enterprises." The image of club members as part of a forgotten middle class appeared more frequently in club rhetoric as the decade proceeded. The 1938 Kiwanis convention listened to club member Roy Smith describe the "first breadline in America . . . during the Republican Administration, when bankers and corporation presidents lined up in front of the RFC [Reconstruction Finance Corporation] tellers' windows." At the same convention, Senator Burton Wheeler talked of corporate control producing an "economic system much more susceptible to government domination." [32]

But only infrequently did club members express resentment toward big business. In part this was because of small business aspirations—many club members worked continually for expansion of their own businesses. Their entrepreneurial dream, to join the ranks of the large firms, muted one possible line of social criticism, that opposing big business domination. The proclamations of the 1938 Conference of Small Businessmen in Washington, D.C., revealed that, while quite conscious of their differences, small businessmen felt a strong identity with big businessmen. [33]

Furthermore, the contribution of corporations to local economies and the participation of corporate representatives in local institutions such as service clubs encouraged a sense of common enterprise. When threatened with federal and state tax legislation like the Robinson-Patman Act of 1937, chain stores sent representatives to present their case to local clubs.

This local lobbying paid dividends by disarming club hostility and guaranteed that members' distrust of federal regulation prevailed over their concern about outside competition. Early in the decade a favorable article on chain stores in the *Rotarian* drew several pages' worth of angry letters. But by the later thirties other pieces treated the anti–chain store Robinson-Patman Act with indifference, and the act received no attention at club conventions. Roger Babson's 1938 article in the *Rotarian* arguing that "little business will never come back by trying to handicap big business" met with broad approval.[34]

In contrast to their response to big business, club members did express their hostility to organized labor, where a more obvious clash of interests prevailed. Even more, the apparent success of "big unionism" threatened to disrupt community consensus. It appeared to club members that the big unions represented another large bureaucracy undermining local business autonomy.

The clubs' narrow-minded attitude toward unions was completely predictable, given the long history of business hostility toward unionization. Yet club members' interpretation of 1930s unionism accurately characterized its bureaucratic thrust. Labor itself experienced broad-based industrial unionism and the encouragement of the New Deal as an additional intrusion of bureaucracy. Of course, for many within the working class that bureaucracy represented a chance for progress. It allowed a mediating of ethnic hostilities and promoted a class solidarity that enabled them to win significant concessions from employers. Large organizations helped unify and politicize the working class.[35] The small businessmen in Rotary, Kiwanis, and Lions saw instead just another outside threat to their interests.

Speeches at Rotary and Kiwanis conventions in the thirties continued to call for a harmony with the employee as part of "vocational service." They continued to champion a friendly paternalism, which seemed to have satisfied workers in the twenties. That such vocational service was failing now could only be due to the interference of "international unionism" and the "politicians." By the late thirties club members could read articles in the *Kiwanian* that decried the influence that big government had given big labor, "greater in power than monopolies of trade and commerce ever dared to be." Rotarians who attended the 1939 convention vigorously applauded Cornelius Garretson as he lamented that "government with the labor leaders seem to have succeeded in driving a wedge in between the employer and his employee," but, he warned labor, that "if in this country we keep drifting on the way we have been doing, we will have no labor organizations. We will have a government that will dictate to business, and we will become only a part of the machine."[36]

Despite the occasional stridency of the clubs' response to unionism and the perceived threat of a dictatorial government machine, however, few club members advocated political action, and, indeed, the clubs continued to stress fellowship as a remedy to organization-bred antagonism. At the same convention at which Rotarians listened approvingly to the railing of Garretson, other Rotarians proposed a remedy—invite union representatives to enjoy the fellowship and forum of a Rotary meeting and, through personal contact, overcome the hostility bred by despair, confusion, and outsiders.[37]

Thus, in sharp contrast to the politicizing effect that the further advance of organization had on workers, local businessmen responded to the incursions of labor and government with attempts to reinforce consensus through their clubs. This contrast comes not just from the dramatically different circumstances of club businessmen and labor; it also displays the values at the center of club life. From the beginning of the club movement, the members had adopted cooperation, paternalism, and stewardship as a defense of their status and community. Now as economic hardship and continued bureaucratic encroachment further undermined their occupational standing, they did not suddenly turn to confrontation, but rather sought to reinforce social cohesion. For club members, preserving consensus in the community and the nation might not remedy already-lost authority, but it could prevent further upheavals and preserve what influence remained.

Therefore Kiwanis International secretary Fred Parker urged the clubs to take a more active role in "molding public affairs," even if that meant that members had to temporarily "endanger their business profit [and] their professional standing." In the *Rotarian,* Stephen Bolles described local clubs' reluctance to engage in controversial public issues as "the Oregon Boot on the Service Club." "We have too many clubs that are afraid of topics," he wrote.[38] Calls for a more prominent role in public affairs, however, did not mean that leaders sought to transform the club's function in the community. As quickly became clear, when Rotary, Kiwanis, and Lions leaders talked of moving into the discussion of controversial issues, they meant that clubs should act to defuse controversy and assert their leadership just as they had in the twenties, by laying grounds for compromise and consensus.

To set an example for local clubs, in the early thirties the *Rotarian* began a series of impartially presented monthly debates on topics such as socialism, the death penalty, gun control, and public health insurance. For this series, the editors solicited articles from Rotary antagonists, among them H. L. Mencken, Clarence Darrow, and Norman Thomas. This change in editorial policy made interesting reading. Compared to the other clubs' magazines, the *Rotarian* attracted by far the most thoughtful analysis of both in-house and worldwide events. But, except for letters predictably denouncing the more unconventional position in each debate—socialization of medicine and the elimination of the death penalty, for example—the monthly features produced little discernible response at the local level.

Along the same lines as the Rotarian monthly debates, Kiwanis later in the decade adopted a policy of promoting "open forums" for the discussion of civic issues. Here too the club was to serve as impartial arbiter, a "clearinghouse on public affairs" to the "thousands of fine Americans who are seeking for authoritative information on the perplexing problems and issues of the present." The Lions also jumped on the discussion platform by sponsoring "Socratic League Debates" designed to "stimulate thought and create open discussion." [39]

In encouraging local clubs to enter openly into the debate on public policy, leaders saw clubs leading the way out of crisis—and clearing the air of political bitterness—by providing a platform for voicing diverse opinion. To accomplish this goal, however, they turned, as they always had, not to a possibly partisan citizenry but rather to the "scientific" analysis of the expert. Sponsoring public debates among professors, economists, and public administrators, the clubs revealed that their faith in "objective" sociological expertise remained unshaken despite the economic crisis. The board of directors of the Lions illustrated this faith when, in announcing the formation of a "Committee on Economic Guidance," they also expressed doubt that "a permanent and definite plan of procedure can come from the office-holding class; nor does it appear likely that the business world can work out its own salvation." Therefore the board turned to fifty leading economists and political scientists to frame a plan for the control of business cycles.

While the Lions sought business advice, the Rotary Club of Chicago went one step further and commissioned a study of themselves by the University of Chicago sociology department. The resulting relatively critical study, *Rotary?*, was then commended to "all thoughtful Rotarians." [40] Conservative club members might inveigh against the policies of the "brain trust," but they shared the assumptions that led to its formation.

By placing the burden of debate on the shoulders of the expert, clubs could play a vital role in community reconstruction without promoting dreaded "isms." This kind of forum could defuse dissent and build a larger consensus. Public participation in open—yet harmless—debate would demonstrate the general strength of the democratic process and, club spokesmen hoped, produce a wider adherence to democratic values. Rotarians read about Des Moines, Iowa, a "city without a bogey," where citizens could sleep soundly, undisturbed by the "goblins of isms invoked from street corner soapboxes" because they met, with the help of Rotary, to talk things over in the "old New England town hall manner."[41]

The political disposition of the nation's middle-class youth particularly concerned club members. Whereas in the twenties the clubs concentrated on the younger boy, attempting to build his character in order to enable him to withstand the temptations of big-city life, now the clubs' interest shifted to older boys, "coming home from college" and unable to find jobs, "subsequently becoming a fertile field for the inculcation of all sorts of ideas and ideals contrary to our own established order." Kiwanis in the twenties listened to convention speeches calling for a "square deal for the crippled child"; in the thirties the favored topic in youth work was "the citizen of tomorrow." The Philadelphia Rotary Club was one of several that held a "Training Course in Citizenship" for young men, seeking to teach future leaders the value of "enlightened political activity." Club members thus sought to dissuade those closest to them, family members and other middle-class youth, from adopting destructive political tendencies and repudiating the members' own paternal influence.[42]

Although assuring themselves that members "were broad-gauged men who can discuss debatable questions without heat and ill temper," the clubs expressed such an exaggerated fear of "controversy" that the vision of the club as a platform for public policy formation never really materialized. Only some two hundred Kiwanis clubs attempted forums in 1937, and even fewer Rotary or Lions clubs did so. At least one club—the Cedar Rapids Rotary Club—reported reluctance to continue because of public impressions of the speakers as "radicals."[43] Local club behavior in the thirties suggests an attempt to avoid such a shift in course. Since political and economic controversy could easily evolve into clashes of personality, to serve as a forum for debates risked disrupting the surface conviviality upon which club fellowship depended. The clubs' concern for community consensus appears even in this failure to play a more broad-based politically prominent role.

In retrospect, the clubs' apolitical fellowship appears as an important, if socially conservative, achievement. Gathering local businessmen, corporate representatives, and even a few participants in New Deal agencies in an atmosphere of friendly cooperation, clubs helped moderate middle-class resentment of difficult circumstances. Reflecting members' genuine ambivalence about social and political change, club fellowship also demonstrates why few members joined an insurgency from the far right. In contrast to their counterparts in continental Europe, who expressed class antagonism in political upheaval, clubs in the United States sought refuge in consensus.[44]

On the other hand, the clubs' emphasis on consensus—on supporting an economic and political order that continued to undermine their local interests—reveals a declining sense of unique community experience and an increasing alignment with a corporate-influenced mass culture. Clubs no longer saw themselves merely as local boosters; now they were bulwarks of the American Way.

From Boosting to Adjustment

One additional development helped to produce a consensus in club life and to integrate members more completely into national society. As the number of clubs began once again to rise rapidly in the late 1930s, growth increasingly took clubs into suburban, primarily residential communities. Although the majority of the clubs remained in communities with populations under ten thousand, 60 percent of clubs founded after 1934 lay in metropolitan districts, as defined by the 1940 census. Clubs in areas such as Chicago and Los Angeles underwent multiplication by division; by 1938 the Los Angeles metropolitan area had more than twenty Rotary clubs in close proximity to one another.[45]

For these clubs, which were based on residential divisions, community spirit did not inhere primarily in balancing interdependent, at times competing, business interests. Instead it depended on adjusting personal concerns and assuring the psychological solidarity of neighbors. Similarly, in this type of community personal definition in terms of occupation became less important than a life-style of consumption and leisure.

As the decade proceeded, clubs placed more and more emphasis on conformity. In 1936 Kiwanis International began pursuing an objective to "support churches in their spiritual aims." Members were to "stand by churches in promotion of special days" such as Loyalty Day and Easter, and they were to see that "every man woman and child goes to church some day." Little difference existed between this campaign and the "Buy your hometown products" days, except here the pressures were applied more to conform in appearances rather than spend money to support local merchants.[46]

Similarly, a change in emphasis occurred in the clubs' educational work. Their interest shifted from preadolescent boys to high-school and college-age youth, and club concerns in education went from playgrounds to extra-curricular school programs. During times when school budgets were often the first public expense trimmed, club members defended "fads and frills" such as music, dramatics, and vocational training as essential to a complete education. The 1935 Kiwanis club secretary described the unnecessary slaughter of hogs as nothing "compared to the unnecessary slaughter of the finest development of our youth which has resulted from so-called economy in public education." In 1933 the *Rotarian* ran a debate between H. L. Mencken and John Dewey, "Shall We Abolish School Frills?." Mencken argued the affirmative, that the "new pedagogy places too much stress upon play activities and too little upon the immemorial fundamentals," and Dewey responded that "frills are a legitimate and practical response to social conditions and needs." In the reader reaction published for months after the article, sentiment ran overwhelmingly in favor of Dewey, largely on the grounds that for the coming generation, "a complex age such as we have now" requires "instruction in public health, music, art, or physical education at the public expense."[47]

In their study of public schools during the Depression, Tyack, Lowe, and Hansot argue that sentiment supporting Dewey's philosophy did not necessarily reflect realities in local school districts. Many communities paid lip service to progressivism in public education, but often that meant only, as in Middletown, new courses like business English and a small guidance program. The determining factor in the adoption of new educational techniques remained the wealth of the school district and the homogeneity of its students. Districts in rural or industrial areas, the ones that needed money most during the twenties, were also the hardest hit during the Depression.[48]

Whether or not club members translated their rhetorical defense of progressive education into financial terms probably also depended on local conditions. What their verbal support of new programs definitely demonstrated was a new sensitivity to psychological adjustment, particularly among youth, but also among the citizenry as a whole. The club conception of guidance programs for youth in the thirties went beyond the vocational counseling the clubs pursued in the twenties to begin to meet the boy's emotional and psychological needs. Expressing a concern that a disenchanted youth might not properly integrate into the social order, articles in club magazines described the "new teacher" as "well trained in psychology, sociology, in health. Many of us would rather have a teacher who isn't an expert in his subject but is an expert in dealing with boys and girls." Articles displayed a new consciousness of the psychological importance of adolescence, recognizing the "powerful influence of developing sex-interest." Convention discussion cited the lack of personal counseling as one of the causes of juvenile delinquency. Club members had always subscribed to environmentalism in their youth work, believing "there are no bad boys, only good boys in bad circumstances." Now, instead of changing community conditions to better serve youth, members proposed to train youth to better adapt to society.[49]

The supposed insights of popularized psychology abounded in club magazine articles. Rotarian Amos Squire wrote on the "Psychology of Fellowship," explaining Rotary's appeal in terms of the "so-called gregarious drive" and "the drive of the desire for approval." Kiwanian Clyde Hissong defined "true Freedom" in terms of the "individual's adjustment to his environment." Personality tests replaced community surveys as evaluative tools, with members being encouraged to "see yourself as others (the customer, the boss, the family) see you."[50] As Warren Susman notes in a penetrating analysis of the middle-class culture of the thirties, this kind of psychologizing attempted to place responsibility on the individual—who could achieve success by self-adjustment—rather than suggesting the necessity of larger social reform. Linked with the withdrawal from ideology, it illustrated again the profoundly conservative trends present in the thirties.[51]

Yet the new psychological emphasis also shows the clubs themselves adjusting to new conditions. Discussions of "the promise of the new leisure" became more frequent as the decade proceeded—perhaps in response to the economic slowdown, which was forcing a "new leisure" on thousands of businessmen, perhaps in response to the Social Security Act and as an encouragement for older club members to retire. But in addition, it reflected the less occupationally oriented role clubs played in suburban locations. "When men are working," Rotarian Billy Phelps told the 1933 convention, "they all look alike. If you want to know anything about individuals you must find out what they do with their leisure time." Leisure thus became an outlet for individual fulfillment and spiritual growth. "Leisure," said Kiwanian Harry Holmes, "means time to pursue our ideals." "Living all your life," to Kiwanian Fred McCallister, meant balancing work and leisure and cultivating consumption "to awaken markets, revive production, create higher standards of living and an increased measure of human happiness."[52]

Thus, as the thirties came to a close, clubs found themselves once again advocating consumption to escape the Depression. Yet this philosophy of consumerism did not just seek to restore the prosperity of the business community, it also stressed the satisfactions of conformity, leisure, and varied schooling. All these elements proved highly compatible with suburban life. By adapting to the thirties' cultural conservatism and the decade's changing communities, clubs had also laid the foundation for growth in the suburbs of the forties and fifties. Club expansion, rapid during the later years of the Depression, would accelerate in postwar America.

Of course, the clubs needed to take only a relatively small step from stressing community cooperation and "boosting, not knocking" to an emphasis on personal "adjustment." To their critics, service clubs seemed from the beginning to deemphasize individual autonomy and work for conformity. But the differences in club style and emphasis between 1920 and 1939 should not be overlooked.

In the twenties club fellowship displayed heightened small business and small community awareness. Club service activities specifically attempted to defend town interests and preserve local business autonomy. But for established clubs, the Depression and the New Deal undermined that autonomy, and the majority of new clubs were organized in communities where local interests seemed less distinct. Although most members remained locally oriented, many of their clubs no longer expressed a sharply defined sense of community.

In the depths of the Depression the very existence of service clubs had appeared threatened. That Rotary, Kiwanis, and Lions left the decade once again growing rapidly showed they still supplied necessary opportunities for business growth, camaraderie, and service. But while the essence of club appeal remained the same, the thrust of club life shifted perceptibly. By the late thirties and into the postwar decades, the emphasis of club leaders lay on integration into a national, and even worldwide, social order. As the vague internationalism increasingly pursued by the clubs demonstrated, the service ethic remained expansive, but its goals became more diffuse.

CHAPTER **6**

Serving the World

Residents of Butler, Pennsylvania, a small city outside of Pittsburgh, probably would not have identified their local tire merchant, Charles Miller, as an ambassador of world peace. Yet in 1927 his photograph appeared on the cover of the *London Sunday Herald* as one of the thousands of Rotarians arriving in Belgium for the International Rotary Convention. Representing thirty-eight countries, the delegates were replacing "hatred between nations with friendship." Miller was taking part in this "world service." He was also embarked with his wife on a rigorous two-week tour of Europe, from Brussels to Paris via Wiesbaden and Venice. It was an experience the Millers would never forget.[1]

The story of the clubs' expansion abroad involves two equally significant aspects of twentieth-century American culture. The first is the impulse of local businessmen like Charles Miller to meet men of differing nationalities and share with them discussions of business and service. This impulse was, in Miller's case, perhaps spawned more by a tourist's curiosity than any idealistic dream of "one world." But as expressed by other men in Rotary, Kiwanis, and Lions, there was also behind this expansionism a belief in the essential unity of human concern and a faith in fellowship's power to overcome conflict. This side of the club's expansionism was founded on the presupposition that all people in all countries conform or should conform to a similar pattern of behavior and values.[2]

Implicit in club overseas growth was an often-provincial assumption that events that concerned American businessmen should concern the world, but also visible was a genuine concern for international understanding. Thus the club members' internationalism paralleled their attitudes toward their community; like their local service, the roots of the clubs' internationalism lay in the consensual ethos of businessmen working for community betterment.

The second aspect of club world growth demonstrates the influence of the American economy and the burgeoning power of multinational corporations based in America. It was this growing influence—and the liberal "corporatist" order that high-level businessmen and makers of American government policy sought to put into place—that laid the groundwork for service clubs outside the United States. Businessmen the world over sought to integrate themselves into the U.S.-based network of trade alliances and financial agreements. Beneath the dignified negotiations of business diplomats, American commercial mass culture flooded into world markets, needing little translation to transform taste and fashion. The more snobbish European cultural arbiters fumed over the Americanizing of European manners, art, and sports and, more often than not, saw the clubs as yet another American incursion—Babbitt overseas. But European and Asian businessmen welcomed service clubs as part of their Americanization and as a door to other American opportunities.[3]

The personal impulse to promote international harmony and consensus and the institutional momentum of American economic expansion were closely linked in U.S. relations with the world. Long before the cold war, businessmen worked to extend the benefits of the American system of capitalist idealism beyond the United States' borders. Club leaders—often calling "internationalism" what is better seen as an attempt to "Americanize"—sought to act as ambassadors of the American dream.[4]

While the success of service clubs abroad illuminated transnational similarities in twentieth-century middle-class culture, variations in club life also demonstrated differences in style and tradition among businessmen of separate countries and revealed the deep conflicts between nations. Unfortunately, their consensual ethos left organization leaders unprepared for this conflict. Struggling to meet the crises of the 1930s, the clubs' international program ultimately suffered from the combined limitations of their service ideal and an organizational timidity that avoided controversy at all costs.

Nevertheless, the clubs' international growth was one of the great successes of the American service organizations, providing a vivid example of Americans' interest in and impact on foreign cultures during a period often characterized as isolationist. Although Rotary was the club that was most active internationally, even Lions and Kiwanis clubs (though their foreign involvement during the twenties and thirties was confined to Canada and Latin America), played up the prestige of international service. Their international programs demonstrated that club preachment could awaken in small-town businessmen an awareness of world citizenship. Eventually international involvement would transform the entire service club movement, creating an organization with a scope and membership far beyond its American origins.

Rotary's Early International Expansion

The first service organization was also the first to charter a club in another country. Canadians who were friends of a Chicago Rotary Club member formed the seventeenth Rotary club in Winnipeg in 1909. Rotary at the time made much of its new international character, but close business and family connections of American club members from the upper border states facilitated northern expansion, and the outlook of Canadian businessmen appeared to differ little from their American counterparts'.[5] More significant international growth occurred later the same year, when Stuart Morrow, a promoter unaffiliated with Rotary, discovered that businessmen in the British Isles would pay to join this new American organization. He quickly formed unauthorized clubs in Belfast, Dublin, Edinburgh, and Glasgow, milking the members for as much of their dues as he could before moving on, often in considerable haste. Meanwhile, Rotary's official representative, Arthur Sheldon, was simultaneously setting up a London branch of "Sheldon's School of Salesmanship" and forming Rotary clubs in England. By 1912, due to the combined efforts of these two hucksters, Rotary could claim ten clubs in the British Isles.[6]

Shortly after, Rotary piggybacked its way into non-English-speaking countries when American businessmen carried the movement south into Cuba, Mexico, Panama, Argentina, and Uruguay and east to the Philippines, China, India, and Japan. Only World War I delayed its further expansion into Europe. Soon after the armistice, as Paul Harris described it, Rotary followed "the dove of peace" to aid in reconstruction of the continent. Businessmen in France, Germany, and Italy, while they did not flock to membership with the enthusiasm of those in the British Isles, nevertheless formed Rotary clubs in nearly all their major cities. As it entered the 1920s, Rotary was truly a worldwide movement.[7]

The international expansion of Rotary owed a great deal to its founder. When he was organizing Rotary, Harris did not plan an international club, but his world travels as a youth had been a crucial formative experience. When the opportunity for worldwide expansion presented itself, he quickly pressed forward, despite early opposition from other influential members. Still, growth such as that fostered by Morrow occurred almost spontaneously, surprising even Harris.[8] Rotary's quick spread around the world demonstrates the degree to which it coincided with the growth of American business's international interests and influence.

Economic connections between England and America, of course, had always been close; but early in the twentieth century the flow of goods out from America aroused in England both fear and a grudging admiration of "the Americanization of the world." In 1901 William T. Stead wrote his often-quoted article describing the "all-American" routine of a British businessman:

> He sits on a Nebraskan swivel chair, before a Michigan roll-top desk, writes his letters on a Syracuse typewriter, signing them with a New York fountain pen, and drying them with a blotting-sheet from New England. The letter copies are put away in files manufactured in Grand Rapids. At lunch time he hastily swallows some cold roast beef that comes from the Mid-West cow, and flavours it with Pittsburgh pickles, followed by a few Delaware tinned peaches, and then soothes his mind with a couple of Virginia cigarettes.

Twenty years later, this same businessman would be enjoying his lunch at a Rotary meeting. When Rotary held its first convention out of America, in Edinburgh, the local press, in the words of C. E. Hewitt, saw the Rotarian "to be coeval with the pole-squatter, the comic-strip buffoon, and the man who propelled a pea-nut from New York to Detroit with the tip of his nose." Yet public ridicule of this American fad did not prevent its increased presence; by the end of the 1920s, there were over four hundred clubs in Great Britain.[9]

In other European countries, where economic connections were less direct, the numbers still testified to a growing cultural influence, with over three hundred clubs on the Continent by the 1930s. Elsewhere the international expansion of Rotary was so closely connected with the widening sphere of American business influence that the first clubs in Brazil, Argentina, Chile, and Peru were all considered "a fine tribute to the American business spirit." In the Middle East and Orient, Rotary emissary Jim Davidson won new clubs by blatantly emphasizing the economic advantage of association with American prosperity—hoping later to convert the clubs to true Rotary principles.[10] One of the nonwestern countries that proved most receptive to Rotary was Japan, which during the first three decades of the twentieth century imported technology and American business techniques to aid its fledgling electronics industry while westernizing its popular culture with movies and baseball.[11] Membership in Rotary meshed nicely with this Americanization.

The Impact of Corporatism

While the growing internationalism of American business served as a vehicle for Rotary expansion, Rotary's internationalism displayed characteristics that historians associate with a philosophy of liberal international development based on expanding economic organizations—a corporatism similar to the economic organization that some big business leaders advocated for the American economy. Many leaders of the American business community placed their faith in voluntary international agreements between business, encouraged but not regulated by friendly governments. If voluntary cooperation succeeded in tempering economic competition, and if nations discarded divisive and wasteful political rivalries, then capitalism could bring about an efficient and peaceful world community. Although not all in government or business shared the corporate vision, America's foreign policy in the 1920s enjoyed a good deal of success following this general direction.[12]

As an international voluntary association, Rotary had many antecedents—most prominently those inspired by missionary Christianity, but also secular organizations like fraternal orders and scholarly societies. Rotary, however, following the reasoning of those advocating corporate economic development, claimed that because businessmen of all countries shared common capitalist concerns, their organization was uniquely placed to foster a broad international understanding. As a 1915 editorial described Rotary's "plans and dreams," if Rotary could unite "a large number of representative businessmen of every nation and every race under the banner of Service," it would thereby ensure "the prevalence of a spirit of International Peace and Good Will." These sentiments were the basis for the "sixth object" of Rotary, to encourage "a world fellowship of business and professional men united in the ideal of service."[13]

Rotarians expressed these sentiments more and more often as American involvement in World War I increased. The prosperity businessmen enjoyed as a result of the conflict heightened their consciousness of international economic interdependence. At the same time, America's position apart from the conflagration gave them a sense of moral superiority, which became inflated with the nation's timely intervention in the war. Postwar leaders of Rotary felt that business transcended national interest and that businessmen—particularly American businessmen—carried the responsibilities of a moral mission to rebuild international order, where politicians had failed. "I earnestly commend the duty of pressing the organization of Rotary clubs into prostrate Europe," President John Poole told the 1919 convention. "Let us help to there unfold the blessings for liberty and peace in the same spirit that brought victory to the world. Any effort that makes for healthy industrial progress is always welcome. . . . And Rotary, standing apart from all hindering alignments, is happily situated to render a great public service."[14]

Rotarians who spoke of the world as "one great interlocking business" and who called for business and professional men to sit down "without kings or congresses" to try "to devise a plan which means safety and permanency" revealed the broad influence of a corporate perspective. In the international sphere, however, just as at home, there were limits to the American Rotarians' associationalism. The Americans were primarily concerned with the sociable aspects of international interaction, and their movement only indirectly aligned itself with the economic tenets of this corporate world order. They couched their calls for economic cooperation in a vague idealism and eschewed direct action. Reluctant to take stands controversial at home, as members of an organization they refused time and again to endorse specific measures like the World Court, an International Board of Arbitration, or the reduction of war debts or tariffs, even though convention discussion and magazine articles indicated a significant amount of support for positive action on all these issues.[15]

This inaction on the part of Americans frustrated the European Rotarians, who often sponsored resolutions proposing a concrete international program. Much of the Europeans' greater interest in this aspect of the Rotary program had to do with their proximity to other nations, but the European Rotary also had its corporate element. Charles S. Maier has contended that Western Europeans, even more than their American counterparts, were moving toward a social order that could be termed corporatist—in which organized social groups exerted their private power at the expense of parliamentary authority. The middle classes, Maier argues, played the primary role in this transformation, turning to corporatism in their search for stability after World War I.[16]

Rotary obviously never became a primary vehicle for this transformation. But the action of Europe's Rotary clubs suggests that Rotary there could align itself, more than was possible in America, with this corporatist tendency. Not only did Europeans place more hope than Americans in Rotary as the basis for international agreements between businessmen, they also demonstrated a greater interest in Rotary's vocational program. In England, for example, British Rotarians listed as service projects the establishment of pension schemes, the revival of apprenticeship, the allocation of profits for staff welfare and sports, and the sponsorship of industrial and workers' councils. In Italy Rotarians became enthusiastic fascists, and in Germany they reached agreements with Hitler. Rotarians everywhere in Europe were more amenable than Americans to welfare capitalism, whatever its political stripe.[17]

Class and Rotary in Europe

This greater accommodation to corporatism demonstrates also a greater willingness among European Rotarians to acknowledge class interest.

Americans neglected the employee relations programs discussed as part of vocational service partly because they felt uncomfortable acknowledging labor and capital as two permanent interest groups. Sample rosters from England, France, and Italy show approximately the same type of business- men as in America, and in their speeches European Rotarians also talk paternalistically of the unity of labor and capital. But European Rotarians expressed much more openly their position in the social structure. In Ger- many and Italy Rotary assumed a more aristocratic tone, adapting itself to the character of the bourgeois elite in those countries. Membership became something of a badge of social distinction. (Members in Italy included the Duke of Aosta, the Duke of the Abruzzi, the Prince of Piedmont, the Count of Turin, and the Prince of Udine, King Victory Emmanuel III.) In England, on the other hand, Rotarians complained of their inability to attract the "big men of their community." According to C. E. Hewitt, as they saw "big bosses negotiate price rings and cartels," Rotarians "were antagonized. The Rotarian's ideal of service above self became more and more the ideal of the small businessman." In America, to be sure, certain elements of Rotary fellowship demonstrated a heightened class awareness, but in these European countries the club served much more openly as a social vehicle for class interest.[18]

Since Americans dominated the leadership of Rotary and set its policies, the frank acknowledgment of class did not alter the structure of European clubs. Nevertheless, the slightly different place Rotary assumed in Euro- pean middle-class life did create an obvious difference in the fellowship at club meetings. In fact, though social affairs could dominate European club life (particularly, it appears, in Italy and France), "fellowship," in the American sense of the word, did not play an important role in European Rotary meetings. By all accounts, the meetings of foreign Rotarians en- couraged little backslapping, no "get-acquainted" stunts, and few practical jokes—in some clubs even first names were rare. At the 1927 conven- tion in Ostend, Belgium, American Rotarians embarrassed their European counterparts when they serenaded King Albert with "he's a jolly good fel- low." By the same token, on a tour of European clubs, Paul Harris was offended when German Rotarians took little notice of his presence at one of their meetings.

The difference was perhaps most dramatically illustrated at the 1921 convention in Edinburgh. Immediately after a speech by Rotarian Alfred Peters of Sheffield, England, recommending dignity in the initiation of members, Rotarian Frank W. Warden of Syracuse, New York, stood up. "The highbrows have had their chance," he called out. "Now its time to loosen up!" and he led the convention in singing "Old MacDonald's Farm."[19]

As noted earlier, informal fellowship was one of Rotary's distinguishing and frequently satirized characteristics in America. American Rotarians defended behavior considered undignified even by the less decorous standards of their country because of the good feelings they felt it created. Yet this most important American trait was the one aspect of Rotary that did not translate successfully to foreign Rotary clubs. Judging from their convention remarks, Rotarians in other countries felt such noisy gregariousness beside the point. The sociability of European clubs either acquired the exclusiveness of aristocratic privilege, or it stressed the practical purposes of middle-class stewardship and the infusion of the spiritual into daily occupational life.

The novelist Thomas Mann, a member of the Dresden Rotary Club during the twenties, was one of several Europeans who eloquently expressed this latter appeal of Rotary. Speaking in 1930 before the Rotary International Conference of Directors, he noted Germany's precarious situation "between two fires"—one on the political right, the other on the left. Rotary suggested itself as part of a middle way: "In the Rotary Club men of all tongues and of all climes have united, men who know well the eternal values in the sphere of the individual, in the sphere of art and culture, men who are determined to defend it against the accusation of materialism— men, however, who are equally determined that they will permit no false romanticism to interfere with their will to serve and to work for a better human organization." [20]

Beside such a grand conception of Rotary's purpose, the glad-handing American club man, with his stunts and sing-alongs, appears pathetically frivolous. Yet it was not necessarily lack of profundity but rather a response to a different social system that accounts for much of the Americans' stress on informal fellowship. Geography and sprawling urban growth shaped an American class structure that differed from its Old World counterpart. The origins of Rotary as a small-town native's response to city life, and its close ties with boosterism in small towns and cities across America, added the concerns of community harmony to class solidarity. If foreign Rotarians saw their clubs primarily as a means of establishing or reinforcing their social position within a more restrictive class structure, then dignity and seriousness of purpose would best assert their standing. On the other hand, American Rotarians, concerned more with tightening the bonds of community, in what they perceived as their open social system, sought a common denominator—unifying affability, without titles or even surnames. [21]

Of course, the American stress on community does not mean a complete lack of class awareness. Given the homogeneity of the communities in which service clubs thrived, class and community feelings were often equivalent. The Americans' class interest remained present, but it was most often expressed in community service projects, activities far less important to European clubs. "Rotary in my country means the same as Rotary in yours—an organization trying to develop in the individual a social consciousness," Rotarian William De Cock Boning of the Netherlands told the 1936 convention. But he went on to note the "marked differences in the character of service." In describing Rotary's middle-class social consciousness, "community spirit" was an Americanism.[22]

The International Service of Kiwanis and Lions

As Rotary learned the lessons of foreign relations in Europe, the other service organizations slowly began to extend their version of community spirit to the international scene. Both Lions and Kiwanis sought the prestige of claiming to be international organizations, and they expanded into Canada shortly after their founding—the Lions even called themselves international before they actually had a club outside of American borders. Yet in the twenties and thirties neither club followed the course of Rotary and aggressively pursued worldwide expansion. Kiwanians considered further international expansion several times during the twenties and thirties but ultimately decided to concentrate on "the frontier of community service." (They reversed their decision in 1959.)

The Lions, usually open to membership expansion of any type, held back from full-scale internationalism in the 1920s—their hesitation perhaps due to the heavy emphasis on Americanization and "Our Nation's Safety" in their domestic program. They did acquire clubs, made up mostly of transplanted Americans, in China, Mexico, and Cuba. In the late thirties, reflecting a nearly faddish concern for Pan-Americanism begun with Roosevelt's good-neighbor policy, they established a foothold in Central America, founding clubs in Panama, Costa Rica, Colombia, and Puerto Rico. The genuine worldwide expansion of Lionism, however, came after World War II.[23]

If the Lions and Kiwanis organizations had merely expressed their reluctance to expand worldwide and then had moved back to local community service, they might have served as isolationist counterexamples to Rotary internationalism. But instead spokesmen made sure to affirm their commitment to world involvement. "A Lions convention is a lesson in world understanding, where you can meet representatives of every nation, race, and creed," claimed a 1926 editorial about the San Francisco convention, which perhaps had an Asian, a sampling of Jews and Catholics, and a few Canadians in attendance. In 1929 the Lions added to their list of objectives, in imitation of Rotary, a pledge "to create and foster a spirit of generous consideration among the peoples of the world through a study of the problems of international relationships from the standpoint of business and professional ethics."[24]

Kiwanis, without such a wide-ranging international objective, went to great lengths to stress their particular internation connection with Canada. Their somewhat strained effort at international service led to the celebration of some unusual symbols. The 1818 Rush-Bagot treaty establishing a peaceful basis for U.S.-Canada relations received a yearly commemorative as "the first great treaty of disarmament." President Harding, perhaps because he died just after he gave a speech on Canadian-American friendship, was memorialized as a man "who blazed new trails in the interest of concord and harmony among nations." And the unarmed border between Canada and the United States became "an object lesson of peace . . . to all the world," a symbol of "the tie that binds more firmly each year, ever-increasing acquaintance and comradeship."[25] Thus Kiwanis and Lions in the twenties and thirties joined Rotary in pursuit of the ideal, if not yet the genuine practice, of international fellowship.

Local Internationalism

Foreign expansion carried prestige and the attraction of the exotic, but American service clubs appeared to pursue international service as an extension of their community spirit. Club spokesmen often discussed the world as if it were "across the backyard fence." "International service is simply to develop between nations the same spirit that operates between neighboring families," wrote William Osborne in the *Rotarian* in 1930. The key to such a spirit, said Kiwanian C. King Woodbridge, was cooperation and trust, born of "world fraternization." As Leland Case put it in the *Rotarian,* international friction would dissolve if "the friendly understanding that unkinks local club problems" was applied to the world movement.[26]

In such a view of world affairs, the problem of war arose through miscommunication, national hostility resulted through ignorance, and peace became a realization of common purpose. "The [international] anarchy is in men's minds," wrote a Rotarian. Lion Frank Miles thought that "the idea of Lionism spread to all the world . . . would make a warless world. Let Lions take the leadership in mobilization of thought for honorable peace." Since essential human nature was everywhere the same, conflict of interests, when examined rationally, disappeared. "That the whole world rides in Fords and laughs at Charlie Chaplin is not without meaning," argued Rotarian George Pope Shannon. If the mere externals of life could all be made uniform, then "the essential human spirit everywhere the same shall hold communion over the earth, unhampered by impertinent local divergences."[27] As a way of facilitating communication, and eliminating "divergences," all service clubs supported the study of Esperanto as an international auxiliary language, so that "language will no longer block peace."[28]

Visible behind the hyperbole that surrounded international service were the same assumptions that motivated clubs' community service projects. Clubs could help unify the world the way they could communities, by creating public sentiment for peace. International problems dissolved into apolitical questions of personality, and sociability became the key to world understanding. Obviously these assumptions made the clubs, as international sociable associations, central to the resolution of world affairs. More significant, however, this outlook gave small businessmen and professionals a rational and comforting way of viewing a tangled world. They could tell themselves, as did Rotary president Will Manier, in 1937, that "the problems of Rotary clubs of Kentucky are the same as the problems of Rotary clubs of Europe."[29]

By reducing world conflict to a local scale, international service not only provided a reassuring familiarity to foreign involvement, it also helped expand the horizon of the local club. Not that international service ever occupied a central place on the local club program. Most clubs shared the dilemma of the Mitchell, Indiana, Rotary club; though they believed themselves "far from provincial in spirit," as a "small club located inland, we seem to not approach the International feature of Rotary with any definite results."[30]

Yet local clubs did find ways at least to acknowledge their membership in an international association. A popular program that was adopted by clubs of all three organizations was to choose a designated sister club and exchange letters, memorabilia, and visiting members. Slightly more ambitious, the Rotary Club of Winnetka, Illinois, in 1930 persuaded the community's high school to allow students in language classes to write letters to new foreign clubs. Combining, as Winnetka did, the themes of youth and international service proved popular. Several Lions clubs during the twenties sponsored children as part of a Near East relief program, while all clubs were eager to treat exchange students to at least a luncheon meeting. One Kiwanis club made a point of inviting every foreign student it encountered to its meetings to discuss peace, for "had we taken in 1917 all the boys and girls of kindergarten age [and] started a program in international peace, today we would have a group of children in the age of twenty to twenty-five years old who would have peace as their foremost thought."

Developing international understanding and goodwill "in the minds of the community at large" also spurred the Rotary club of Nashville, Tennessee, which set up "an Institute of International Understanding"—a several-week program of speeches and discussion.[31]

While these efforts of local clubs must surely be credited with awakening, for at least a short time, the members' international consciousness, most of the activities retained a local orientation. The Princeton, Illinois, club listed as one of its international programs a discussion of the nationalities of members' ancestors. Similarly, the Lincoln, Nebraska, Rotary club's special meeting, "A Night in Bohemia," celebrated local ethnic origins as well as promoting international awareness. Members dressed in authentic costumes, served Czechoslovakian dishes, and sang Czech songs.[32]

This type of contact with foreign cultures allowed local interest to mingle with a type of escapist internationalism. Such meeting programs as "slide shows of Europe," promoted as international service, carried an appeal akin to tourism, briefly exposing members to exotic climes. On the national level, the club magazines often ran National Geographic–style pictorial reviews of Canada or Latin American or European countries, particularly prior to foreign conventions. "Crystal clear laughter, the rhythm of dancing feet, the soft strumming of guitar," an advertisement for the 1935 Lions convention described Mexico City, "where every day is a holiday." This emphasis added interest and appeal to international activity. At the same time, however, it distorted members' understanding of important economic and political distinctions between countries, by ignoring harsh realities and reducing foreign practices to quaint custom.[33]

Local club programs utterly failed to consider seriously the heightening international crisis in the late twenties and early thirties. While their neglect undoubtedly had an element of provincial isolationism, programs discussing international conflicts risked the same divisiveness as programs focused on internal political developments, and perhaps they were avoided for that reason. The Elgin, Illinois, Rotary chapter, to take one small example, suffered the loss of one of its most prominent members because of what he perceived as Rotary's support of lowered tariffs for Swiss watches. More serious, because of its genuine international implications, was the hostility with which the Seattle Rotary greeted the 1934 talk by Tsune-jiro Miyaoka, of the Tokyo Rotary Club, in which he defended Japan's expansionism.[34]

Rotary and International Conflict in the Thirties

The consensual methods of international service received their most severe test in the 1930s, when conflict between countries in the Rotary fold gradually ripened into war. These conflicts put Rotary in an untenable position. Primarily a social organization, Rotary had no means of responding to deep political crises. It would be unrealistic, therefore, to expect Rotary to have responded adequately to the conflict eventually resulting in World War II. On the other hand, the organization's absolute refusal to judge— to "take sides"—reveals limitations that angered even some Rotarians.

The Depression, while it caused Rotary difficulties at home, did not lessen the association's commitment to international service. If anything, Rotary increased its level of world involvement. The 1931 convention, held in Vienna, the first organized by Europeans, witnessed a "frank and courageous" discussion of the tariff question at an international roundtable. As Rotarians congratulated themselves on the "new atmosphere of friendliness" between French and German Rotary clubs, a portent of what was to come appeared in the Far East. China's difficulties, abetted by Japan, brought a letter to the August *Rotarian* asking if "the Rotary clubs are going to sit down idly and not do something." The answer perhaps was provided in the next issue, when an editorial entitled "Rotary in the Orient" praised the Japanese feudal code, "the Bushido," finding it comparable to the Rotary code of ethics.[35]

The intentions of Japan could still, in the early thirties, appear benign. Not so with those of Hitler, who, shortly after he rose to power, threatened to eliminate the German Rotary clubs, along with all other voluntary associations not sponsored by the state. The president of Rotary, however, sought an audience with the Führer, and was able to assure Rotarians in November 1933 that when "the real character of Rotary" was explained to "Germans in posts of high responsibility, a satisfactory understanding was reached." Rotary, as a result, continued in Germany "without change in its fundamental features and with the approval of the Hitler Administration." Still, "some of our Jewish Rotarians terminated their membership under varying conditions."[36]

While tensions rose in the East and Europe, Rotarians, mostly from Europe, attempted without success to strengthen Rotary's support of international justice. Even such a mild and vaguely worded resolution calling on Rotary to "amplify its characteristics as regards international service" aroused much debate and was tabled. Rotary had already clarified its official stand on international politics. "Rotary in its corporate capacity does not attempt to interfere with forms of government nor with political systems or schools of thought." Thus the organization attempted to preserve an absolute neutrality, "offering its good offices" to both Japan and China as they began their undeclared war.[37]

Faced with a troubled international scene, officials in the Rotary administration tried to offend no one. When Hitler finally forced Rotary in Germany to disband completely in 1938, the president of Rotary, Maurice Duperrey, praised the German Rotarians for "their example that the first duty of every Rotarian is to be a loyal citizen of his own country, even though one is devoted to the cause of international understanding." Yet some Rotarians, like the governor of the Swedish district, Harald Tolle, felt Rotary's actions "too few and too faltering." Answering those critics, the chairman of the 1938 session on international service first stated the case of those supporting strong stands on international issues: "There are those who think in times like these Rotary's present procedure is inane and meaningless. These friends of Rotary believe that it is time that the high-minded, right-thinking Rotarians of all nations rise as one man in denunciation of offending nations in order that the hand of justice throughout the world be sustained and international lawlessness be banished." But the Chairman rejected this "high and moral concept of Rotary," because in following it, "Rotary would be blown in a thousand pieces."[38]

Yet by this time, most of the "offending nations" had disbanded their Rotary clubs, ending with the Italians in 1939. Even then, an editorial noted that since Italian Rotarians reached a decision "only after earnest study" and "with regard to their obligations as good citizens of their country," Rotarians should avoid criticizing them because it would "most likely embarrass them." This fine and paralyzing sensitivity disgusted some leading British Rotarians, particularly as they found themselves being bombed by Hitler. "Are we to wait and again be contemptibly kicked out, as in Germany, for lack of courage to leave?," asked the editor of the British magazine *Rotary Service,* W. W. Blair Fish, in 1940. Rotarian Wilifred Andrews, in the same publication in 1941, wrote contemptuously of the Rotary organization's assertion that a Rotarian must be a good patriot above all. By that principle, "only those Germans who exalt the state above humanity can be good Rotarians."[39]

Rotary's refusal to take a stand undoubtedly reflected official U.S. neutrality and the concern of leading American Rotarians that statements condemning the Axis countries would involve the club in controversies at home. Unfortunately, it appears that a bureaucratic concern for organizational continuity clouded some of the club leaders' moral vision.

Nevertheless, the failure of Rotary to condemn international lawlessness, even when fellow members were put at risk, also demonstrates the inadequacy of the Rotarians' sociable service ethic in the face of true conflict of interest. "To deal with conflicting ideologies is and always has been Rotary's specialty," claimed Paul Harris optimistically before the 1939 Rotary convention. Yet that is exactly what Rotary as an organization could not do. Despite assertions to the contrary, the organization existed more to reinforce international goodwill than to create it, and it had no mechanisms to arbitrate disputes between members, or even to censure clubs that supported obvious violations of international law.

While Rotary in the midst of the Depression could not have been expected to alert Americans to the impending crisis in world affairs, the organization might have supported more strongly—even only with resolutions—those foreign Rotarians in the 1930s who were themselves willing to take a stand. The fact that fear of controversy disabled Rotary's ability to act—even with direct evidence of fascism's terrors—constitutes a serious moral failing of the service ethic.

Service Clubs and the "New" Internationalism

It was almost with relief that service clubs turned away from the moral dilemmas of internationalism and the economic pressures of the Depression to immerse themselves in the war effort. Here was an activity for which their organizations were ideally suited—mobilizing a united population to support a patriotic cause. A joint meeting of Kiwanis, Rotary, and Lions clubs adopted a resolution "that we reaffirm the purposes for which we exist, rededicate ourselves to them and pledge ourselves to an intensification of our efforts in meeting such exigencies as may arise." It also urged "energetic cooperation with all other agencies which are now seeking to meet the present need of civilian warfare and civilian morale."[40]

In efforts similar to those they made in World War I, club members gave blood, supported war bond drives, collected scrap metal, helped with rationing, grew victory gardens, and assisted the United Service Organizations (USO) in entertaining the boys at home. Rotarians corresponded with club members in allied countries and did what they could to send packages of food and supplies. Most of all, their morale-building activities helped preserve "mental hygiene" in what the *Lion* saw as "the war of nerves the Axis is waging on civilization through threats, fatigue, and rumors."[41]

The successful conclusion of the war once again brought businessmen the world over flooding into service clubs. "Consciously or unconsciously, the entire world is clamoring for Rotary," international president S. Kendrick Guernsey announced to the San Francisco convention in 1947 as he reviewed a record of growth that had placed Rotary in more than a hundred countries. The Lions could also claim that "the spirit of Lionism can cure the world's ills" while they chartered, worldwide, more than one club daily.[42] As American government policy pursued an increasingly international emphasis, so too did the clubs continue to make internationalism a keynote of their service programs. Rotary and the Lions received flattering invitations to send representatives to the United Nations advisory conference in San Francisco in 1945, as "voluntary associations with an international membership," and from its beginning the United Nations received the support of all the service clubs.

Support of the institutions and committees of the U.N. was in harmony with the clubs' conviction that peace required an internationally minded community. Rotarians made little mention of the failures of their efforts at goodwill in the thirties; indeed, Paul Harris, in his last message before his death, told the 1946 convention that "Rotarians are deeply thankful that governments of the world are following the trail blazed by Rotary forty-one years ago."[43] Even more than before the war, it appeared to service club members that "the world is shrinking—today we are all neighbors" and that world unity depended upon "mutual understanding based on a fuller and more intimate knowledge of our fellow men in foreign lands." The theme of the 1947 Rotary International Convention was "living together in friendship and understanding."[44]

With the world as one big neighborhood, the United Nations became a community institution. The Kiwanis club of Middletown, Ohio, was one of many clubs that discussed the U.N. as an "international town meeting," defusing aggression through debate and thereby promoting their own common interest.[45] Such a view, widely shared among Americans, tended to trivialize the United Nations, making it simply an organizational expression of international goodwill. When any genuine clash of interests occurred in U.N. deliberations, American club members, like most of their fellow citizens, assumed that the goals of the United States should prevail.[46]

In general, however, service club organizations after World War II attempted to avoid excessive patriotism in their international dealings. Organizational leaders were certainly aware that, as Melvin Jones put it, their fellowship might "counteract the harmful ideologies through which enemies of democracy divide men," although they did not implement any explicitly cold war international programs.[47] They displayed, in the late forties and early fifties, great concerns about the threat of communism, both in the United States and around the world, and it is perhaps no accident that enormous postwar service club growth occurred in developing countries, first in Latin America and then the Far East, corresponding with massive infusions of U.S. aid and carefully cultivated economic ties. But all clubs carefully avoided any suggestions that Americans "owned" the service club movement, and both Rotary and the Lions—and later, in the 1960s, Kiwanis—self-consciously elected their officers from a wide range of countries.

Worldwide Service

The clubs' international expansion came on the coattails of the American drive for power and shared some of the presuppositions of official American policy. Like other Americans, club members often failed to comprehend the world in its complexity. Even as they exposed members to foreign cultures and new experiences, the clubs discounted the differences; theirs was not primarily an ethic of pluralism. Rather, they gathered under the banner of benevolent capitalism, promoting a worldwide neighborliness, always hoping that unity lay just a handshake away.

Nevertheless, the worldwide growth of service clubs should not be discounted. The same organizational dynamic that spawned club expansion at home pushed forward international growth, as business interests combined with the missionary impulses inherent in service. Individual American businessmen helped to promote club growth overseas, but once established, these clubs were rapidly incorporated into a unified association. American headquarters quickly urged what Paul Harris called "international good manners" upon even the most provincial American clubs. In a process that deserves more historic recognition, in less than two decades service club officials had fashioned a smoothly functioning international organization.

After World War II, Rotary, Kiwanis, and Lions clubs underwent explosive growth abroad. The clubs continued to encourage personal fellowship—sponsoring international scholarships, encouraging club exchanges, or, in the case of Rotary, sending members as "Paul Harris Fellows" to visit "as many foreign Rotary clubs as possible." But this continuity is less dramatic than the new scope of the club movement. Foreign expansion soon exceeded growth within the States. By the 1960s, more service club members lived outside the United States than inside it, and by the 1980s the membership in the clubs of the Far East alone nearly exceeded American membership.[48] Although they continued to converse in what Rotary called "the universal language of service," the massive international operations that emerged in the fifties and sixties represented organizations removed in both membership and motives from the small-town American clubs of the twenties.

CHAPTER 7

Serving the Suburbs

Grandfather: And this is only the beginning, son. Because men will always
yearn for fellowship—communities will always need service—
business must always have high standards—and the world more
than anything else needs understanding and brotherhood.
Grandmother: Rotary gives us a glimpse of humanity as we would like it to be.
Grandfather: Yes, Jimmy, in the future Rotary will go as far as each Rotarian
will let it go.

*Stage darkens. . . . Boy scouts appear carrying flags of all nations in which there
are Rotary clubs, while an unseen voice proclaims:* Nineteen-o'five—one
country, one club, a handful of members; nineteen-fifty-five—ninety countries,
eighty-seven hundred clubs, almost half a million members.

—concluding scene, "The Anniversary Album" pageant,
1955 Rotary convention

Rotary and its two kindred organizations had good reason
to celebrate in 1955. World War II, like the first World War, had inaugu-
rated another period of rapid expansion in club membership. Suburbanization fueled club growth; a majority of new members came from the rapidly
multiplying suburban enclaves, where familiar club programs in education,
traffic safety, and recreation acquired a new relevance and local significance. Foreign expansion for the Lions and Rotary was equally rapid, and
their student exchange and foreign aid programs gave both organizations
a sense of worldwide prestige.

Despite the clubs' apparent compatibility with postwar life, members
in the early 1950s expressed more openly than ever before their resentment of institutional growth in American society. Linking this resentment
with anticommunism, members continued to attack big government and
big labor as representative of the excesses of an organizational America—
and continued to celebrate Rotary, Kiwanis, and Lions as true representatives of the "American Way." Of course, since the headquarters of the
service organizations themselves required large bureaucracies, spokesmen

could hardly denounce all corporate organization. Instead, they increasingly described the clubs as part of the independent sector of American institutional life, pursuing the voluntarism that kept the democratic tradition alive.

In their hostility toward unions and the welfare state, the clubs' statements again echoed corporate spokesmen. But unlike the 1920s, club members no longer organized in defense of a distinctive style of life. They spoke much less of "bringing a dead town to life" or of "restoring a sense of craft" to their businesses. They remained as concerned as ever about local issues; if anything, suburban living induced a greater resident parochialism than did living in a small-town community. Nevertheless, suburban development had undermined local businesses' sense of overarching community unity.

As the turbulent sixties and seventies shattered the sense of a national middle-class consensus, the service club's brand of sociability no longer seemed quite relevant to the experiences of small businessmen. What had begun as relatively progressive associations of local clubs dedicated to community service had become mature organizations following a familiar round of fellowship and philanthropy—but, despite the hopes of their founders, never quite achieving the status of central American institutions.

Local Businessmen in a Big Business World

Although the service clubs recruited over three hundred thousand new members in the decade following World War II, the infusion of new businessmen did not bring in the flood of corporate officers that some club leaders hoped would join. Throughout the 1930s, with small business suffering hard times and in apparent jeopardy from continued economic centralization, Rotarian spokesmen worried that the club did not attract the corporate executive. Young executives, who were highly mobile as they stepped up the corporate ladder, did not seem to share the civic concerns of well-rooted small businessmen.[1]

Postwar expansion did increase executive membership in all the clubs. "Many of our employees in the communities where we operate are members of Lions Clubs," Clifford Hood, vice president of U.S. Steel condescendingly told the 1951 Lions convention. But one club survey, taken of Rotarians in 1947, found 44 percent owned their own business, while another 35 percent were corporate officers and executives in smaller firms. As a further indication of these Rotarians' involvement in small business, 66 percent belonged to their local chamber of commerce. Another survey of Kiwanians ten years later reported that 86 percent either owned their business or else made a significant portion of their business's purchases.[2]

As a number of sociological studies convincingly establish, the involvement of large corporations in community associations such as the service clubs seldom extended above middle-management representatives, who joined mainly to establish community goodwill. Surveys done by research firms for organization headquarters confirmed that expansion had not significantly changed the membership's locally oriented business and professional character. In 1947 an article in the *Kiwanis Magazine* hopefully predicted "fine results" if "large corporations joined the community" and local clubs. As was already quite apparent, however, top-level corporation executives would not involve themselves in the type of sociable voluntary activity the clubs represented.[3]

That club membership retained its local business character did not bode well for the future influence of service organizations. Immediately after the war, however, club prospects looked bright. In both retail and manufacturing sectors returning veterans swelled the ranks of small businessmen. Until a downturn hit small business in the mid-fifties, prosperity reigned amid an outpouring of editorial support linking small businessmen and civic virtue. Clubs themselves were praised in popular periodicals: *Colliers* ran a laudatory article in 1948, and *Life* did a pictorial on the 1949 Lions convention. As in the twenties, club members could depend on the *Saturday Evening Post* to tell the "truth about service clubs"—that during their meetings, members' analyses of national politics "were as informed and intelligent as anything I'd read" and that, given the chance, they "could run the country handily."[4]

With membership expanding rapidly, no new Mencken or Lewis to torment them, and the American public seemingly convinced of the virtues of small businessmen and service organizations, clubs could feel they enjoyed a rightful prestige as representatives of American principles. "The democratic way is the Rotary way," Rotarian Walter Williams told the 1950 convention. "America's great dynamic strength exists because out of the grass roots each citizen has been a dynamic producer, planner, and doer," and nothing exemplified this strength better than "Rotary community service."[5] Kiwanian O. Sam Cummings echoed these sentiments in a 1952 *Kiwanis Magazine* editorial. As "articulate representatives of the great middle class," club members "most vigorously champion the cause of the private enterprise system" essential for "the preservation of our way of life."[6]

Resentment of Socialist Trends

Yet even though they expressed confidence in their mission, club members also appeared convinced that the American Way was under siege.

The clearest threat came from outside American society—the great communist powers and their agents of subversion. But communists were not the only group working to undermine American traditions. "Big government" and "big labor" had also abandoned the American Way and were careening out of control down an unfamiliar path. Club members, certain they represented true democratic principles, but aware of their lack of influence over the major forces shaping American society, lashed out with uncharacteristic resentment at the "sinister forces trying to muscle in on Libertyville."[7]

Club members supported wholeheartedly the anticommunist crusades of the late forties and early fifties, although they generally avoided the paranoia associated with the extremes of McCarthyism. The cold war, the Rosenberg case, and the pervasiveness of anticommunism among politicians and big business leaders made members' anxieties seem plausible. The Soviets represented a significant threat and, even worse, a Soviet reporter had ridiculed the service clubs as places "where full grown men, merchants of suspenders or electric ranges, roared upon command."[8]

In their eagerness to defend "American democratic capitalism," club members at times exaggerated the presence of the red menace in ways that today strain credulity. An article in the *Kiwanis Magazine* worried about the "one half-million of our people gullible enough to follow the pied pipers of international communism." To show how easy it would be for communists to take over a Kiwanis club, a member secretly enrolled himself in a mock communist party and then won election to the presidency. More than one club pulled this stunt, which always ended with "shocked Kiwanians" arriving for a luncheon in a room with a picture of Stalin on the podium and signs on the walls proclaiming "Down with Capitalistic Kiwanians" and "The United Soviets of America."[9] Lions president Harold Nutter told the 1951 convention that though he did "not believe any Lion is a Communist," it was always possible that they would "associate with an organization such as ours to cause confusion and distrust." He reassured convention attendees that "neither I nor any of the members of my own club in Camden, New Jersey, would tolerate for a moment a communist among our members."[10]

Club members, though, did not appear obsessed with fears of communist takeover. As Samuel Stouffer observed in 1954, "The picture of the average American as a person with the jitters, trembling lest he find a Red under the bed, is clearly nonsense."[11] While Lions president Fisher warned the 1949 convention that communism "creates decay from within, using the spores of discontent and disillusionment to break down the supporting fiber of our Christian democratic way of life, and reduce it to a worthless

mass of rotten ineptitude," he knew the antidote: "Lionism is a purify-
ing force." An editorial in the *Kiwanis Magazine* also downplayed the
red menace. "Certainly the communist internationale hasn't been able to
place an average of 67 agents in every one of 2,650 communities and win
for them positions of leadership in business and the professions." Hugh
Stevenson's 1949 *Kiwanian* article, "Why Is Anyone a Communist?," provided an interpretation of communism's appeal that explained this sinister
menace in familiar terms. According to Stevenson, communism met the
psychological needs of those not integrated in the community, giving "re-
lease to resentment," supplying a "scapegoat for failure," and "flattering
the ego." A little counseling could remove any shade of pink.[12]

The clubs' response to the threat of communism reveals less a deep-
seated fear than a desire to protect the free enterprise system on all fronts—
or, as one of the 1951 Kiwanis International objectives put it, to "resist
all trends toward socialization." Ultimately, clubs worried most about
the "socialism" that emanated from within American society. Members
had complained during the Depression of the growth of government but,
uncertain in crisis conditions, had considered "government interference"
perhaps necessary. Now, as prosperity seemed assured, it appeared the
federal government had capitulated to indulgent paternalism—something
a Rotarian clergyman called "the greatest threat yet advanced against the
American Way." In trying to satisfy the unreasonable demands of lazy and
dissatisfied Americans, government had "slammed the door in the face of
the average man." Once begun on its socialistic course, government began
to expand of its own accord, and so, as Senator Wallace F. Bennett told the
1951 Rotary convention, "the common citizen is of less importance than
the maintenance of the [government] organization and its functions."[13]

One beneficiary of government's growth—a group apparently not
among the "average men" hurt by federal bureaucracy—was the labor
union. "Labor has cried and schemed for power," wrote Harry Adams in
the *Kiwanis Magazine* in 1947. "Well, it has it now. Labor has the power
to take all Americans to even higher standards of living or to new and un-
charted depths of disaster." Adams left no doubt that the latter possibility
would be more likely.[14]

Behind the overwrought club rhetoric lay the economic reality of small
business interests. Both the federal government and the union appeared in
the forties and fifties to be large organizations hostile to small businessmen. Despite lip service paid to small business as the foundation of the
free enterprise system, the federal government granted the largest share of
government contracts during World War II and after to large firms. From
the 1950s into the 1960s government actually encouraged conglomeration

in the name of competition. Small business, then, had a real grievance against government interference beyond the nuisance of red tape.[15]

To a certain degree, government intervention also helped foster postwar union growth, particularly with Korean wartime spending, although the power of unions remained more of a possible threat to small business than a real one. The passage of the Taft-Hartley Act in 1947 curtailed the large-scale organizing drives of the late thirties. Despite the much-publicized postwar "social accord" reached between several large industries and their unionized workers, union success never reached far into medium and small firms.[16]

The very fact that unions never really achieved blanket nationwide organizing, however, meant individual small firms that did experience strikes, or did have to meet union demands, would be at a competitive disadvantage in the domestic marketplace. Therefore the threat of unions remained a matter of legitimate economic concern to small business.[17]

The Symptoms of Pop Psychology

Still, in retrospect, club members vastly exaggerated the power of both the welfare state and the union. Much of their reaction seems due to the ideological context provided by big business strategies, which linked the anti-communist crusade and an emotional defense of the free enterprise system with an attack on unions and federal prolabor policies. Club spokesmen also borrowed heavily from the psychological approach of corporate personnel departments, which attempted to employ a variety of methods from the behavioral sciences to overcome the appeal of unions.[18]

Clubs fully shared the interest in the "science of human relations" that swept corporate industry after the war. A *Lion* article called personnel management "a new art bringing a revolution to industry." An official Rotary publication, *Service Is My Business,* gushed that "each store, each office, each workshop, each factory is a laboratory of human engineering, where vital knowledge is waiting to be organized."[19]

In this psychologized context, club spokesmen stressed that both the welfare state and the union capitalized on men's emotional weaknesses. *Service Is My Business* argued that labor's power, although aided by government paternalism, had a psychological basis—similar to communism's appeal as identified in other club publications. Membership in unions gratified "feelings of inferiority caused by [automated] conditions in modern employment," as when workers won strike victories over employers. Unfortunately, the book argued, this psychological compensation drives an "unnatural wedge" between employees and managers that "decreases production and threatens the whole structure of society." Like unions, government growth could also indicate a society-threatening mental laxity. Government restrictions and regulations were "bred in apathy." The "welfare state is only a state of mind," the editor of the *Kiwanis Magazine* argued, as he called for an alert citizenry.[20]

Thus the psychological mode of analysis that first appeared in the thirties became more pervasive after the war, as club spokesmen analyzed "socialistic trends" in terms of apathy or resentment, supplying "compensation" for "feelings of inferiority." All levels of American culture had shifted from a primarily sociological analysis to a predominantly psychological one by the fifties. Intellectuals led the way in speaking of "status anxiety," "identity crisis," "inferiority complex," and "transferral."[21] The clubs' psychological terminology drew more directly from popular writers such as the honorary Rotarian Norman Vincent Peale, who explained his "positive psychology" before the 1949 Rotary convention and also published articles in *Kiwanis Magazine* and the *Lion*.[22]

Club members might have found this way of thinking particularly appealing because it downplayed the genuine conflict of interest small businessmen might feel with government bureaucrats and labor unions. As local controversy was soothed with club fellowship, so might these national tendencies be therapeutically solved with proper scientific applications of service.

Yet beyond these traditional booster concerns for social consensus, the psychologizing of club social analysis in the early fifties revealed how deeply members themselves had been influenced by the corporate way of life. As they moved through the twentieth century, the clubs' spokesmen went from promoting cooperation in order to advance community interest to talk of individual adjustment to the social order, and finally to touting human engineering as a balm for worker discontent. Each of these rhetorical positions displays a conservative impulse to preserve social unity. Yet each moves closer to what could be termed a bureaucratic perspective of human action—stressing psychological manipulation in the interest of organizational stability and fretting over the difficulties of personal fulfillment amid a shadowy institutional world beyond individual control.[23]

As club leaders began to express a corporate perspective—even in their complaints about bureaucratic life—it became apparent that club ideology no longer expressed the tension between the urban bureaucratic way of life and cooperative small-town values. To be sure, resentment of bureaucratic impersonality and a desire to recapture communal intimacy continued to hold great appeal in the early fifties—the clubs' ability to rally small businessmen concerned about socialistic tendencies might explain the clubs' rapid growth. But once members' more pressing fears about the survival of the American Way subsided, local clubs found themselves struggling to recapture the town-oriented values upon which they once based their service activities. Not only was corporate thinking proving difficult to resist, another powerful social trend, suburbanization, was also undermining the clubs' rationale.

Success in Suburbia

In 1955 Rotary's North American membership stood at 268,136, Kiwanis's had grown to 228,905, and the Lions had solidified their newly gained position as the largest service organization, with a total of 325,640 American and Canadian members. Yet these international organizations could still claim that 70 percent of local clubs served communities with populations under 20,000. These new club communities were not the small towns on the defensive that had provided such fertile club ground in the twenties; instead they were expanding newly settled suburban communities. From 1945 to 1955 more than 70 percent of new clubs formed fell within census-defined Standard Metropolitan Areas.[24] This growth showed the service clubs playing an important role in the suburban experience, as several of the multitude of associations that attracted the suburban "joiner."

Most of the suburbanization during the forties and fifties resulted from migration out of the cities, generated by returning servicemen searching for affordable family-style housing. Many national associations regarded these new communities as territory ripe for organization. As Herbert J. Gans showed in his well-known study of one of the later Levittowns, the original impulse to join often came from external sources—representatives from the national organizations recruiting members to form new clubs. For the service clubs, with their emphasis on expansion, this procedure had already been well established by the 1940s. Expansion followed a set bureaucratic process, involving the proposal of possible new club communities by the district governor, a survey of potential members, a sponsoring club, and a representative from headquarters to coordinate the final formation.[25]

Of course, club recruiters could only do so much to attract new members; not all demand for clubs was created externally. An important motive for joining service clubs remained the possibility of business contacts, particularly important in a new locale. Sociologists have also established that suburban conditions, while they do not create the urge to join, do enhance other motives for community participation. A sociological study of suburban attitudes found that the relative affluence of residents, the homogeneity of their backgrounds and interests, and the community's location as a slightly isolated subarea of the city encouraged neighboring and local involvement similar to that found in small-town culture. Gans observes that organizations allowed a new and largely homogeneous population to sort itself by interests and prestige. In addition, as members of a new residential area, Levittowners felt particularly anxious to establish the trappings of a genuine community, including associations like service clubs—whether or not these associations proved important to their lives as a whole. In the suburbs, then, the service organizations benefited both from small-town-like conditions and from the desire to emulate small-town community.[26]

On the basis of these similar conditions, service clubs could continue pursuing many of the same kinds of projects they did in the twenties. Projects involving youth work, education, and traffic safety continued to occupy their service agenda. All the while, service club interests shifted noticeably, displaying the impact of the clubs' suburban locations. Club activities centered even more on leisure facilities, such as building parks and swimming pools. Youth work often involved close cooperation with the Parent-Teacher Association. For example, the Kiwanis Club of Torrington, Connecticut, cosponsored lectures on child psychology with the Parent-Teacher Association. Other Kiwanis clubs sought to "teach community living" to youngsters, delving into problems such as "zoning, sewerage disposal, church attendance—in fact all of the things people face today." Club fund-raising activities, though still directed to traditional service themes such as the helping the blind, aid for crippled children, and college scholarships, turned more and more to weekend, non-business-oriented events, such as pancake breakfasts and chicken barbecues, and to door-to-door solicitation, selling such items as light bulbs, fruit cake, and even monosodium glutamate in a "three shaker set."[27] Noticeably missing in these activities are the booster incentives so clear in earlier club community service. In fact, the clubs responded to suburban residence with a gradual deemphasis on the element of community in the club's service ethic.

The Community of "Limited Liability"

Suburban life did not, as many early commentators feared, mean the complete loss of gemeinschaft. Even in recent years, analysts of suburban life note the persistence of neighborly behavior and local allegiance.[28] Despite the enthusiasm for service clubs that resulted from these concerns, however, suburban localism did not mean that the clubs could draw on a reservoir of community spirit. William Whyte noted in Park Forest, Illinois, tremendous pressures to participate in neighborly activity. So strong was this pressure to conform, Whyte felt, that the residents he studied often avoided the broader community interest organizations (such as service clubs) for more intimate blockwide associations—so as not to alienate the neighbors.[29]

Whyte had an axe to grind, hoping to stimulate individuals to resist such conformity, but other observers with different themes have worried that suburban life does not encourage broad community awareness. In his study of Philadelphia and its suburbs, Sam Bass Warner, Jr., argues that most suburban dwellers wish to live "informally among equals," free of responsibilities and demands. Throughout the twentieth century, he believes, disregard of public responsibility, though endemic to metropolitan Philadelphia, best characterized the suburbs.[30]

In a more recent appraisal of suburban culture, Barry Schwartz adds a third critical perspective, finding suburban sociability "diffuse." A wide variety of organizations form, but, drawing on a small number of very similar people, they cannot sustain a specialized purpose. The result is a "confusion of means and ends" that creates an active but shallow associational life. As an example, Schwartz cites the suburban church, which, more than its urban counterpart, serves general socialization functions, sponsoring activities such as bingo, singles dances, and scout troops—and perhaps losing its spirituality in the process.[31]

These observations of suburban life echo earlier criticisms of small-town culture—the conformity enforced by excessive neighboring, the insularity of the narrow-minded provincial, and the loss of leisure-time fulfillment caused by overorganization. It is precisely these community vices that service clubs claimed to have successfully overcome in small towns all over the country, where members testified that they "pulled a town together." But a crucial element of small-town service club life, and the focus of small-town boosterism, failed to appear in postwar suburbia. These largely residential communities did not foster a sense that individual business interest required a stake in overall community success.

The suburbs' general failure to develop a booster ethic can be traced to the pattern of metropolitan development established as early as the twenties. During this first suburban boom period, suburbs sprawled from the city in configurations determined only by developers' landholdings and the automobile. Retailers, keeping pace with their customers' migration, quickly distributed their outlets into the new residential areas, taking advantage of low rents and easy accessibility by car. The result—the infamous suburban commercial strip and later, spreading quickly after World War II, the shopping center—not only destroyed the retail function of the cities' central business district, it also failed to generate suburban business centers akin to the small town's Main Street.[32] The scattering of the suburbs' commercial interests meant that a sense of a business community based on location did not emerge, no matter how strong a loyalty suburbanites felt to their residential locality. A small retailer, who on Main Street might have helped his service club "sell Jonesville to itself," would, in a shopping center location, fund club projects by selling products from national manufacturers door to door.

Service clubs in the postwar suburb thus appeared in an anomalous position. Residents flocked to membership; club growth was as rapid in this type of community as in the twenties' small town. But as an institution that at its best combined social, business, and civic concerns, the clubs occupied a far less influential position than in the small town, for these concerns often existed separately in the suburb and seldom worked together to form a broad sense of community.

A revealing study of Forest Park, a suburb of Cincinnati, accounts for its patchwork pattern of community interest—intense in some areas, indifferent in others—by drawing on Morris Janowitz's concept of a "community of limited liability." Forest Park residents in the fifties and sixties saw themselves as members of several different communities—business, professional, religious, or social—of which Forest Park was only one. Only when an issue arose of concern to all these interest groups, such as a development plan affecting property values, did residents display a wider civic concern.[33]

Operating in the suburbs, the service clubs could draw on a number of these limited communities. They could still be vehicles for expressing local interest, displaying altruism, or making business contacts. But suburban clubs could not tap a civic loyalty created by a confluence of business interest, residential anxieties, and community pride. Community spirit was less deeply rooted for a fast-food franchise owner joining to show his public-mindedness than it was for a local businessman joining to defend the autonomy of his town and his business.

The "Independent Sector"

As local clubs felt diminished incentives to boost the community, national leaders responded and no longer spoke so fervently of community service. In 1926 Lions president W. B. Todd argued that the club's "prime purpose" is "to make its hometown a better place to live." Thirty-five years later, the president of Kiwanis International thought it disillusioning "that we have so usually read [service club objectives] as a community improvement association advertisement." Anyone who believes that "community charities form the first business of civic clubs in the second half of the twentieth century is still living in the first half of it." He thought Kiwanis members should start acting and thinking as world citizens. Beginning in 1965, Rotary also sought to promote world community service. Club charity would no longer meet home-town insufficiencies; rather it would go where it was most needed around the world.[34] Demonstrating the increasing significance of the clubs' international membership, this new thrust of service also shows the influence of the Peace Corps, Vista, and other United States government-sponsored voluntary agencies.

The rhetoric of club leaders, in fact, appeared more characteristic of a large-scale charitable agency than a club promoting fellowship. Spokesmen now talked of the clubs as organizers of America's volunteer spirit, in contrast with, and at times in competition with, the bureaucracy of government welfare agencies. Rotarians worried in the early sixties about the "civic stagnation" caused by government paternalism. But they reassured themselves that "most of the good work of this nation is done by the millions of people engaged in voluntary work." Lions president Edward Lindsey also felt that the nation was "crying for a resurgence of independent individualism," which the Lions could provide. The clubs belonged to the "independent sector" represented by millions of "dedicated individuals quietly working to tear down old walls of prejudice and misunderstanding." [35]

Businessmen seemed less inclined, however, to join the independent sector than they had been with a hometown service club. The slow but steady growth that the service clubs experienced from 1955 to 1965 leveled off. The number of members still remained substantial—the Lions American-Canadian membership was over 500,000; Rotary's and Kiwanis's, over 300,000 and 200,000, respectively. But as the sixties proceeded, the clubs found themselves observing protests, riots, and political turmoil that shattered the national consensus that the clubs now worked to support.

Clubs and the Collapse of Consensus

The clubs responded to the problems in the late sixties as they always had to social difficulties, with a call for "one-to-one" interaction and increased cooperation. Just as in the twenties and the thirties, they focused on youth and prescribed organizational remedies. At a panel discussion on "Youth, Law, and Order" at the 1968 convention, Rotarians heard that Judge Lester Loble had "never had before [him] an active Boy Scout, Camp Fire Girl, 4-H Member, or member of a similar group or a youngster who was a regular attendant of Sunday school or church." Lions at the 1969 convention listened to their president, W. R. Bryan, prescribe a remedy for "racial disturbances, student eruptions, lack of family discipline and decline of religious influences"—an "unprecedented emphasis on youth" in Lionism via youth camps and "Leo" clubs for young men. "Never has there been a better method to promote person-to-person understanding." Lions also read small-college president Miller A. F. Ritchie's prescription for campus troubles—what he called a "staculation" committee combining students, faculty, and administration, meeting once a month to "discuss and work out grievances, hone new ideas for improving interpersonal relationships and sharpen the spirit of community on campus."[36]

In their attempts to renew consensus, club members echoed their predecessors in the 1930s. Back then, the clubs' stress on personal, nonpolitical interaction had struck a sympathetic chord with many in the middle class who sought security and cohesion in the face of the Depression. In the late sixties and early seventies, however, the threat to middle-class self-definition came from within that class's own ranks. The civil rights movement, Vietnam, a changing economy, a shift in sexual morality, and a seeming decline in law and order—all opened generational and cultural rifts that clubs were unable to bridge.

As they themselves recognized, service club members belonged on one side of the divide—that of the "establishment," or, in Richard Nixon's terms, "the silent majority." A few members lamented the clubs' identification with a stodgy and repressive older generation. John T. Trutter argued in the *Rotarian* that young people have a negative image of older people, "and by association, service clubs," because many members "blame everything on the new generation and in trying to solve the problems of the community and the world, refuse to face up to the fact that the activities of the past will not fulfill the needs of the present."[37]

On the whole, club members felt they represented responsibility and historic achievement, standing, just as they had in the twenties, against those youthful critics who would tear down and not build up. "We must not forget our heritage and the blood, sweat and tears which were shed to give this country a solid foundation. Now why would some, from the inside, want to destroy it?," asked the Whiteville, North Carolina, attorney J. Bruce Eure in a letter to the *Rotarian* about campus unrest.[38]

Unfortunately for Rotary, Kiwanis, and Lions, despite frequent references to the service clubs' ability to "build bridges between people," their ideal of consensus appeared to a growing segment of the middle class to be antiquated and inadequate. In a 1971 article in *Newsweek* club leaders expressed concern about the clubs' ability to "project a meaningful image to socially conscious young adults." Kiwanian R. P. Merridew dismissed those fears at the convention that year, pointing back to the Kiwanians of 1938, who passed resolutions condemning drug trafficking and pollution. Even back then, he told the convention, "Kiwanis had been 'relevant.' "[39]

If Merridew hoped to suggest that the clubs had been in advance of their time, then of course he was guilty of convention hyperbole. The clubs' position on each decade's issues could be taken as a solid barometer of middle-class opinion. The continuities between the Kiwanis resolutions of 1938 and those of 1970 simply show the constancy of American middle-class concerns in the twentieth century. Yet Merridew could not be faulted in claiming relevance for the clubs through those years. For a significant section of that middle class, Kiwanis and the other service clubs have provided a way of meeting the transformations of the twentieth century. For a white middle class of local businessmen and professionals, the clubs' fellowship served as a link between work and leisure, private enterprise and social responsibility, and local, national, and international concerns.

The problem the clubs faced in the sixties and seventies, and the reason their relevancy to U.S. society declined, did not stem from their failure to keep pace with the issues of the day. Articles in club magazines throughout those decades discussed not only youth protests, pollution, and drug addiction and also demonstrated ongoing concern with urban renewal, world hunger, care for the elderly, and the impact of high technology on small business. Despite this admirable attempt to address current problems, club voluntarism struggled to mediate between business, personal, and community concerns. In recent decades service organizations have once again attempted to adapt to changes in club life and community life.

A New Sociability?

From their inception, service clubs showed themselves willing to accommodate many of the changes that economic development brought to local life. Members found it less easy to discard the personal prejudices that affected their sociability. But an incident at the 1971 Kiwanis convention gave a clear illustration that the changed context for club activity required new attitudes. Addressing the assembled delegates, Stephen E. Kolzak, the seventeen-year-old president of the Key Club (the youth group sponsored by Kiwanis) did not merely express gratitude for club assistance, mouthing the usual platitudes about learning the necessity of responsibility and public service. Instead, he gave a speech describing how several local Kiwanis clubs had refused to sponsor youth chapters at a school because it was racially integrated. Sharply critical of his elders, he asked how their prejudice squared with the clubs' service ideal.[40] Kolzak's brash oration exposed a contradiction within club life. Although members talked of toleration and "breaking down traditional prejudice" through their fellowship and service, such efforts did not extend much beyond the prosperous white businessmen who might normally socialize with each other outside of club life. Particularly glaring were race and gender restrictions that barred women and African Americans active in local business, men and women who were otherwise eligible, who shared most of the same professional and community interests as the businessmen welcomed to membership.

African Americans had been excluded for years on the grounds that they would disrupt the camaraderie of white businessmen. By the 1950s, however, a significant number of Americans could no longer accept discrimination in the name of fellowship. In some respects the service clubs proved themselves more flexible in adapting to this new climate than many other sociable associations. Although their long-standing segregation is no credit to the clubs, in Rotary, at least, individual members had always expressed concern at the hypocrisy of club segregation.[41]

Still, integration of African Americans proved difficult to achieve. The first American black admitted to service clubs was apparently Smith Robinson, a head of hospital maintenance who joined the Healdsburg, California, Rotary Club in the early 1950s. Under the pressure of the civil rights movement and concerned members, African Americans were gradually admitted to all the large city clubs. As one Rotary official wrote in in 1954, however, "one would be naive not to recognize that individual Rotary clubs do, openly or quietly, practice discrimination of one kind or another." As late as 1967 a controversy that drew national attention occurred when the Decatur, Illinois, Rotary club refused to admit an African American minister. But with the strong encouragement of the national associations, even clubs in provincial small cities began to open their membership. In the 1990s, while local discrimination undoubtedly remains a problem for service clubs, no national racial barriers remain.[42]

The 1980s witnessed another breach in the bulwark fortifying club sociability—the rule preventing women from joining. American service clubs had always been willing to cooperate in community activities with women's clubs and employ women as "essential cogs"—secretaries and headquarters operatives. They had also set up women's auxiliaries—"Rotary-Annes," "Ki-Wives," and "Lionesses"—although these had never been as integral to service clubs as they had been for lodges. But occasional proposals to welcome women as full-fledged members had always been quickly dismissed.

Despite this tradition, in a time of gender transformation and slowing membership growth clubs were forced to change their practices. In

May 1987 the U.S. Supreme Court ruled that the clubs now had to allow women access to all the privileges and pleasures of serving the community through fellowship. Although lawyers for Rotary International argued against the admission of women, the suit that resulted in the decision was in fact brought by a local Rotary club from Duarte, California, which was ejected by the international organization when it admitted women to bolster a declining membership. The process showed that some of the tension observable in the twenties between local clubs and the organizational bureaucracy remains—one of the women members responsible for the suit was quoted in the *Los Angeles Times* as saying, "I don't feel I was fighting for the rights of women; it was the right of the club to determine the matter for itself."[43]

But even those at organizational headquarters could not be entirely displeased by the result of the case. The majority opinion by Justice Brennan testified to the degree to which the clubs had integrated themselves into middle-class life. Brennan ruled that Rotary was a public institution since it was highly publicized, and it had a large membership and a high turnover rate, promoting the participation of nonmembers. Except for the high turnover rate, club leaders have long attempted to sell these qualities to members. Furthermore, removing gender restrictions allows clubs to bolster declining membership. Except for pockets of local resistance, all three service organizations have begun to recruit women, just as all three have increased black membership in recent years.[44]

In one sense, this relative inclusiveness represents the fulfillment of the ideal of service, which, as the clubs expressed it, had always claimed to destroy "age-old barriers to friendship." In other ways, this extension of membership represents a new brand of sociability. If clubs can successfully accommodate women, African Americans, and the ever-increasing international membership as equals in club life, Rotary, Kiwanis, and Lions will be expanding personal as well as club consciousness. Through a genuinely all-encompassing membership, one that truly operates in a global community, the clubs could indeed discover, as the *Lion* would have it, "A New Opportunity to Serve."[45]

Conclusion

Throughout the 1970s into the early 1980s, as club growth in the United States slowed, worried club officials commissioned studies on club purpose and image. "Where are we? Where are we going?" Rotarian president William Robbins asked readers of the *Rotarian* in 1975, calling on members to "renew the spirit of Rotary" and send their views on the purpose and objective of Rotary.[46] Even though six months later Robbins had concluded that "Rotary can be one of the greatest forces for good this world has ever known," and although club expansion overseas continued to boom, club growth in the United States remained stagnant.

As befits the large corporate organizations the clubs have become, club leadership has responded to changes with a series of public relations campaigns. In 1986, facing the first net loss of members since the Depression, Lions International commissioned a study by the consulting firm of Savlin/ Williams and Associates. Its findings described an aging membership, a continuing preponderance of Lions clubs operating in economically suffering small communities in the North and Midwest, and, apparently most galling, an ignorance of, if not outright contempt for, Lions clubs among members of the major media. The response was to promote a series of public service announcements. Kiwanis and Rotary followed with their own campaigns. Apparently these efforts have had some effect in improving the image of the clubs. Five years later an international committee studying attitudes toward Rotary concluded that thanks to a new sophistication about public relations, "members of the media have finally realized they aren't dealing with a local 'luncheon' group. They are now dealing with an influential international organization of more than 1.1 million members."[47]

It remains unclear whether public relations and recognition by the national media can overcome the conditions militating against local club voluntarism. The difficulty that the service clubs have encountered in the contemporary United States does not lie in unsuccessful public relations, but rather in the new types of communities, the changing patterns of sociability, and the general economic uncertainty affecting the country's middle class.

In the late nineteenth century, when the middle class was experiencing a crisis of self-definition caused by social turmoil, many middle-class men and women withdrew into more restrictive neighborhoods and associations, yet many others also affirmed their position through stewardship and activist cooperation. Businessmen's service clubs represented this latter response. Confident that they represented the community interest, they pursued a civic voluntarism that often promoted growth and development, but they also supported a form of community betterment that attempted to preserve local autonomy. At their peak of popularity in the 1920s, the clubs attracted a group of small businessmen and professionals determined to accommodate modern life without abandoning local pride and civic responsibility.

As Rotary, Kiwanis, and Lions clubs developed through the middle decades of the twentieth century, their concerns and activities changed to reflect the increasing influence of bureaucratic organization upon their members' lives. After experiencing the nationalizing impact of the New Deal and World War II, clubs in provincial towns and small cities continued to play their accustomed boosting role, but most members, especially those in suburban locations, pursued a slightly different brand of voluntarism, raising charitable contributions in nationally organized candy sales, supporting United Way drives, and sending money for international good works partially funded by government agencies. By the early 1960s clubs had become a familiar part of a philanthropic organizational sector.

The disruptions of the last twenty-five years, however, have generated a different middle-class response than that which carried the clubs through the first half of the twentieth century. As the sixties and seventies brought political protest, the middle class became more conscious of the broad range of competing interests challenging its view of a good society. Many in the middle class began to question whether growth and development represented unqualified progress. At the same time, consumerism, bureaucratic encroachment, and sprawling metropolitan expansion continued to shape the values of work, individual responsibility, and community solidarity. Whatever the long-term impact of these trends in the United States, in the 1980s and 1990s, when combined with economic uncertainty, they encouraged middle-class retreat and privatism, disrupting the operations of the organizational sector in many areas of American life. As Rotary, Kiwanis, and Lions clubs struggled to ensure their place in new middle-class communities, the middle class as a whole also became less confident that its vision defined the nation and less certain how it might serve the community.[48]

In 1988 Austin P. Jennings, the president of Lions International, noted the large suburban influx of a "New Breed" of "results-oriented" individuals who "see little need to join a Lions Club—as a matter of fact, these people see little need to join anything."[49] Yet Jennings was only partially accurate. Recent sociological studies have suggested an explosion in the number of grassroots organizations and neighborhood associations. What the new breed of middle class does not appear to join as often are more broadly based community service organizations.[50] Presumably, if this trend continues, the clubs could suffer the fate of the lodges in the twentieth century—hanging on through sheer social inertia, attracting a hard core of dedicated members but few others, ending with even their public insignias unintelligible except to the initiated.

Hinting at a more hopeful scenario is the fact that overall club membership in the United States grew (albeit slowly) from the mid-1980s into the 1990s. Other developments also suggest the clubs can continue to mediate between business, personal, and community concerns. As local businesses find themselves confronting the global marketplace, the international scope of Rotary, Kiwanis, and Lions could increase the attraction of membership. In "postsuburban" settlements, where talk of community becomes a marketing ploy, there endures a hunger for the local connectedness that the clubs can provide. Amid the often competing welter of charitable agencies sponsored by churches, nonprofit organizations, and government, clubs offer a philanthropy enriched by personal involvement. Thus, a century after their founding, Rotary, Kiwanis, and Lions could remain appealing for those men—and now women—interested in combining business, fellowship, and service.

In 1941 Rotary secretary Chesley Perry, who had done nearly as much as founder Paul Harris to shape the service club movement, gave a valedictory address to the Rotary Executive Committee. Soon he would retire, after more than thirty years of service to Rotary, and he felt slightly disgruntled with his recent experiences in club life. Businessmen, he believed, had not responded well to the Depression. Faced with a crisis, they had not acted in "the spirit of unselfish service." Neither had the Rotary Club accomplished much with its international program. Rotarians, Perry felt, needed to keep in mind that "our Rotary movement has existed for more than a quarter-century on the thesis that business should be service, that is to say above the acquisition of great wealth and power." The need still remained, as it did when Rotary was founded, for a group of businessmen, "a hardy core of citizenry in every country who are clear in their thinking, energetic in their action, pervasive in their influence. Theirs is the task of invoking the spirit of tolerance, respect for others, and cooperation."[51]

If the clubs' influence in twentieth-century America was less than pervasive, it was not for lack of effort. In thousands of projects, members demonstrated their energy. Virtually no community in America is without a park, clinic, or scholarship program sponsored by service clubs. Ultimately, the clubs, designed primarily for economic benefits and fellowship, could do little to intensify club members' impact on twentieth-century social trends. But by stressing public responsibility and community action, clubs mobilized small businessmen who might otherwise have been quietly absorbed in the corporate mainstream, and they pressed members to look beyond private interest.

It appears that in the 1990s Perry's hope that the service club movement could provide an inspirational "core of citizenry" may not be realized. Yet for all their limitations, for all their occasional descents into naivete, buffoonery, and prejudice, these "men of vision," as Mencken sarcastically referred to them, still express a worthwhile ideal. In a society in which corporate responsibility usually means no one takes the blame, in which private enterprise is often accompanied by public loss, perhaps the best we can hope for are professionals and business leaders willing to share the philosophy, if not the fellowship, of the service club.

Notes

Introduction

1. Several community studies discuss the clubs briefly, but only two works besides those written or commissioned by club members have focused on the clubs exclusively—one a useful book written in the 1930s by the sociologist Charles F. Marden, *Rotary and Its Brothers: An Analysis and Interpretation of the Men's Service Clubs* (Princeton, N.J.: Princeton University Press, 1935), and the other an unpublished doctoral dissertation by Howard Bahlke, "Rotary and American Culture: A Historical Study of Ideology" (University of Minnesota, 1956).

2. I do not want to minimize the significant and meaningful differences in club status that exist at the local level; nevertheless, seen from a national perspective, the membership similarities outweigh these local distinctions.

3. Of course, one might cite differences in other regions that had a significant impact on the development of service clubs, including the newness and rapid twentieth-century growth of western cities and the relative isolation of the old middle class on the northern plains. But Illinois provides a range of communities that allows for some comparative study. For a discussion of Illinois and the service club movement, see chapter 3 below. For a discussion of service clubs and the 1920s' business ethos in southern cities, see Blaine A. Brownell, *The Urban Ethos in the South, 1920–1930* (Baton Rouge: Louisiana State University Press, 1975); on the West, see Marden, *Rotary and Its Brothers,* 120–73; on the northern plains, see Catherine McNicol Stock, *Main Street in Crisis: The Great Depression and the Old Middle Class on the Northern Plains* (Chapel Hill: North Carolina University Press, 1992).

4. Like many historians, I believe the central event in modern American history has been the rise of large-scale organizations—industrial corporations, government agencies, and labor unions. Nevertheless, I am not so much interested in the institutional side of this story—a story of increasing rationalization and standardization—as in the less rational reactions and motivations and the tensions and ambivalence that invariably accompany the inexorable march of bureaucratic structures. The frequently cited central works in this field include Samuel P. Hays, *The Response to Industrialism, 1885–1914* (Chicago: University of Chicago Press, 1957), Robert Wiebe, *The Search for Order, 1877–1920* (New York: Hill and

Wang, 1967), and the two summaries by Louis Galambos, "The Emerging Organizational Synthesis in Modern American History," *Business History Review* 44 (Autumn 1970): 279–90, and "Technology, Political Economy and Professionalization: Central Themes of the Organizational Synthesis," *Business History Review* 57 (Winter 1983): 471–93. Olivier Zunz adds sophistication and human interest to this interpretation in *Making America Corporate, 1870–1920* (Chicago: University of Chicago Press, 1990).

5. I accept in general the distinction that historians of the organizational synthesis have drawn between the old middle class and a new middle class of corporate managers and bureaucrats—a distinction that involves differences in values as well as in occupational composition. I also recognize that the range of occupations and levels of business in club life, while not extraordinarily broad, does make it problematic to attempt generalizations about the members' place in an old or a new middle class. Nevertheless, this very difficulty confirms my sense of the service clubs as transitional organizations. The clubs could be identified with old values by one sociologist working in late twenties—Marden in *Rotary and Its Brothers*— and at the same time be identified with the values of the new middle class by others—the Lynds in *Middletown*. Zunz provides a brilliant description of the transition between an old and new middle-class order in *Making America Corporate*. For a discussion of the relationship between an old and new middle class as it stood in a provincial region in the 1930s, see Catherine McNicol Stock, *Main Street in Crisis*.

6. Reuel Denney, "Feast of Strangers: Varieties of Sociable Experience in America," in Herbert J. Gans et al., *On the Making of Americans: Essays in Honor of David Riesman* (Philadelphia: University of Pennsylvania Press, 1979), 251–69. Despite their many business and charitable activities, the Rotary, Kiwanis, and Lions clubs' prime concern was fellowship and social solidarity rather than any specific reform—in sociological terms, they are "expressive" rather than "instrumental" associations. I prefer the term "sociable," understanding that sociability always carries with it—"expresses"—crucial concerns of status, class, ethnicity, and gender. Of the large sociological literature on voluntarism, see in particular Constance E. Smith and Anne Freedman, *Voluntary Associations: Perspectives on the Literature* (Cambridge, Mass.: Harvard University Press, 1972), and James Q. Wilson, *Political Organizations* (New York: Basic Books, 1973).

7. Robert S. and Helen Merrell Lynd, *Middletown: A Study in American Culture* (1929; repr., New York: Harcourt, Brace and Co., 1956); William Whyte, *The Organization Man* (New York: Doubleday and Co., 1956); and David Riesman, *The Lonely Crowd: A Study in Changing American Character* (New Haven, Conn.: Yale University Press, 1950). Two historians who relate the change in personal identity to consumer capitalism are Warren Susman, in "From Character to Personality," in *Culture as History: The Transformation of American Society in the Twentieth Century* (New York: Pantheon, 1984); and T. J. Jackson Lears, especially in *No Place of Grace: Antimodernism and the Transformation of American Culture, 1880–1920* (New York: Pantheon, 1981), 32–58; and Lears and

Richard W. Fox, eds., *The Culture of Consumption: Critical Essays in American History, 1880–1980* (New York: Pantheon, 1983). Only *Middletown* refers to the clubs directly; the others are more concerned with the change in manners and style with which the clubs are associated.

Chapter 1: From Fraternity to Service

1. Harris wrote three autobiographies, all of which carried this account. The quoted phrases are drawn from *The Founder of Rotary* (Chicago: Rotary International, 1928), 38–107. The other autobiographies are *This Rotarian Age* (Chicago: Rotary International, 1935), and *My Road to Rotary* (Chicago: A. Kroch and Son, 1948).

2. The literature on fraternalism has expanded a great deal in recent years as historians have discovered its centrality to nineteenth-century male life. In this chapter I draw extensively on the studies of three historians. Mary Ann Clawson's book *Constructing Brotherhood: Class, Gender, and Fraternalism* (Princeton, N.J.: Princeton University Press, 1989) encapsulates the findings of two articles, "Fraternal Orders and Class Formation in the Nineteenth-Century United States," *Comparative Studies in Society and History* 27 (June 1985): 672–95, and "Nineteenth-Century Women's Auxiliaries and Fraternal Orders," *Signs* 12 (Autumn 1986), 40–61, and establishes her as the general authority on American fraternalism. Mark Carnes thoroughly explores the relationship between gender and fraternal ritualism in *Secret Ritual and Manhood in Victorian America* (New Haven, Conn.: Yale University Press, 1989). Also useful is Lynn Dumenil's persuasive study of Masonry in *Freemasonry and American Culture, 1880–1930* (Princeton, N.J.: Princeton University Press, 1984). Finally, John S. Gilkeson's exhaustive study of changes in one city's voluntary activity, *Middle-Class Providence, 1820–1940* (Princeton, N.J.: Princeton University Press, 1986), covers some of the transitions I will be discussing.

3. Thoreau, "Resistance to Civil Government," in *Reform Papers,* ed. Wendell Glick (Princeton, N.J.: Princeton University Press, 1973), 70–71; Alexis de Tocqueville, *Democracy in America,* ed. J. P. Mayer (Garden City, N.Y.: Doubleday, 1969), 509–13.

4. This process is best described in Mary P. Ryan, *Cradle of the Middle Class: The Family in Oneida County, New York, 1760–1865* (New York: Cambridge University Press, 1981), and Stuart M. Blumin, *The Emergence of the Middle Class: Social Experience in the American City, 1760–1900* (New York: Cambridge University Press, 1989). The sizable literature describing the role of gender in the middle-class cultural configuration is reviewed by Linda Kerber in "Separate Spheres, Female Worlds, Women's Place: The Rhetoric of Women's History," *Journal of American History* 75 (June 1988): 9–39.

5. On the role of voluntary associations, see Ryan, *Cradle of the Middle Class;* Blumin, *The Emergence of the Middle Class;* and Gilkeson, *Middle-Class Providence.* John F. Kasson describes the rise of behavior codes that came with the

emergence of a class society in *Rudeness and Civility: Manners in Nineteenth-Century Urban America* (New York: Hill and Wang, 1990). Covering some of the same ground is Karen Halttunen, *Confidence Men and Painted Women: A Study of Middle-Class Culture in America, 1830–1870* (New Haven, Conn.: Yale University Press, 1982).

6. The Manchester Unity of Odd-Fellows was created from a collection of local funeral benefit societies in 1810 and became one of England's first and largest affiliated orders. P. H. J. H. Gosden, *Self-Help: Voluntary Associations in Nineteenth-Century Britain* (New York: Harper and Row, 1974), 27–29; Robert W. Moffret, *The Rise and Progress of the Manchester Unity of the Independent Order of Odd-Fellows, 1810–1904* (Manchester: Board of Directors, Manchester Unity, 1905).

7. John Bodnar briefly discusses these associations in "Ethnic Fraternal Benefit Associations: Their Historical Development, Character, Significance," in *Records of Ethnic Fraternal Benefit Associations in the U.S.: Essays and Inventories* (St. Paul: University of Minnesota Press, 1981), 5–14. See also Lizabeth Cohen, *Making a New Deal: Industrial Workers in Chicago, 1919–1939* (Cambridge: Cambridge University Press, 1990), 64–75.

8. Paul Goodman, *Towards a Christian Republic: Antimasonry and the Great Transition in New England, 1826–1836* (New York: Oxford University Press, 1988); Dorothy Ann Lipson, *Freemasonry in Federalist Connecticut* (Princeton, N.J.: Princeton University Press, 1977); Kathleen Smith Kutolowski, "Freemasonry and Community in the Early American Republic: The Case for Antimasonic Anxieties," *American Quarterly* 34 (Winter 1982): 543–61.

9. Quoted in Theodore Ross, *Odd-Fellowship: Its History and Manual* (New York: M. W. Hazen, 1888), 98. Other measures are described in James L. Ridgely, *History of American Odd-Fellowship: The First Decade* (Baltimore, Md.: Published by author, 1878), 42–47, and Rev. B. B. Hallock, "History of Odd-Fellowship," in *The Odd-Fellows' Offering* (New York: Samuel A. House, 1842), 40.

10. The changes in fraternalism conform to other evidence of the "spread of gentility" supplied by Kasson in *Rudeness and Civility.*

11. Ritual from Past Grand Patriarch, *Revised Odd-Fellowship . . . Illustrated* (Chicago: Ezra A. Cook, 1886), 49; Dumenil, *Freemasonry and American Culture,* 88–111.

12. When the American Odd-Fellows formulated a ritual, they made the English Odd-Fellow ceremony more elaborate, adding dramatic scenes and lengthening the sacred oaths. This elaboration of ritual came at a time when the Manchester Unity was simplifying its own, focusing instead on efficiency in its benefits program. As a result of disagreements over ritual, the American Odd-Fellows split with the English fraternity in the early 1840s. In 1878 the Odd-Fellow historian James Ridgely wrote condescendingly of the Manchester Unity as "chiefly a life and health insurance company," while in the American order "we find stirring appeals to the higher nature and those moral and divine principles which elevate it almost to the dignity of a religion." *History of American Odd-Fellowship,* 10.

Dumenil finds similar sentiment among Freemasons. *Freemasonry and American Culture,* 31–71.

13. Carnes, *Secret Ritual and Manhood in Victorian America,* 146–57.

14. "Address before the Members of Illini Lodge #4, Independent Order of Odd-Fellows, Jacksonville, Ill., 20th day of July 1848," Illinois State Historical Archives.

15. Clawson, *Constructing Brotherhood,* 178–210.

16. On the efforts of orders to assuage fears and capitalize on the emotions of the Civil War, see Clawson, *Constructing Brotherhood,* 118–29, and Dumenil, *Freemasonry and American Culture,* 8–9.

17. A broad survey of fraternal orders in America, along with data on their membership and founding, can be found in Alvin J. Schmidt, *Fraternal Organizations* (Westport, Conn.: Greenwood Press, 1980). To the dismay of their white counterparts, blacks insisted on forming their own lodges of fraternal orders, such as the Masons, the Odd-Fellows, and the Elks, creating within them self-help communities. For a study of black Masonry, see William N. Muraskin, *Middle-Class Blacks in a White Society: Prince Hall Freemasonry in America* (Berkeley: University of California Press, 1975). Late in the nineteenth century Catholics won dispensation to organize the Knights of Columbus, a story told in Christopher Kauffman, *Faith and Fraternalism: The History of the Knights of Columbus, 1882–1982* (New York: Harper and Row, 1982).

18. For an illuminating discussion of the importance of fraternalism to the working class, see Richard Jules Oestreicher, *Solidarity and Fragmentation: Working People and Class Consciousness in Detroit, 1875–1900* (Urbana: University of Illinois Press, 1986), 16–118. Clawson offers a slightly different perspective in *Constructing Brotherhood,* 87–110.

19. The best general study of working classes and fraternalism is Clawson, *Constructing Brotherhood.* Gilkeson finds a cross-class membership in Providence, Rhode Island, Odd-Fellows lodges in *Middle-Class Providence,* 155–57. The mixed constituency of the Baltimore, Md., lodge is described in Ridgely, *History of American Odd-Fellowship.* John T. Cumbler discusses the working-class Odd-Fellows lodges in Lynn and Fall River, Massachusetts, in *Working Class and Community in Industrial America: Work, Leisure, and Struggle in Two Industrial Cities, 1880–1930* (Westport, Conn.: Greenwood Press, 1979), 44–50, 157–64. And Brian Greenberg focuses on laborers in Albany lodges in "Worker and Community: Fraternal Orders in Albany, New York, 1845–1885," *Maryland Historian* 8 (Fall 1977): 38–53. The discovery of the importance of fraternalism for the working class has led inevitably to a discussion of the relationship of fraternalism to working-class consciousness. Clawson makes a convincing argument that the fraternal ideology discouraged it. Richard Jules Oestreicher argues that fraternal orders in Detroit "led two ways—toward alliance with the middle class and toward radicalism." *Solidarity and Fragmentation,* 42–88. But the radicalism seems less due to fraternalism than to a hearty dose of socialism that Oestreicher also finds in Detroit working-class subculture.

20. Clawson, "Fraternal Orders and Class Formation," 689–93.

21. James M. Patton, "Odd-Fellowship," *Odd-Fellow World* 7 (Jan. 1900): 23.

22. David Thelen, *Paths of Resistance: Tradition and Dignity in Industrializing Missouri* (New York: Oxford University Press, 1986), 156–72.

23. Ross, in *Odd-Fellowship: Its History and Manual*, 240–70, makes reference to these troubles. Evidence is also in Grand Sire's Report, Independent Order of Foresters, *Fifty-first Annual Communication, Sovereign Grand Lodge*, 1875.

24. Quoted in Viviana A. Rotman Zelizer, *Morals and Markets: The Development of Life Insurance in the United States* (New York: Columbia University Press, 1979), 95.

25. Ross, *Odd-Fellowship: Its History and Manual*, 236. For a sampling of fraternal oratory, see Hallock, *The Odd-Fellows' Offering*, and *Fraternity: A Compilation of Historical Facts and Addresses Pertaining to Fraternalism in General and the Fraternal System in Particular* (Rochester, N.Y., 1910).

26. Zunz, *Making America Corporate*, 90–101.

27. Schmidt, *Fraternal Organizations*, 5–6; Clawson, *Constructing Brotherhood*, 211–42.

28. On this transformation, see Blumin, *The Emergence of the Middle Class*, 263–97; Zunz, *Making America Corporate*, 125–48; and Jurgen Kocka, *White-Collar Workers in America, 1890–1940: A Social-Political History in International Perspective* (Beverly Hills, Calif.: Sage Publications, 1980). On interdependence, see Thomas Haskell, *The Emergence of Professional Social Science: The American Social Science Association and the Nineteenth-Century Crisis of Authority* (Chicago: University of Chicago Press, 1977), 1–47, 234–40.

29. On the cultural impact of consumption, see Lears, *No Place of Grace*, and Lewis Ehrenberg, *Stepping Out: New York Nightlife and the Transformation of American Culture, 1890–1930* (Chicago: University of Chicago Press, 1981). On the middle-class "crisis," see Alan Dawley, *Struggles for Justice: Social Responsibility and the Liberal State* (Cambridge, Mass.: Belknap Press, 1991), 63–172.

30. James Gilbert notes that while members of the middle class were "inventing new vocations and acting in different ways, they did not entirely cast off older notions of behavior, propriety, and culture—thus the troubled, even divided consciousness of self at the turn of the century." *Perfect Cities: Chicago's Utopias of 1893* (Chicago: University of Chicago Press, 1991), 7. Catherine McNicol Stock argues that middle-class Dakotans clung to traditional conceptions of family and community into the 1930s. *Main Street in Crisis*, 41–85.

31. Gilkeson, *Middle-Class Providence*, 148–57. On urban upper-class associations, see Frederic Jaher, *The Urban Establishment: Upper Strata in Boston, New York, Charleston, Chicago, and Los Angeles* (Urbana: University of Illinois Press, 1982).

32. What it meant to have a mixed-sex work force is discussed by Cindy Sondrik Aron in *Ladies and Gentlemen of the Civil Service: Middle-Class Workers in Victorian America* (New York: Oxford University Press, 1987). See also Dawley, *Struggles for Justice*, 85–97, and Zunz, *Making America Corporate*, 126–48.

33. Margaret Marsh, *Suburban Lives* (New Brunswick, N.J.: Rutgers Uni-

versity Press, 1990), 32–40. See also Steven Mintz and Susan Kellog, *Domestic Revolutions: A Social History of American Family Life* (New York: Free Press, 1988), 107–31.

34. Carnes, *Secret Ritual and Victorian Manhood,* 153–55.

35. Editorial in *Odd-Fellow World* 7 (May 1900): 15.

36. *The Sons of Malta Exposed: By One Who Was "Sold"* (New York: Published by author, 1860); Grand Sire's Report, *Sixty-ninth Annual Communication, Proceedings of the Sovereign Grand Lodge,* I.O.O.F., Baltimore, Md., 1892.

37. Quote and description of the order's changing character in Charles Edward Ellis, *An Authentic History of the Benevolent and Protective Order of Elks* (Chicago: B.P.O.E., 1910), 197–200.

38. James R. Nicholson, *History of the Order of Elks, 1868–1952* (Chicago: B.P.O.E., 1953), 230–400; John W. Wilks, "The Uplift of the Order of Elks," *American Elk* 14 (Jan. 15, 1915): 5.

39. Editorial, *Elks Magazine* 6 (Sept. 1927): 39.

40. Davis wrote an autobiography, *The Iron Puddler* (New York: Grosset and Dunlap, 1922), which describes his early laboring life but quickly passes over his Moose organizing work to discuss "Mooseheart." Slightly more detailed, but utterly adulatory, is a biography by fellow Moose Joe Mitchell Chapple, *Our Jim* (Boston: Chapple Publishing Co., 1928). The clearest picture of Davis's Moose activities comes from a more complete in-house history, Warner Oliver, *Back of the Dream: The Story of the Loyal Order of Moose* (New York: E. P. Dutton and Co., 1952). Davis's personal papers, containing his speeches and addresses as secretary of labor, as well as correspondence concerning the Moose in the thirties, are housed in the Library of Congress.

41. David W. Harter, *Historical Souvenir of the Loyal Order of Moose* (Chicago: Published by author, 1915), 33–73; Guy H. Fuller, ed., *Loyal Order of the Moose and Mooseheart* (Mooseheart, Ill.: Mooseheart Press, 1918), 36–52.

42. "James Davis Appeals to Our Women," *Mooseheart Magazine* 2 (Nov. 1916): 99.

43. Davis, "Address to the National Association of Catholic Charities, Sept. 17, 1922," MS, Box 38, James Davis Papers, Library of Congress; "Pittsburgh Speech," MS, Box 39. Davis's appointment book shows more meetings with corporate heads such as Armour, Babson, and J. B. Bonner of U.S. Steel than with labor leaders. Box 1, James Davis Papers.

44. Roger Babson, "What the Moose Can Do for Business," *Proceedings,* Loyal Order of Moose, Thirty-fifth Annual Convention, Supreme Lodge of the World, Toledo, Ohio, 1921, 86–93. Davis ignored an appeal in 1931 to respect a Cleveland hotel strike by holding the convention elsewhere in 1931. See William Green to Davis, Feb. 19, 1931, Correspondence, Box 3, James Davis Papers.

45. On the move to masculinize religion, see Gail Bederman, "The Women Have Had Charge of the Church Work Long Enough": The Men and Religion Forward Movement of 1911–1912 and the Masculinization of Middle-Class Protestantism," *American Quarterly* 41 (Fall 1989), 432–63.

46. Richard T. Ely, "The Social Law of Service," in Robert T. Handy, ed., *The*

Social Gospel in America, 1870–1920 (New York: Oxford University Press, 1966), 221–34. Susan Curtis places the social gospel and its key practitioners within the context of new middle-class values, particularly those concerning work, domesticity, and consumerism, in *A Consuming Faith: The Social Gospel and Modern American Culture* (Baltimore, Md.: Johns Hopkins University Press, 1991).

47. See Anne Firor Scott, "Women's Voluntary Associations in the Forming of American Society," *Making the Invisible Woman Visible* (Urbana: University of Illinois Press, 1984), and her fuller treatment of women's clubs in *Natural Allies: Women's Associations in American History* (Urbana: University of Illinois Press, 1991), 111–40.

48. Mrs. Jane Cunningham Croly, *Sorosis: Its Origin and History* (1886; repr., New York: Arno Press, 1975). An excellent discussion of women's study clubs is Theodora Penny Martin, *The Sound of Our Own Voices: Women's Study Clubs, 1860–1910* (Boston: Beacon Press, 1987). For a study of the women's club movement focusing on its activism in the 1890s and 1900s, see Karen J. Blair, *The Clubwoman as Feminist: True Womanhood Redefined, 1868–1914* (New York: Holmes and Meier Publishers, 1980).

49. "Mrs. Brown's Final Address," in Mary I. Wood, *The History of the General Federation of Women's Clubs* (New York: Norwood Press, 1912), 329 (hereafter cited as *The History of the GFWC*).

50. Clawson, *Constructing Brotherhood,* 178–210.

51. Martin, *The Sound of Our Own Voices,* 142–81.

52. Turn-of-the-century dissatisfaction with domesticity is discussed in Annegret S. Ogden, *The Great American Housewife: From Helpmate to Wage Earner, 1776–1986* (Westport, Conn.: Greenwood Press, 1986), 135–70.

53. Quoted in Wood, *The History of the GFWC,* 250.

54. Henriette Greenbaum Frank and Amalie Hofer Jerome, eds., *Annals of the Chicago Woman's Club* (Chicago: Chicago Woman's Club, 1916), 62; Mrs. Ellen Henrotin, *Official Proceedings,* GFWC, Third Biennial Convention, Louisville, Ky., 1896, 23–37. In cities members of the federated clubs appear to have been mainly fairly wealthy upper-class women; in small towns the membership was less wealthy, but solidly middle class. Blair, *The Clubwoman as Feminist,* 95–96; Gilkeson, *Middle-Class Providence,* 162.

55. Quoted in Helen McKay Steele, *The Indianapolis Women's Club, 1875–1940* (Greenfield, Ind.: Wm. Mitchell Printing Co., 1944), 27. The concern expressed by Mrs. Brown, that "mismanagement [or] inefficiency might wreck our Federation fleet" (Wood, *The History of the GFWC,* 324), appears in even the smaller clubs. The Friday Afternoon Club, of Farmington, New Hampshire, discussed parliamentary practice once a month. *Topics, 1905–06* (Farmington, N.H.: Privately printed, 1905).

56. Sarah Platt Decker, "Opportunity of Women's Clubs to Improve the Usefulness of Public and Private Institutions," *Official Proceedings,* GFWC, Third Biennial Convention, Louisville, Ky., 1896, 182–85; Decker quoted in Wood, *The History of the GFWC,* 109.

57. Greenbaum and Jerome, eds., *Annals of the Chicago Woman's Club, 1876–1916*, 278–301; Blair, *The Clubwoman as Feminist*, 278–301. Blair, anxious to establish the feminist credentials of club women, stresses the city clubs' important role in the Progressive movement. However, women's clubs in smaller cities and towns, like the men's service clubs that were soon to follow, worked to strengthen, not disrupt, communal unity and avoided the controversies progressive politics might raise.

58. For the fate of the clubs in the twenties, see Stanley J. Lemons, *The Woman Citizen: Social Feminism in the 1920s* (Urbana: University of Illinois Press, 1973), 54–55, 123–24. On women's movements in the twenties, see Nancy Cott, *The Grounding of Modern Feminism* (New Haven, Conn.: Yale University Press, 1987).

59. Paula Baker describes the role of rural New York women's organizations in creating a new conception of public life—and also their failure to profit from this new conception—in *The Moral Frameworks of Public Life: Gender, Politics, and the State in Rural New York, 1870–1930* (New York: Oxford University Press, 1991).

60. Harry Emerson Fosdick, *The Meaning of Service* (New York: Association Press, 1920).

61. Although lodge membership lists proved difficult to obtain in the Illinois communities where most local research for this study was done, work through local obituary or biography files suggests that about one-third of the service club members were members of fraternal orders, mostly Masonic lodges. A detailed roster of the Montgomery, Alabama, Rotary Club of 1922 lists 36 percent of the members as Masons, 22 percent as members of the Elk, and lesser percentages in other orders. Charles Marden in a survey done in 1929 found a similar percentage—159 of 421 men, or 37 percent, belonged to the Masonic order. Marden, *Rotary and Its Brothers*, 67.

62. Frank L. Mulholland, "Women and Rotary," *Rotarian* 27 (Jan. 1925): 14–15. The formation of businesswomen's service groups—Soroptimists, Zonta, and Quota—with the aid of Stuart Murrow, a professional organizer tangentially affiliated with Rotary—helped bolster the arguments of those opposed to women's membership. The material in the "Women and Rotary" file at Rotary Headquarters shows, however, that individual members continued to take the possibility seriously. See below, chapter 7.

63. Harris article in the *Rotarian* 31 (Nov. 1927): 10–12; Will Manier to Jas. Carmichael, Cape Town, South Africa, Jan. 22, 1925, "Rotary and Blacks" file at Rotary International.

64. Rabbi Steven Wise, for example, received a standing ovation at the 1924 Rotary convention. He praised the organization for "standing like a rock against every attempt of class or group or clan to divide America." *Proceedings* Fifteenth Annual Convention, Toronto, 1924, 272. Service clubs were overwhelmingly Protestant, although exact statistics are difficult to establish, since religious affiliation was not listed on membership applications and only infrequently in rosters. In a

survey of 500 club members in New Jersey, Marden found that 319 were Protestant (64 percent), 68 were Catholic (13 percent), and 19 were Jewish (4 percent). *Rotary and Its Brothers,* 64. Anecdotal evidence, however, supports the contention that religious prejudice was not one of the pervasive faults of the clubs. Social and political life in Herrin, Illinois, was in the twenties disturbed by conflicts over Klan activity. By the early thirties the town's Rotary club had as an active member a Roman Catholic priest from Italy, and it boasted a Jewish president, and at least one visitor credited the club with pulling the community together in hard times. Visit of James H. Roth to Herrin Illionis, Feb. 19, 1934, Herrin Club File, Rotary Headquarters.

65. This assessment of the Klan is based on new studies establishing that the Klan represented a cross-section of the community, united more by a reactionary vision than by economic or status grievances. For a summary of these studies, see Stanley Coben, *The Rebellion against Victorianism: The Impetus for Cultural Change in 1920s America* (New York: Oxford University Press, 1991), 136–56. Among the most significant representatives of the new works are William D. Jenkins, *Steel Valley Klan: The Ku Klux Klan in Ohio's Mahoning Valley* (Kent, Ohio: Kent State University Press, 1990), and Leonard J. Moore, *Citizen Klansmen: The Ku Klux Klan in Indiana, 1921–1928* (Chapel Hill: University of North Carolina Press, 1991).

66. See especially Moore, *Citizen Klansmen,* 106–50, and Coben, *Rebellion against Victorianism,* 141–50. While some of their revisionist portrait of the Klan is convincing, the portrayal of Klansmen as victims, heroically fighting the cold-hearted business interests out to destroy their community, is objectionable. Moore in particular puts this slant on the Klan. He begins his chapter on the local efforts of the Klan by quoting the Lynds on the loss of democracy, the increase in corruption, and the impersonality of greed that now prevailed in a community dominated by business elites. The Klan, in contrast, was a populist organization, involving women and children in their picnic outings and generally paying attention to the needs of the average person. Of course, Moore has to admit that Catholics and blacks felt a great deal of fear at the cross burnings that also took place. But because no actual violence occurred and the real enemy was the economic elite, this aspect of Klan membership is downplayed.

67. An example of this contrast is the relative lack of concern club members displayed about Prohibition, which was a central issue for the Klan. Occasionally members paid lip service to "obeying the law of the land," particularly in relation to boy's work and "setting an example for America's youth." But the mayor of Atlanta felt no qualms about welcoming the 1923 Kiwanis convention by saying, "I trust you delegates to the great International Kiwanis convention have discovered ere this time that Atlanta is wet. If you have not, when you go back to your hotels just ask the bellboy." Kiwanis International, *Proceedings,* Atlanta, 1923, 57. Later, in the 1930s, the repeal of Prohibition was scarcely noted in convention proceedings.

68. On the status of fraternal orders in the thirties, see Robert S. and Helen

Merrell Lynd, *Middletown in Transition: A Study in Cultural Conflict* (New York: Harcourt, Brace, and Co., 1937), and W. Lloyd Warner et al., *Democracy in Jonesville: A Study in Quality and Inequality* (New York: Harper and Row, 1949). The Eagles are described in Schmidt, *Fraternal Organizations,* 65.

69. Dumenil, *Freemasonry and American Culture,* 115–20; "Report of the Grand Sire," I.O.O.F., *Eighty-fifth Annual Communication, Proceedings, Sovereign Grand Lodge,* Toronto, 1921, 10–81.

70. Dumenil, *Freemasonry and American Culture,* 185–221.

71. Lucien J. Eastin, "Report of the Grand Sire," *One-hundredth Annual Communication, Proceedings, Sovereign Grand Lodge,* Jacksonville, Fla., 398–99; Herbert A. Thompson, "Report of the Grand Sire," *One-hundred-and-first Annual Communication, Proceedings, Sovereign Grand Lodge,* Portland, Ore., 1925, 30; Clawson, *Constructing Brotherhood,* 241–42.

72. Thomas G. Andrews, *The Jericho Road: The Philosophy of Odd-Fellowship* (Oklahoma City: William Thomas Co., 1937), 426.

Chapter 2: Serving Business

1. Owen Young quoted in Wallace B. Donhom, "The Emerging Profession of Business," *Harvard Business Review* 5 (July 1927): 401.

2. George W. Dudderer, "Membership in Trade and Professional Organizations," Rotary International, *Proceedings,* Third Annual Conference, Twenty-fourth District, Clarksburg, W.Va., 1925, 99.

3. For a concise overview of small business's role in the American economy, see Mansel G. Blackford, *A History of Small Business in America* (New York: Twayne Publishers, 1992).

4. Roland Berthoff, "Independence and Enterprise: Small Business in the American Dream," in Stuart Bruchey, ed., *Small Business in American Life* (New York: Columbia University Press, 1980).

5. C. Wright Mills, *White Collar: The American Middle Classes* (New York: Oxford University Press, 1953), 34–59.

6. Virgil Jordon, "The Business Psychle," *Freeman* 8 (Dec. 5, 1923): 298–300.

7. Advertisement in *National Rotarian* 2 (Mar. 1912): 14.

8. Arthur F. Sheldon, *The Science of Efficient Service, or the Philosophy of Profit Making* (Chicago: Sheldon Business Schools, 1915).

9. Harris, pamphlet dated 1908, Rotary History File, Rotary International.

10. "The Story of Rotary," *Rotarian* 34 (Feb. 1929): 21.

11. Of the 253 members listed on the 1910 Chicago roster, 175, or approximately 70 percent, were in the retail or service sector, supplying goods and services to local markets. Only 11 percent were manufacturers, who presumably had customers beyond city limits, while the others were professionals, railroad or utility executives, and handlers of agricultural products (such as stockyard owners) who also clearly had outside clients. The same figures hold for clubs in San Francisco—53 of 75, 70 percent in the commercial sector (San Francisco also had seven rail-

road executives); Los Angeles—177 of 252, 70 percent in local retail and services (with the bulk of the remainder belonging to shippers and suppliers of agricultural products); Seattle—132 of 193, 68 percent (Seattle had a relatively high percentage of manufacturers, 32, or 16 percent); and New York—79 of 105, 75 percent, serving primarily local markets.

12. A. M. Ramsay to Charlie Newton, Aug. 7, 1923. Chicago Club File, Rotary International.

13. Annual Report of the Chicago Association of Commerce, 1909; *Chicago: The Great Central Market: Its Representative Merchants and Factors* (Chicago Commercial Association, 1905), 10; Vilas Johnson, *A History of the Commercial Club of Chicago* (Chicago: Privately printed, 1977).

14. Daniel Cady to German Emory, May 13, 1910, New York Club File, Rotary International.

15. Harris, *My Road to Rotary,* 232. In a survey taken of charter members in 1920, most admitted they found profits the greatest incentive to join the club (and mentioned the great deal of business they did in fact receive), but four of the ten responding spoke of sociability as an additional incentive. All went on to say they now valued the fellowship more. Rotary History Files, Rotary International.

16. Rotary Club of Oakland, *Rotarily Yours: A History of the Rotary Club of Oakland* (Oakland, Calif.: Rotary Club of Oakland, 1969), 34; M. H. Diffenbaugh to Chesley R. Perry, Jan. 12, 1912, and H. C. Winslow to Chesley Perry, Dec. 21, 1910, Lancaster, Pa., Club File, Rotary International.

17. "E.G." [Emerson Gauss?], "History of the Rotary Club of Chicago," Rotary History File, Rotary International, 66–70; *Bulletin of the Chicago Association of Commerce* 3 (Oct. 25, 1907): 3.

18. National Association of Rotary Clubs, *Proceedings*, Second National Convention, Portland, Ore., 1911, 11.

19. Association of Rotary Clubs, *Proceedings*, First National Convention, Chicago, 1910, 98.

20. John R. Knutson, "Rotary and Christian Ideals," *Rotarian* 4 (Jan. 1914): 5.

21. Rotary International, *Proceedings*, Seventh Annual Convention, Atlantic City, N.J., 1917, 42; E. J. Skeel, "Greater Rotary," pamphlet issued by the Seattle Rotary Club, Seattle Club File, Rotary International.

22. On the interaction of law and corporate ideology, see Martin Sklar, *The Corporate Reconstruction of American Capitalism, 1890–1916* (New York: Cambridge University Press, 1988), 166–74; Louis Brandeis, *Business—A Profession* (Boston: Small, Maynard, and Co., 1914), 7. Thomas L. Haskell examines the thought of Tawney and Durkheim in "Professionalism versus Capitalism," in Haskell, ed., *The Authority of Experts* (Bloomington: Indiana University Press, 1984), 180–225; Paul Harris to Mac Martin, Feb. 23, 1910, Minneapolis Club File, Rotary International.

23. Allan Albert, Address, *Proceedings*, Fourth Annual Convention, Buffalo, New York, 1913, Rotary History Files, Rotary International.

24. Close analysis of the urban constituencies of progressivism appears in the

case studies compiled in Michael H. Ebner and Eugene Tobin, eds., *The Age of Urban Reform: New Perspectives on the Progressive Era* (Port Washington, N.Y.: Kennikat Press, 1977).

25. Thomas James Riley, *A Study of the Higher Life of Chicago* (Chicago: University of Chicago Press, 1905), 54; Chicago Club File, Rotary International.

26. Kevin Starr, *Inventing the Dream: California through the Progressive Era* (New York: Oxford University Press, 1985), 228.

27. Judith Sealander, *Grand Plans: Business Progressivism and Social Change in Ohio's Miami Valley, 1890–1920* (Lexington: University of Kentucky Press, 1988); Sally Griffith, *Hometown News: William Allen White and the Emporia Gazette* (New York: Oxford University Press, 1988). The classic work on the relationship between business and progressivism is Robert H. Wiebe, *Businessmen and Reform: A Study of the Progressive Movement* (Cambridge, Mass.: Harvard University Press, 1962). On business involvement in progressive municipal reform, see Martin J. Schiesl, *The Politics of Efficiency: Municipal Administration and Reform in America, 1800–1920* (Berkeley: University of California Press, 1977), esp. 133–48 and 171–88. As an example of club involvement in progressive reform, the Seattle Rotary Club participated in a broad reform program led by the city's municipal league, but the reforms involved not so much fundamental institutional change as nativist measures promoting social order. Lee F. Pendergrass, "Urban Reform and Voluntary Association: The Municipal League of Seattle, 1910–1916," in Ebner and Tobin, *The Age of Urban Reform*, 62.

28. See Crummey's recollection is in Rotary History File, Rotary International.

29. Zunz, *Making America Corporate*, 176–97.

30. Mettler to Mr. W. E. Whittlesey, June 19, 1936, Davenport, Iowa, File, Rotary International.

31. The development of Kiwanis is detailed in L. A. Hapgood, *The Men Who Wear the K* (Indianapolis, Ind.: Kiwanis International, 1981), and Oren Arnold, *The Widening Path: An Interpretative Record of Kiwanis* (Chicago: Kiwanis International, 1949.

32. The standard in-house history of Lionism is Robert J. Casey and W. A. S. Douglas, *World's Biggest Doers* (Chicago: Wilcox and Follett, 1959).

33. Wilson and his advisors, hoping to avoid excessive expansion in the scope of the federal government, inspired widespread voluntarism through a campaign of propaganda and support of local activity. David M. Kennedy, *Over Here* (New York: Oxford University Press, 1980).

34. Rotary International, *Proceedings,* Eighth Annual Convention, Atlanta, 1918.

35. President John Poole's Address, Rotary International, *Proceedings,* Ninth Annual Convention, Salt Lake City, 1919, 24; Walter Kern, in "The Rotarian Open Forum," *Rotarian* 14 (Mar. 1919): 69.

36. Statistics compiled from published club directories, 1920–29.

37. "Brief History of Rotary," in Rotary International, *Manual of Procedure for Rotarians* (Chicago: Rotary International, 1920), 5.

38. Statistics compiled by comparing yearly lists of new clubs with the U.S. Census of 1930. Statistics concerning total membership from Charles Marden, *Rotary and Its Brothers,* 121.

39. Harry D. Kitson, "Growth of the 'Service Idea' in Selling," *Rotarian* 20 (Feb. 1922): 56; Gerald Swope, "What Big Business Owes the Public," *World's Work* 53 (Mar. 1927): 556. See also Morrell Heald, "Big Business Thought in the Twenties: Social Responsibility," *American Quarterly* 25 (Mar. 1962): 223–46.

40. Rotary International, *Proceedings,* Fourteenth Annual Convention, St. Louis, 1923, 231.

41. *The Weekly Letter* 9 (Sept. 21, 1925), Rotary International.

42. Herbert Hoover, *American Individualism* (New York: Doubleday and Co., 1922), quotes from 27–30, 71–72.

43. Ellis W. Hawley, in J. Joseph Huthmacher and Warren I. Susman, eds. *Herbert Hoover and the Crisis of American Capitalism* (Cambridge, Mass.: Schenkman Publishing Co., 1973), 4–5. In her biography of Hoover, Joan Hoff Wilson also notes the attempt to reconcile old and new economic values in a "philosophy of vague corporatism." *Herbert Hoover: Forgotten Progressive* (Boston: Little, Brown and Co., 1975), 35–40.

44. Hawley provides an excellent summary of corporate liberalism in his article, "The Discovery and Study of a 'Corporate Liberalism,'" *Business History Review* 52 (Autumn 1978): 309–19. See also, in the same issue, Kim McQuaid, "Corporate Liberalism in the American Business Community, 1920–1940."

45. In fact, Mansel G. Blackford notes that small business owners in the early twentieth century "participated less fully than most other Americans in the organizational life of the United States, even when such participation would have been in their best economic interest." *A History of Small Business in America,* 60. I would argue, however, that Blackford does not pay enough attention to small business participation in service clubs and chambers of commerce.

46. Kiwanis International, *Proceedings,* Eleventh Annual Convention, Memphis, Tenn., 1927, 159.

47. Editorial, *Lion* 4 (Mar. 1922): 338; Crawford McCullough, "The Expression of the Rotary Idea through Its Rules and Regulations," in *Proceedings,* Seventeenth Annual Convention, Ostend, Belgium, 1927, 166. "Report of the Committee on Classification," Kiwanis International, *Proceedings,* Seventh Annual Convention, Atlanta, 1923, 84.

48. Guy Gundaker, President's Address, Rotary International, *Proceedings,* Fifteenth Annual Convention, Toronto, 1924, 31. Other information from the Gundaker Biographical File, Rotary International.

49. Poe Fulkerson, "Public Service and Scientific Management," *Kiwanis Magazine* 10 (Mar. 1925): 134. Not all club members held this view, including one Kiwanian who blamed the faults of his club on "attorney domination" and complained, "I have never been to a convention yet but what there has been a preponderance of professional men running it." His comment went unremarked because

the four men directing the discussion were all lawyers. *Proceedings,* Eleventh Annual Convention, Memphis, Tennessee, 1927, 187.

50. Statistics compiled using club directories, 1920–29.

51. Wiebe notes the leading role of professionals in advancing the network of national associations. *The Search for Order,* 111–32.

52. Edward A. Silberstein, "Improving the Relationship between Competitors," Rotary International, *Proceedings,* 1925, Sixteenth Annual Convention, Cleveland, Ohio, 392–93.

53. Codes of ethics were prominently displayed in each club magazine and in many local club rosters.

54. Kiwanis International, *Proceedings,* Thirteenth Annual Convention, Milwaukee, 1929, 277.

55. Rotary International, *Proceedings,* Tenth Annual Convention, Salt Lake City, 1919, 219.

56. Rotary International, *Proceedings,* Sixteenth Annual Convention, Cleveland, Ohio, 1925, 105.

57. Susan Curtis makes a slightly different, but I think equally valid, point—that those who combined business and religion helped sanctify the corporate consumer economy. *A Consuming Faith: The Social Gospel and Modern American Culture* (Baltimore, Md.,: Johns Hopkins University Press, 1991), 228–78. Rolf Lunden discusses club religiosity in *Business and Religion in the American 1920s* (Westport, Conn.: Greenwood Press, 1988).

58. From Rotary club files, it appears that the smaller towns were the least likely to obey classification rules and had the most difficulty coming up with vocational service programs. Examples include Jefferson, Ohio, Rocky Mount, N.C., and Indianola, Iowa. Kiwanis Club vocational service is discussed in *Proceedings,* Ninth Annual Convention, St. Paul, Minnesota, 1925, 69. The Lions Club placed considerably less stress on classification and vocational service; thus, in the Lions' case this conflict between national aims and club practice was less noticeable.

59. Address of Raymond J. Knoeppel, *Proceedings,* Thirteenth Annual Conference of Rotary Clubs, Second District, Sacramento, 1928, 46.

60. Kiwanis International, *Proceedings,* 1925, 69. Evidence for this inactivity also appears later, in the correspondence of the 1935–36 Kiwanis district governor, Elmer Embree. Letters urging club projects in the area of "improving business standards" were to no avail, and finally Embree had to write an official at Kiwanis headquarters. "This activity [business standards] has not gone so hot. Guess the subject is like the weather-'dry.'" Elmer Embree to Mr. George H. Alfa, Aug. 1, 1936, Embree Papers, Box 9, File 44, Northern Illinois Regional History Center.

61. Raymond J. Wheeler, speech in *Proceedings,* Twelfth Annual Conference, Second District Rotary International, Stockton, 1927; Kiwanis International, *Proceedings,* Thirteenth Annual Convention, Milwaukee, Wis., 1929, 22.

62. "A History of De Kalb Kiwanis Club, 1921–1967," Northern Illinois Regional History Center, Collection 18, Box 1.

63. Of these three, the individual attendance requirement caused the most diffi-culty. It was aimed at the common problem of members joining clubs but then not bothering to attend meetings. It also created an extremely high membership turn-over—members would join, miss the requisite meetings, and be expelled, perhaps to join again later. To create more incentives for attendance, all three organizations held yearly attendance contests, awarding the winners prizes and also publishing the names of the clubs with the lowest percentages.

64. David Smith Reichlin, "From Civic Duty to Psychological Reward" (Ph.D. diss., University of Pittsburgh, 1981), 56.

65. Gilkeson describes a similar standardization for federated women's clubs in *Middle-Class Providence,* 250.

66. Quoted in "A History of Lionism" (unpublished MS, Lions International), 38. The Lions were the first to use paid organizers to expand from town to town. Until the mid-twenties Rotary and Kiwanis either relied on indigenous organiza-tion or on older clubs to father new groups in nearby communities. As a result, the Lions grew far more rapidly than the other two, but, sometimes lacking true local grounding, it also had a greater club failure rate. See Marden, *Rotary and Its Brothers,* 127.

67. Harris paid Chesley Perry high tribute, calling him "the builder of Rotary International." Perry had worked as a bank clerk and as secretary of a fraternal association before becoming Rotary's first general secretary in 1910, a job he held until 1942. From all accounts, he was an aloof but dedicated worker, with a high conception of Rotary's purpose.

68. Perry to Glenn Mead, June 6, 1914, Philadelphia Club File, Rotary Interna-tional; Raymond M. Harris to Roscoe Taylor, July 20, 1922, Lincoln, Nebr., Club File, Rotary International.

69. Rotary International, Minutes of the Board of Directors Meeting, Oct.–Nov., 1922, 16.

70. Editorial, *Kiwanis Magazine* 9 (July 1924): 373; Kiwanis International, *Proceedings,* Eleventh Annual Convention, Memphis, Tenn., 1927, 138.

71. Writing of local opposition to federal education reform, Lynn Dumenil notes a pervasive fear of federal bureaucracy in the 1920s combined with a relative complacency about the bureaucratic impact of private organizations. "'The Insa-tiable Maw of Bureaucracy": Antistatism and Education Reform in the 1920s," *Journal of American History* 77 (Sept. 1990): 499–524. The complaints of club members show that they were aware that although private associations could also bring some standardization and loss of local control, the local rewards of club presence were compensation.

72. Lizabeth Cohen, *Making a New Deal: Industrial Workers in Chicago, 1919–1939,* 53–158.

Chapter 3: Serving the Community

1. "Great Rotary Meeting Comes to a Brilliant Finale at Big Dinner," *Bloomington Pantagraph,* Apr. 9, 1920, 2.

2. Though he slights the Midwest in *Rotary and Its Brothers,* Marden makes some interesting speculations about the appeal of service clubs to the West and Southwest. He explains the prominence of clubs in California and Texas by the newness of many of the towns there, which generated a desire to establish "community" quickly through organizations. Studies of new suburbs in the fifties support this reasoning. See below, chapter 7. *Rotary and Its Brothers,* 120–73.

3. Timothy Mahoney, *River Towns in the Great West: The Structure of Provincial Urbanization in the American Midwest, 1820–1870* (New York: Cambridge University Press, 1990).

4. *Ottawa, Old and New: A Complete History of Ottawa, Illinois, 1823–1914* (1912–14; repr., Ottawa, Ill.: *Republican Times,* 1984).

5. On midwestern manufacturing, see William N. Parker, "Native Origins of Modern Industry: Heavy Industrialization in the Old Northwest before 1900," and David Klingaman, "The Nature of Midwest Manufacturing in 1890," in David C. Klingaman and Richard K. Vedder, eds., *Essays on the Economy of the Old Northwest* (Athens: Ohio University Press, 1987), 243–98.

6. These struggles are described in *Ottawa, Old and New;* Louise Kessler, *Hometown in the Cornbelt: A Source History of Bloomington* (Bloomington, Ill.: Privately printed, McClean County Historical Society, 1950); and Louis Scott Gard, *A Centennial History of Jacksonville, 1825–1925* (Jacksonville, Ill.: Privately printed, Jacksonville Public Library, 1925). The lengths Princeton, Illinois, went to avoid acquisition of its power plant by a Chicago syndicate in the first three decades of the twentieth century—continued operation in the red, more expensive service, and limitations on peak load use—shows the degree to which outside control of utilities was disliked by local residents. However, as the historian of Princeton points out, "Few cities, if any, operating their own electric light and power plants have more successfully weathered the opposition to municipal ownership or withstood the luring inducements of corporations." George Owen Smith, *A History of Princeton* (Princeton, Ill.: Matson Public Library, 1966), 118.

7. *Ottawa, Old and New,* 144.

8. On the interurban, see George W. Hilton and John F. Due, *The Electric Interurban Railways in America* (Palo Alto, Calif.: Stanford University Press, 1960), 335–432. On local attitudes to the interurban, see Norman Moline, "Mobility and the Small Town, 1900–1930: Transportation Change in Oregon, Illinois" (University of Chicago Department of Geography, Research Paper No. 132, 1971); Smith, *A History of Princeton,* 122; Louise Scott Gard, *Centennial History of Jacksonville, 1825–1925,* 86.

9. Carl Carlson, *Aurora, Illinois: A Study in Sequent Land Use* (Private edition, distributed by University of Chicago Libraries, 1940), 20–50.

10. Sterling Merchants Association Ledger and Minute Book, entry Nov. 20,

1912, Northern Illinois Regional History Center, Collection 171, File 1. Apparently Peoria businessmen were also encouraged by Chicago's Association of Commerce to form their own association. "Peoria's Association of Commerce," *Peoria Journal*, Feb. 2, 1948, 3.

11. Scrapbook, Sterling Chamber of Commerce, Northern Illinois Regional History Center, Collection 171, 1.

12. Sally Griffith describes this process in Emporia, Kansas, in *Hometown News*.

13. Burl Noggle, *Into the Twenties: The United States from Armistice to Normalcy* (Urbana: University of Illinois Press, 1974), 155. For a favorable contemporary evaluation of these efforts, see Jesse F. Steiner, "An Appraisal of the Community Movement," *Journal of Social Forces* 7 (Mar. 1929): 333–42.

14. Edwin Lord to Chesley Perry, Jan. 29, 1914, Ottawa, Ill., Club File, Rotary International.

15. Perry to Elwood R. Kroos, Dec. 30, 1913, Ottawa, Ill., Club File, Rotary International.

16. Crawford McCullogh, "The Expression of the Rotary Idea through Its Rules and Regulations," 166; Frances Hazelton Williams, "What Lionism Has Accomplished in Small Cities," *Lion* 11 (Jan. 1928): 38–39.

17. Carl Metzger to Chesley Perry, Dec. 20, 1913, and James Collins to Perry, Dec. 16, 1913, Ottawa, Ill., Club File, Rotary International.

18. R. M. McClure to Perry, June 19, 1913, Morris, Ill., Club File, Rotary International; F. Wayne Graham, *Sixty-five Years of Devotion and Accomplishment: A Brief History of the Rotary Club of Morris* (Morris, Ill.: Rotary Club of Morris, 1980).

19. Fred High, *Making Service Pay,* distributed by the Community Development Association, 1922, Local History File, Jacksonville, Ill., Jacksonville Public Library.

20. District governor's memo, 1929, Jacksonville, Ill., Club File, Rotary International.

21. Tom Davis to Cecil B. Harris, Jan. 17, 1922, and D. S. Wentworth to Mr. Phillips, 1924, Aurora, Ill., Club File, Rotary International.

22. The rosters of the Bloomington, Illinois, clubs are on file at the McClean County Historical Society.

23. On Funk, see Hellen M. Cavanagh, *Seed, Soil, and Science: The Story of Eugene D. Funk* (Chicago: Lakeside Press, 1963); on Lanphier, see Robert C. Lanphier, *Sangamo: A History of Fifty Years* (Springfield, Ill.: Privately printed, 1949), Local History Collection, Springfield Public Library; on Smith, "E. E., A Memorial Booklet," Northern Illinois Regional History Center, Smith Papers, 2.

24. For sociological studies concerning community influence, see Michael Aiken and Paul E. Mott, eds., *The Structure of Community Power* (New York: Random House, 1970). Also see Donald A. Clelland and William H. Form, "Economic Dominants and Community Power: A Comparative Analysis," *American Journal of Sociology* 69 (Mar. 1964): 511–16, and a study by C. Wright Mills and

Melville J. Ulmer, "Small Business and Civic Welfare," which was published by the United States Senate Select Committee on Small Business as *Small Business and the Quality of American Life*. For a historical perspective, see David Hammack, "Problems in the Historical Study of Power in the Cities and Towns of the United States," *American Historical Review* 83 (Apr. 1978): 323–49, and "Small Business and Urban Power: Some Notes on the History of Economic Policy in Nineteenth-Century American Cities," in Bruchey, ed., *Small Business in American Life*, 319–37.

25. *Program* for the 1930 Conference of the Rotary Clubs of the Forty-fifth District of Rotary International, Murphysboro, Ill., 68, 143.

26. "Community Service—A Clinic," Rotary International, *Proceedings, Twenty-first Annual Convention*, Chicago, 1930, 101.

27. "Report of the Major Committee on Activities," *Lion* 9 (Aug. 1926): 17–19; *Kiwanis Activities, vol. 4*, 1925 (Chicago, 1925). Each club's monthly magazine listed local club activities sent to them by local secretaries.

28. Charles Stewart, "What Local Commercial Organizations Can Learn from the Moline Study," MS copy, File 208, Box 7, Urbana Association of Commerce Papers, Illinois Historical Survey.

29. Chapin to Mr. Godfrey M. Lebhar, *Chain Store Age*, Dec. 6, 1927, Box 1, File 17; Chapin to S. P. Evans, Sept. 27, 1928, Box 3, File 105, Urbana Association of Commerce Papers, Illinois Historical Survey.

30. Thorstein Veblen, "The Country Town," in Wesley C. Mitchell, ed., *What Veblen Taught: Selected Writings* (New York: Sentry Press, 1967), 394. Veblen's caustic essay belongs among the classic excoriations of American provincialism and, like others in the same vein, depends upon a certain degree of caricature for its effectiveness.

31. For descriptions of this relationship, see Lewis Atherton, *Main Street on the Middle Border* (Bloomington: Indiana University Press, 1954), 49–57; and Richard Lingeman, *Small-Town America: A Narrative History, 1620 to the Present* (New York: Putnam's, 1980), 326–36.

32. Kiwanis International, *Proceedings, Twelfth Annual Convention*, Memphis, Tenn., 1927, 615. For lists of activities concerning the farmer, see *Kiwanis Activities, vol. 4*, 1925, 30–33; Brooks Hays, "Farmers Find Lions Good Friends," *Lion* 6 (Oct. 1923): 6; and R. D. Stitzel, "The Brainerd, Minn. Lions Club and the Farmer," *Lion* 6 (Mar. 1924): 26.

33. David Brody, "The Rise and Decline of Welfare Capitalism," in John Braeman, Robert Bremner, and David Brody, eds., *Change and Continuity in Twentieth-Century America: The 1920s* (Columbus: Ohio State University Press, 1968), 147–78. Paternalism came naturally to club members because the majority of them, as small employers, conducted labor relations on a personal scale. Nevertheless, controversy erupted when Rotarians at their convention in 1919 attempted to vote on a resolution making specific proposals concerning compulsory arbitration and wage legislation. Discussion became quite heated, and the resolution was dropped. See *Proceedings*, Salt Lake City, 1919, 139–50.

34. Anecdotal evidence concerning clubs and labor relations presents a mixed picture, but it appears unlikely that service clubs appreciably altered business sympathies, either toward greater understanding or toward increased conflict. See below, chapters 5 and 7, for further discussion of club members' attitudes toward labor relations. Marden found club rhetoric had no impact either on labor relations or general business standards. *Rotary and Its Brothers*, 43–60.

35. Glen White to Dean C. M. Thompson, [Sept.?] 1925, File 221, Box 8, Urbana Association of Commerce Papers, Illinois Historical Survey; Dixon Chamber of Commerce Minutes, Mar. 9, 1928, File 7, Box 1, Dixon Chamber of Commerce Collection; Sterling Chamber of Commerce Minutes, Monday, Jan. 31, File 1, Box 4; Rockford Chamber of Commerce, *Member's Bulletin*, Mar. 1927, File 5, Box 1, Northern Illinois Regional History Center.

36. Board of Director Minutes, Dixon Chamber of Commerce, Nov. 9, 1928, File 7, Box 1, Dixon Chamber of Commerce Papers, Northern Illinois Regional History Center. Much later, as companies were bought and relocated south by corporate conglomerates, some of these owners would be remembered fondly for the paternal interest they took in employees. "In my family, God was first and (Rotarian) R. C. Lanphier was second, recalled a former employee. "Sangamo was a company with a heart." "When the Lights Went Out at Sangamo," *Springfield State Journal Register* (Sept. 25, 1981). The death of E. E. Smith also called forth employee homages. "E. E., A Memorial Booklet," Northern Illinois Regional History Center, Smith Papers, 2.

37. Ed S. Voight, "Will the Civic Club Endure?" *Lion* 11 (Sept. 1928): 20–21.

38. The Los Angeles Rotary project is described in Rotary Club of Los Angeles, *History of the Rotary Club of Los Angeles* (Los Angeles: Rotary Club of Los Angeles, 1955), 115–16; and the Lions' work for the blind is detailed in "History of Lionism" (unpublished MS, Lions International), 137–46.

39. Urbana Rotary Club, *Annual Financial Report*, 1927. The Cairo Kiwanis Club's work is described in "Efficiency Contest Spurs Activities," *Kiwanian* 10 (Mar. 1925), 523. The Lions clubs' work is described in *Lion* 7 (Feb. 1925): 32–34.

40. Marden, *Rotary and Its Brothers*, 149.

41. Dist. Gov. Graham, "What Lionism Is and What It Is Not," *Lion* 6 (Oct. 1923): 5; speech of Gov. Everts at Rotary International, Sixth Annual Conference of Rotary Clubs of the Twenty-third District, 1921, 15. At the 1923 Rotary convention delegates passed a resolution designed to serve as a guideline for clubs undertaking service projects. It advised clubs that "activities which enlist the individual efforts of all Rotarians are generally more in accord with the genius of Rotary than those that require the mass action of the club," a statement soon echoed by other service organizations. On the other hand, if actions were undertaken by the club as a whole, the "club should endeavor to secure the cooperation of all other organizations that ought to be interested, and seek to give them full credit." The club's "most successful" role was that of "propagandist." "A Rotary club discovers a need, . . . [and] does not seek alone to remedy it but to awaken others to the necessity of the remedy, seeking to arouse the community to its responsibility."

42. The Aberdeen, N.C., Kiwanis Club, listed in *Kiwanis Activities, vol. 4,* 1925, 81.

43. The Chicago club was the first to undertake such a survey, employing a young researcher out of the University of Chicago to take a "survey of the boy situation" in 1919 (which is on file at Rotary Headquarters). Los Angeles and Salt Lake City surveys of "boys' life" in their communities were undertaken in 1928. The Los Angeles survey was published in 1928 under the title *The City Boy and His Problems.* Health surveys were sponsored by the Kingsport, Tennessee, Kiwanis Club and the Richmond, Virginia, Rotary Club in 1925. General community surveys were recommended by the Lions' "major committee activities report" and the Kiwanis' "report on public affairs." *Lion* (Aug. 1926), 17; *Proceedings,* Ninth Annual Convention, 1925. Not surprisingly, given its similar business purposes, the chamber of commerce also adopted the community survey, as it sought to identify strengths and weakness for "community development."

44. Roy Lubove, *The Professional Altruist: The Emergence of Social Work as a Career, 1880–1930* (Cambridge, Mass.: Harvard University Press, 1965), 155–82, quote from 172.

45. Minutes, Urbana-Champaign Community Chest, 1928, Illinois Historical Survey.

46. David Macleod, *Building Character in the American Boy: The Boy Scouts, YMCA, and Their Forerunners, 1870–1920* (Madison: University of Wisconsin Press, 1983), 202. James Leiby discusses the only partially successful attempt among social workers to shift philanthropy from a class to a community basis in *A History of Social Welfare and Social Work in the United States* (New York: Columbia University Press, 1978), 163–90.

47. Joseph Kett's book *Rites of Passage* (New York: Basic Books, 1977) is the essential reference on "the invention of the adolescent" by organizations such as the YMCA and Boy Scouts. David Macleod's more focused study, *Building Character in the American Boy,* deepens Kett's insights.

48. Raymond J. Kneoppel, editorial in *The Boy* 1 (Apr. 1923), New York Club File, Rotary International.

49. William Butcher, "Boy's Week International," Rotary International, *Proceedings,* 1925, 475–81.

50. Detailed descriptions of New York's boy's week appear in *Rotarian* 20 (Nov. 1920) and in the New York City Club File at Rotary International.

51. "Report of the Executive Committee on Public Affairs," Kiwanis International, *Proceedings,* 1922 convention, 55. *Kiwanis Activities* from 1922 to 1929 shows approximately 5,083 activities under the category "handicapped children" but nearly twice that many in the categories of recreation, vocational guidance, boy's work, Boy Scouts, and the YMCA.

52. "Manual of Procedure for Rotarians," *Proceedings,* 1921, 498.

53. Rotary Club of Lancaster, *History of the Lancaster Rotary Club* (Lancaster, Pa.: Rotary Club of Lancaster, 1935), 27.

54. Kiwanis International, *Proceedings,* Twelfth Annual Convention, Seattle, Washington, 1928, 133.

55. "Manual of Procedure for Rotarians," *Proceedings,* Twelfth Annual Convention, Edinburgh, 1921, 498; "Boyhood's Challenge for 1922," *Rotarian* 20 (Jan. 1922): 5–8.

56. For a discussion of the ideas of these men, see Kett, *Rites of Passage,* 215–28; Macleod, *Building Character in the American Boy,* 97–110; and Paul Boyer, *Urban Masses and Moral Order in America, 1820–1920* (Cambridge, Mass.: Harvard University Press, 1978), 246–51. J. Adams Puffer wrote an article for the *Lion* in 1924, in which he was introduced as a "lecturer to service clubs on boy's work." See "Chumming with Boys," *Lion* 7 (Nov. 1924): 8.

57. P. H. Higley, "A Dangerous Age for Fathers," *Rotarian* 28 (Jan. 1926): 18–19.

58. "Lions and the Boy Problem," *Lion* 11 (Nov. 1928): 20–22.

59. Daniel T. Rodgers, "Socializing Middle-Class Children: Institutions, Fables, and Work Values in Nineteenth-Century America," in N. Ray Hiner and Joseph M. Hawes, eds., *Growing Up in America: Children in Historical Perspective* (Urbana: University of Illinois Press, 1985), 119–35.

60. C. P. Segaro, "Vocational Guidance," Kiwanis International, *Proceedings,* 1929, 137–45.

61. Herbert R. Bruner, "Square Pegs and Round Holes," *Rotarian* 22 (Apr. 1923): 192–94.

62. Rotary Questionaire, Feb. 27, 1920, Harrisburg, Ill., Club File, Rotary International. On school consolidation, see Wayne E. Fuller, *The Old Country School: The Story of Rural Education in the Middle West* (Chicago: University of Chicago Press, 1982), 218–91.

63. This report is in *Rotarian* 22 (Jan. 1923): 49. The Lynds also observe the importance of the high school basketball team for Middletown's community spirit. *Middletown,* 484–85.

64. Earle Draper, "Solving the Playground Problem," *Rotarian* 20 (Jan. 1922): 19.

65. This figure is based on the number of projects compiled in *Kiwanis Activities, vol. 4,* 1925, added to those reported monthly to the *Lion* and the *Rotarian;* Rockford, Ill., Club File, Rotary International.

66. Macleod, *Building Character in the American Boy,* 203.

67. *Kiwanis Activities, vol. 4,* 1925, 65.

68. Quoted in Francis Hazleton Williams, "Good Scouts," *Lion* 10 (Nov. 1927): 12.

69. Macleod thinks community concerns masked class anxiety. Because the middle class was more solidly in control in smaller communities, he argues, they identified the fate of their class with that of their community; thus "middle-class defensiveness was transmuted into community defensiveness." The Boy Scouts and YMCA were an attempt to protect the small-town boy from "urban contagion" and also prepare him for later contact with the city. *Building Character in the American Boy,* 224–29.

70. Robert S. Lynd and Helen Merrell Lynd, *Middletown,* 272–80; Albert Blumenthal, *Small-Town Stuff* (Chicago: University of Chicago Press, 1932), 264–71.

71. Robert S. Lynd and Helen Merrell Lynd, *Middletown,* 301–6, 484–95. The Lynds' portrayal of the impact of mass culture on a small city, though insightful throughout, is strongly influenced by the general aversion among cultivated Americans in the 1920s (and after) to the standardization of American life, which they equated with the loss of individual freedom and creativity. Seeing businessmen as agents of that standardization, they exaggerate the "lockstep conformity" among the business class to make their point—ignoring the presence of the very critics they quote and ridiculing the service clubs with imagery straight from *Babbitt.* Historians otherwise extremely careful in their use of evidence have, in my opinion, been too willing to accept without qualification the Lynds' depiction of Middletown's business class (which at times verges on caricature) as accurate not only for Muncie but for all small towns and cities in the 1920s.

Chapter 4: The Clubs and the Critics

1. H. L. Mencken, review of *Middletown: The American Mercury* 16 (Mar. 1929): 379.

2. A notable exception to that impression is an article by Thomas S. Hines, "Echoes from 'Zenith': Reactions of American Businessmen to *Babbitt,*" *Business History Review* 41 (Summer 1967): 123–40, which catalogues the remarkable extent of the reaction to *Babbitt* among American businessmen.

3. The most significant expression of this awareness was Frederick Lewis Allen's *Only Yesterday,* published in 1931. For a recent discussion of Allen, see David M. Kennedy, "Revisiting Frederick Lewis Allen's *Only Yesterday,*" *Reviews in American History* 14 (June 1986): 309–14.

4. Andre Siegfried, *America Comes of Age* (New York: Harcourt, Brace, 1927), 141; Virgil Jordon, "The Business Psychle," *Freeman* 8 (Dec. 5, 1923): 298–300; Harold J. Laski, "The American Scene," *New Republic* 53 (Jan. 19, 1928): 16–17.

5. Quoted in Arthur Hobbes, "Is There Anything Wrong with Rotary?," *Rotarian* 27 (Nov. 1925): 50.

6. Gilbert Seldes, "Service," *New Republic* 43 (July 15, 1925): 207; Duncan Aikman, "American Fascism," *Harper's Magazine* (Apr. 1925): 514–19; Bruce Bliven, "The Babbitt in His Warren," *Scribner's Magazine* (Dec. 1928): 899–901; Ruth Sapin, "Babbitt, Jr.," *New Republic* 48 (Sept. 8, 1925): 68–69.

7. For a perceptive discussion of the "Midwest as metaphor," see Frederick J. Hoffman, *The Twenties* (New York: Collier Publishers, 1962), 327–35.

8. Editorial, *New York Times,* June 19, 1923, 18.

9. Booth Tarkington, "Rotarian and Sophisticate," *World's Work* (Jan. 1929): 41–44.

10. Reported to the *Rotarian* 26 (June 1925). For a catalog of club responses, see Thomas Hines, "Echoes from 'Zenith.' "

11. Raymond Kneoppel, "A Member Replies," *Scribner's Monthly* (Dec. 1928): 954; Arthur Hobbes, "Is There Anything Wrong with Rotary?," *Rotarian* 28 (Nov. 1925): 50–53.

12. Will Garrity, "Menckenitis," *Rotarian* 28 (Mar. 1926): 8–9.

13. Editorial in *Rotarian* 27 (Oct. 1925): 26.

14. William Feather, "The Sire of Kiwanis," *American Mercury* 1 (Mar. 1924): 355.

15. Editorial in *Kiwanis Magazine* 9 (Feb. 1924): 67.

16. Bruce Bliven, "Lower 9, Car 26," *New Republic* 41 (June 10, 1925): 72. A memo from the international president to club secretaries published in the *Weekly Letter* (Dec. 8, 1925) suggested "dignity" in club expression because of "critics on the watch for an occasion to ridicule Rotary." Calls for changes in member behavior and an increased focus on service were made throughout the twenties in articles and convention speeches. Typical was the editorial in *Kiwanis Magazine* 9 (May 1924): 29, "How to Get Good Publicity and Avoid Bad," and the report of the publicity committee at the following year's Kiwanis convention, *Proceedings, Tenth Annual Convention, Atlanta, 1925, 59–63.

17. Hines cites other passages from the *Rotarian* that "rival even the choicest passages in Lewis' novel." "Echoes from 'Zenith,'" 136–37.

18. *Handbook of Entertainment for Rotary Clubs* (Chicago: Rotary International, 1919); Paul Harris, *This Rotarian Age*, 35.

19. Sinclair Lewis, "The Man Who Knew Coolidge," *American Mercury* 13 (Jan. 1928): 20; Kiwanis International, *Proceedings, Eleventh Convention, Memphis, Tenn., 1927, 496. Lewis, it should be said, generally underestimated the amount of intelligent speech making that went on at club conventions, although the Duluth, Minnesota, Lions club in 1964 reportedly responded favorably to a verbatim reading of a speech that Babbitt had given before the Zenith Real Estate Board. David G. Pugh, "Babbittry and Baudelaire," in Warren French, ed., *The Twenties: Poetry, Fiction, Drama* (Deland, Fla.: Edward/Everett and Co., 1975), 90.

20. The quotations are from "Americana" sections in *American Mercury:* 20 (May 1930); 6 (Dec. 1926); 15 (Sept. 1928); and 39 (Mar. 1927).

21. Quoted in Edward Silberstein, "Rotary, from the Outside," *Rotarian* 28 (Jan. 1926): 33.

22. Quoted in Arthur Melville, "Heads or Tails," *Rotarian* 28 (Apr. 1926): 23.

23. Historians and literary critics have also ignored the important distinction between the thought of the two men. See, for example, the otherwise excellent study by Edward Martin, *H. L. Mencken and the Debunkers* (Athens: University of Georgia Press, 1984).

24. George H. Douglas, *H. L. Mencken: Critic of American Life* (Hamden, Conn.: Archon Books, 1978). Douglas's interpretation is particularly convincing when explaining why Mencken quickly fell from favor when the intellectual mood changed from debunking to populist celebration. Mencken did not alter his essential positions; according to Douglas he was never in any but coincidental accord with the trends of twentieth-century social thought.

25. Mencken, *Prejudices, Sixth Series* (New York: Alfred J. Knopf, 1926), 70–71. Compare to Alexis de Tocqueville, *Democracy in America*, 535–38.

26. Mencken, *Prejudices, Third Series* (New York: Alfred J. Knopf, 1922), 109–18.

27. Sinclair Lewis, "The Long Arm of the Small Town," in *The Man from Main Street,* ed. Harry E. Maule and Melville H. Cane (New York: Random House, 1953), 272; Lewis, *Main Street* (New York: New American Library, 1961), 259.

28. Martin Light, *The Quixotic Vision of Sinclair Lewis* (West Lafayette, Ind.: Purdue University Press, 1975); Perry Miller, "The Incorruptible Sinclair Lewis," in *The Responsibility of Mind in a Civilization of Machines* (Amherst: University of Massachusetts Press, 1979), 120.

29. Mencken, *Minority Report* (New York: Alfred J. Knopf, 1956), 178–79.

30. Johan Huizinga, *America* (New York: Harper and Row, 1972), 257.

31. "Rotarian Open Forum," *Rotarian* 30 (Feb. 1927): 67.

32. Robert S. Lynd and Helen Merrel Lynd, *Middletown,* 299–306.

33. Richard Wightman Fox, "Epitaph for Middletown: Robert S. Lynd and the Analysis of Consumer Culture," in Fox and T. J. Jackson Lears, eds., *The Culture of Consumption: Critical Essays in American History, 1880–1980* (New York: Pantheon, 1983), 103–41.

34. Kennedy, "Revisiting Frederick Lewis Allen's *Only Yesterday";* Allen, *Only Yesterday* (New York: Harper and Row, 1931), 178–79.

35. 1931 Chesterton speech quoted in C. P. Hewitt, *Towards My Neighbour: The Social Influence of the Rotary Movement in Great Britain and Ireland* (London: Longsman Green and Co., 1950), 148.

36. Edgar A. Guest, *Collected Verse* (Chicago: Reilly and Lee Co., 1934).

37. A little later, in the early 1930s, the *Rotarian* welcomed as book critic the Yale professor and Rotarian William "Billy" Phelps, who several times a year selected for Rotarians a recommended reading list. In an acute analysis of Phelps's style, Joan Shelley Rubin notes that "his lists and epigrams functioned not to provide literary analysis or aesthetic instruction but to create in listeners the sense that they were culturally 'in the know.' " Rotarians could appreciate this more democratic and communal approach to the "higher culture." *The Making of Middlebrow Culture* (Chapel Hill: University of North Carolina Press, 1992), 281–90.

38. Rotary International, *Proceedings,* Eighteenth Annual Convention, Ostend, Belgium, 1927, 323; I. K. Russell, "H. L. Mencken's Shock Troops," *Lion* 8 (Dec. 1926): 9; Kiwanis International, *Proceedings,* Tenth Annual Convention, Montreal, 1926, 122.

39. International Association of Lions Clubs, *Lions Stunt Book and Toastmaster's Guide* (Chicago: Lions International, 1950), 9.

40. Rufe Chapin, "An Outline of Rotary's Beginings," dated 1925, Rotary History File, Rotary International.

41. Bill Elliot, "The World-Wide View of Rotary," Rotary International, *Proceedings,* 1928, 260.

42. *New York Times* and *Chicago American* articles in "Criticism" File, Rotary International.

43. Rotary Club of Minneapolis, *The Story of Minneapolis Rotary, 1910–1935* (Minneapolis: Rotary Club of Minneapolis, 1935), 97.

44. Oliver L. Cremer, *Rockford Rotary: Fifty Years of Service* (Rockford: Rotary Club of Rockford, 1966), 137.

45. This generalization is based on an impressionistic reading of club histories, but it is a generalization supported by others who have written on the clubs. The Rotary historian David Shelley Nicholl entitled his chapter on the organization in the thirties "Death of the Boy." *The Golden Wheel: The Story of Rotary, 1905 to Present* (Estover, Plymouth, Eng.; MacDonald and Evans, 1984).

46. For thoughts on this cultural transition, see Warren Susman, "Personality and the Making of Twentieth Century Culture" in *Culture as History: The Transformation of American Society in the Twentieth Century* (New York: Pantheon Books, 1984): 271–85.

Chapter 5: Adjusting to Hard Times

1. Three books have had an important influence in my thinking on this chapter: Catherine McNicol Stock, *Main Street in Crisis,* which details the ambivalent adjustment of local businessmen in the Dakotas to New Deal agencies; Alan Brinkley, *Voices of Protest: Huey Long, Father Coughlin, and the Great Depression* (New York: Vintage Books, 1983), which exposes the depth of local resistance to bureaucratic encroachment in the 1930s; and Lizabeth Cohen, *Making a New Deal,* which, as I have already discussed (chapter 2), provides a model for group response to economic integration.

2. Malcolm Brown and John N. Webb, *Seven Stranded Coal Towns: A Study of an American Depressed Area* (Washington, D.C.: U.S. Government Printing Office, 1941), 95–102.

3. Theodore Rosenoff, *Dogma, Depression, and the New Deal: The Debate of Political Leaders over Economic Recovery* (Port Washington, N.Y.: Kennikat Press, 1975), 35–39.

4. "Business Confidence Week Proves Great Boon," *Lion* 13 (Nov. 1930): 8; "Old-Man Depression Killed, Prosperity the Victor," ibid.: 10; "Buy Now—the Key to Better Business," *Ki-Grams* 11 (Jan. 19, 1931): 8; "Muskegon Busts the Buyers' Strike," *Kiwanis Magazine* 15 (Dec. 1930): 577, 608; "Notorious Character Is Gone from Saugus," *Kiwanis Magazine* 16 (Sept. 1931): 267; "Des Moines's 'Hot Dollar Campaign,'" *Rotarian* 37 (Oct. 1930): 44. Craig Lloyd describes the importance of public relations techniques to Hoover's administrative style and their complete breakdown during his presidency in *Aggressive Introvert: A Study of Herbert Hoover and Public Relations Management, 1912–1932* (Columbus: Ohio State University Press, 1972).

5. Urbana Courier Clipping, Jan.(?) 1932, club report, March 1932, Urbana Club File, Rotary International.

6. Report to District Governor Jan. 9, 1934, Jacksonville, Ill., Club File, Rotary International; A. Alonzo Rea, secretary of the Aurora Rotary Club to Chesley R. Perry, Feb. 10, 1932, Aurora, Ill., Club File, Rotary International.

7. Walter Ingram to O. S. A. Hanke, Feb. 2, 1935, De Kalb Kiwanis Collection, Box 3, Folder 3, Northern Illinois Regional History Center.

8. Wallace Austin, Report of Membership Committee, Kiwanis International, *Proceedings,* Sixteenth Annual Convention, Detroit, 1932, 117; Edgar G. Dondria, "The Critical Years Ahead," *Rotarian* 38 (May 1931): 5.

9. Rotary International, *Proceedings,* Twenty-first Annual Convention, Chicago, 1930, 21–33.

10. "1934 Memo of Official Visit of District Governor," Herrin, Ill., Club File, Rotary Headquarters.

11. "Visit of James H. Roty to Benton, Ill., Feb. 19, 1934, Benton Club File. Club files at Rotary International noted, for example, the continued strength of certain clubs despite bank failures and other economic problems, namely, the clubs in Reading, Pennsylvania, Cairo, Illinois, Modesto, California, Muncie, Indiana, and Indianola, Iowa. Clubs that failed because of "impossible economic conditions" were also noted: Shinston, West Virginia, Coaldale, Pennsylvania, Madisonville, Tennessee, Beaumont, Georgia, and Clinton, South Carolina. But even in depressed agricultural areas, clubs found organizing possibilities. In 1937 businessmen formed a Lions club in Cobden, Illinois, in a southern Illinois peach-growing district. There the Depression spurred a renewed attempt to unite representatives of town and country. Jane Adams, "Creating Community in a Midwestern Village: Fifty Years of the Cobden Peach Festival," *Illinois Historical Journal* 83 (Summer 1990): 97–108.

12. Report of club to district governor, Aug. 30, 1934, Macomb, Ill., Club File, Rotary International.

13. Marvin C. Park to R. Wandall, Dec. 27, 1937, Los Angeles Club File, Rotary International. Wandall's reply sounded the universal plaint of the harassed bureaucrat: "I sympathize heartily with all you say about this business of submitting resolutions, but what can I do? Nothing! We in this office are bound by the rules of the constitution."

14. "The Dallas Penny Provider Plan," *Kiwanis Magazine* 17 (Nov. 1932): 507; Leland Case, "Filling in with Soup" *Rotarian* 43 (Mar. 1933): 16–17; "Lions Kitchen, Portland, Ore.," *Lion* 13 (Jan. 1931): 6; "Community Gardens, An Opportunity," *Rotarian* 43 (Apr. 1933); "Old Shoe Drive," *Ki-Grams* 11 (Nov. 30, 1931): 2.

15. Robert S. Lynd and Helen Merrell Lynd, *Middletown in Transition: A Study in Cultural Conflicts* (New York: Harcourt, Brace and Company, 1937), 284.

16. See, for example, David M. Katzman, "Ann Arbor: Depression City," and Bonnie Fox Schwartz, "Unemployment Relief in Philadelphia, 1930–1932: A Study of the Depression's Impact on Voluntarism." Both are in Bernard Sternsher, ed., *Hitting Home: The Great Depression in Town and Country* (Chicago: Quadrangle Books, 1970), 47–84. See also Charles H. Trout, *Boston, the Great Depression, and the New Deal* (New York: Oxford University Press, 1977), 75–100.

17. Quoted in John Finbar Jones and John Middlemist Herrick, *Citizens in Service: Volunteers in Social Welfare during the Depression, 1929–1941* (Lansing: Michigan State University Press, 1976), 11.

18. Michael B. Katz, *In the Shadow of the Poorhouse: A Social History of Welfare in America* (New York: Basic Books, 1986), 206–15.

19. These statistics are drawn from "Club Activities Classified, Lions International, *Proceedings,* Twentieth Annual Convention, Chicago, 1937, 59–335; "Major Activities Committee Report," *Lion* 9 (Aug. 1926): 17; Kiwanis International, *Kiwanis Activities, vol. 4,* 1925, and *Kiwanis Activities, vol. 15,* 1936.

20. Official Communication No. 2 to Secretaries, Feb. 15, 1935. De Kalb Kiwanis Collection, Northern Illinois Regional History Center. On the distrust of federal bureaucracy, see Dumenil, " 'The Insatiable Maw of Bureaucracy,' " and Alan Brinkley, *Voices of Protest,* 142–68.

21. Letter to *Rotarian* (Feb. 1934): 39.

22. Letter to *Rotarian* 43 (Sept. 1933): 2; Editorial in *Rotarian* 43 (Aug. 1933): 37; Chester E. Willard, "Meeting Cut-Throat Competition," *Rotarian* 43 (Oct. 1933): 33–36.

23. Letter, Don Berry to *Rotarian* 44 (Mar. 1934); Letter, Fred Carlson to *Rotarian* 44 (Feb. 1934); "Symposium: Is the New Deal Working?," ibid., "NRA Advisory Committee Discharged," *Rotarian* 45 (Sept. 1934): 9; Melvin Jones, Report of the Secretary, quoted in "A History of Lionism" (unpublished MS, Lions International), 143.

24. William E. Leuchtenburg, *Franklin D. Roosevelt and the New Deal* (New York: Harper and Row, 1963), 69–70.

25. Raymond Knoeppel, "Non-financial Incentives in Business," *Proceedings,* Twenty-fifth Annual Convention, Detroit, 1934, 40. Rockford *Kiwanis News,* Mar. 19, 1935; Kiwanis Collection, Box 1, Northern Illinois Regional History Center.

26. John A. Salmond, *The Civilian Conservation Corps, 1933–1943: A New Deal Case Study* (Durham, N.C.: Duke University Press, 1967), 102–20. "Report on Youth Service," Rotary International, *Proceedings,* 1934, 276–300; Herbert M. Schmidt, "Kiwanis in C.C.C. Camps," *Kiwanis Magazine* 19 (June 1934): 252.

27. Anderson, who went on to have a long career as senator and a strong advocate of environmental conservation, also met other New Dealers through Rotary, including James A. Farley, President Roosevelt's campaign manager, and A. Harry Moore, the governor of New Jersey. Clinton P. Anderson, *Outsider in the Senate* (New York: World Publishing Co., 1970), 25. Anderson's biographer, Richard A. Baker, feels that the "presidency of Rotary International assured Anderson's political success," introducing him to influential men and helping him become a successful speaker. *Conservation Politics: The Senate Career of Clinton P. Anderson* (Albequerque: New Mexico University Press, 1985), 16–23.

28. E. E. Embree to W. D. P. Warren, Mar. 10, 1934, and Embree to Mr. Frank D. Chase, Mar. 3, 1934, Embree Collection, Box 3, Northern Illinois Regional History Center.

29. Catherine McNicol Stock details the complicated relationship between New Deal values and the members of the old middle class in the Dakotas. She argues that for these men and women the New Deal represented a particularly

wrenching cultural crisis: the New Deal meant community transformation that threatened the old middle class's vision, but at the same time its programs contained enough of the old values that they could not be entirely repudiated, particularly in the context of economic need. *Main Street in Crisis,* esp. 86–127.

30. Cornelius Garretson, address to Business Practices Assembly, Rotary International, *Proceedings,* Twenty-fourth Annual Convention, Boston, 1933, 284; Discussion of "Efficiency in Government," Kiwanis International, *Proceedings,* Twentieth Annual Convention, Washington, D.C., 1936, 258–79.

31. Alan Lawson, "The Cultural Legacy of the New Deal," in Harvard Sitkoff, *Fifty Years Later: The New Deal Evaluated* (Philadelphia: Temple University Press, 1985). Richard H. Pells describes the decline of socialist radicalism into an anti-ideological defense of the American Way in *Radical Visions and American Dreams: Culture and Social Thought in the Depression Years* (New York: Harper and Row, 1973), 293–329. Even more than Pells, Warren Susman stresses the ideological innocence of the decade in "The Culture of the Thirties," in *Culture as History,* 150–83.

32. Hendrik Van Loon, "A Credo for a New Day," *Rotarian* 42 (June 1933): 6–8, 51; Clark Clement, "Kiwanis Can Help Find the Answers," *Kiwanis Magazine* 19 (Mar. 1934): 99–100; Kiwanis International, *Proceedings,* Twenty-second Annual Convention, San Francisco, 1938, 18–92.

33. Mills, *White Collar,* 43. For discussions of small business ideology, see Rowland Berthoff, "Independence and Enterprise: Small Business in the American Dream," in Stuart W. Bruchey, ed., *Small Business in American Life,* 28–45, and John Bunzel, *The American Small Businessman* (1955; repr., New York: Arno Press, 1979). Both Berthoff and Bunzel point out small-business dreams of growth. But they also stress small-business independence to the point of ignoring other ideological influences, such as club participation.

34. On small business and chain store legislation, see Mansel G. Blackford, *A History of Small Business in America,* 88–96. Evidence of club response appears in C. O. Sherrill, "Across the Chain Store Counter," *Rotarian* 38 (June 1931): 10–11. Angry letters, most of them accusing chain stores of community irresponsibility, occupied two pages in both the July and August issues. In contrast, dispassionate discussions of the Robinson-Patman Act appear in Walter F. Boye, "The Robinson-Patman Anti-Price Discrimination Law," *Kiwanis Magazine* (Apr. 1937): 76, 114; and "Shackling the Chain Store," *Rotarian* 54 (Feb. 1939): 16–17. Babson remained a club favorite throughout the Depression. Roger Babson, "Is Little Business Coming Back?," *Rotarian* (Oct. 1938): 8–9; reader response the following (Nov.) issue.

35. Lizabeth Cohen, *Making a New Deal,* 251–360. Not all workers experienced the benefits of national organization. Elizabeth Faue argues that the triumph of bureaucracy in the Minneapolis labor movement "closed down" possibilities for leadership among working women. *Community of Suffering and Struggle: Women, Men, and the Labor Movement in Minneapolis, 1915–1945* (Chapel Hill: University of North Carolina Press, 1991), 126–46.

36. Cornelius Garretson, "Lend Me Your Deaf Ear," Rotary International, *Proceedings,* Thirtieth Annual Convention, Cleveland, Ohio, 1939, 101–2; W. Clement Moore, "Business Needs Common Sense, a Tonic, and a Vacation," *Kiwanis Magazine* 23 (Jan. 1938): 67–68.

37. Rotary International, *Proceedings,* Thirtieth Annual Convention, Cleveland, Ohio, 1939, 210–24.

38. Stephen Bolles, "The Oregon Boot on the Service Club," *Rotarian* 36 (Jan. 1930), 11–12, 58; Fred Parker, "The Cycle of Progress," Kiwanis International, *Proceedings,* Seventeenth Annual Convention, Los Angeles, 1933, 68–72. The Rotarian district governor David Reese also urged the approach of "controversial topics" in his address, "New Times, New Methods," *Proceedings,* Twenty-third Annual Convention, Seattle, 1932, 143–47.

39. Walter P. Hepner, "National Forums of Democracy," *Kiwanian* (May 1938): 263–64; Melvin Jones, *Report to the Mexico City Convention* (Chicago, 1935), 23. Leland Case led a discussion of the *Rotarian*'s policy of impartial debates in the 1930s in *Proceedings,* 1939, 150–54.

40. "Board of Director's Report," *Lion* 15 (Apr. 1933): 3–5; *Rotary?* (Chicago, 1934); Allen D. Albert, "Rotary under the Microscope," *Rotarian* 45 (Aug. 1934): 25–27.

41. Wayne Gard, "A City without a Bogey," *Rotarian* 46 (May 1935): 30–31, 50.

42. Discussions of "Youth Work" in Rotary International, *Proceedings,* 1934, 276–311; *Proceedings,* Twenty-eighth Annual, Nice, France, 1937; Kiwanis International, *Proceedings,* Nineteenth Annual Convention, San Antonio, Tex., 1935, 96–117; "Report on Training Course in Citizenship Prepared for the Rotary Club of Philadelphia," Aug. 1938, Philadelphia Club File, Rotary International. Additional programs are described in Phillip C. Lovejoy, "Youth Gets a Hearing," *Rotarian* 49 (Sept. 1936): 23–25. Howard Bahlke discusses the shift to older youth in "Rotary and American Culture: A Historical Study of Ideology" (Ph.D. diss., University of Minnesota, 1956).

43. From the discussion of open forums in Kiwanis International, *Proceedings,* Twenty-second Annual Convention, San Francisco, 1938, 272–84, 326, and from a similar discussion appearing in Rotary International, *Proceedings,* Twenty-seventh Annual Convention, Atlantic City, N.J., 1937, 408–11.

44. Jurgen Kocka makes this point in *White-Collar Workers in America, 1890–1940,* 251–84. See below, chapter 6, for a fuller comparative perspective.

45. These statistics were compiled by comparing club directories from the thirties with U.S. Bureau of the Census, *County and City Data Book, 1940;* record of suburban Los Angeles clubs from Los Angeles File, Rotary International.

46. Kiwanis International, *Proceedings,* Twentieth Annual Convention, Washington, D.C., 1936, 236–38. This objective continued into the 1950s. The obvious criticism—that large attendance is hardly a church's spiritual aim—did not seem to occur to Kiwanian leaders. Perhaps they felt that "to support the churches in their material aims" might seem incongruous.

47. Fred Parker, "The Challenge of Our Special Objectives," *Kiwanis Magazine* 20 (Jan. 1935): 6–7, 44; "Shall We Abolish School Frills: Yes, by H. L. Mencken—No, by John Dewey," *Rotarian* 42 (May 1933): 16–19; quote from letter of response in following (June) issue: 2–4.

48. David Tyack, Robert Lowe, and Elisabeth Hansot, *Public Schools in Hard Times: The Great Depression and Recent Years* (Cambridge, Mass.: Harvard University Press, 1984), 150–86.

49. Dean Lobaugh, "The New Kind of Teacher," *Kiwanis Magazine* 22 (Apr. 1937): 210, 254; Roy E. Dickerson, "What's the Matter with Our Bill?," *Rotarian* 50 (Apr. 1937): 15; Rotary International, *Proceedings,* Twenty-ninth Annual Convention, San Francisco, 1938, 376–414.

50. Amos Squire, "The Psychology of Fellowship," *Rotarian* 47 (Sept. 1935): 13–15, 51; Clyde Hisson, "The Kiwanis Quest for Freedom," *Kiwanis Magazine* 19 (Feb. 1934): 53–55; William Marston, "As the Boss Sees You," *Rotarian* 55 (July 1939): 24–26, 59.

51. Warren Susman, "The Culture of the Thirties," in *Culture as History,* 150–83.

52. William Lyon Phelps, "Building Leisure-time Activities," Rotary International, *Proceedings,* 1934, 79–85; Harry Holmes, "The New Leisure," Kiwanis International, *Proceedings,* Twentieth Annual Convention, Washington, D.C., 1936, 292; Fred G. McAllister, "Live All Your Life," *Kiwanis Magazine* 22 (Jan. 1937): 9.

Chapter 6: Serving the World

1. "With the Rotarians in Belgium," *London Sunday Herald,* Sunday, June 5, 1927. Clipping and story courtesy of Dr. Genevieve Miller.

2. John S. Gilkeson describes these assumptions as part of a "middle-class cultural imperialism." *Middle-Class Providence,* 354.

3. For the relation between economic expansion, foreign policy, and American cultural influence, see Emily S. Rosenberg, *Spreading the American Dream: American Economic and Cultural Expansion, 1890–1945* (New York: Hill and Wang, 1982). A solid summary of current interpretations of foreign policy during the twenties and thirties appears in Michael J. Hogan, "Revival and Reform: America's Twentieth-Century Search for a New Economic Order Abroad," *Diplomatic History* 8 (Fall 1984): 287–310. See also John L. Braeman, "American Foreign Policy in the Age of Normalcy: Three Historiographical Traditions," *Amerikastudien/ American Studies* 26 (Nov. 1981): 125–28. For a contemporary perspective on Americanism and European civilization in the twenties, see Hiram Motherwell, *The Imperial Dollar* (New York: Brentano's Publishers, 1929), 183–221. A historical study focusing particularly on economic and political influences is Frank Costigliola, *Awkward Dominion: American Political, Economic, and Cultural Relations with Europe, 1919–1933* (Ithaca, N.Y.: Cornell University Press, 1984).

4. Rosenberg, *Spreading the American Dream,* 111–12. Rosenberg is virtually

unique among historians in recognizing Rotary as an important manifestation of American cultural expansion.

5. Nicholl, *The Golden Wheel: The Story of Rotary, 1905 to the Present* (Estover, Plymouth, Eng.: McDonald and Evans, 1984), 81; E. C. Russell, *Fifty Years of Rotary in Ottawa, 1916–1966* (Ottawa, Can.: Rotary Club of Ontario, 1966); Victor Lauriston, *History of the Sarnia Rotary Club, 1927–1965* (Sarnia, Ont.: Sarnia Rotary Club, 1966).

6. Nicholl, *The Golden Wheel*, 92–115.

7. Paul Harris, *My Road to Rotary*, 238–40, 254. Descriptions of European clubs found in Rotary Italiano, *Annuario del Distretto Italiano, 1936–37* (translated for me by Nancy McCall); Marcel Chapelon, *Annuaire des Rotary Clubs de France, 1938–39* (Paris: Rotary International, 1938); Henri Diffre, *Histoire du Rotary en France* (Lyon: BOSC Freres, 1959) (translated for me by Cathy Charles); Dr. Erich Heintel, *50 Jahre Rotary Club Wien, 1925–1975* (Wien, Ger.: Rotary Club Wien, 1975); Alfon S. Schler, *25 Jahre Rotary-Club Baden-Baden* (Baden-Baden, Ger.: Ernst Koelblin, 1955).

8. "E. G.," "History of the Rotary Club of Chicago," (unpublished MS, Rotary International), 13.

9. Hewitt, *Towards My Neighbour*, 6. Stead quoted in J. Potter, "America and Europe: Economic Interconnections," in Robin W. Winks, ed., *Other Voices, Other Views: An International Collection of Essays from the Bicentennial* (Westport, Conn.: Greenwood Press, 1978), 149–63.

10. Nicholl, *The Golden Wheel*, 175–230.

11. Yasukichi Yasuba, "American Impact on the Japanese Economy" in Robin Winks, ed., *Other Voices, Other Views*, 164–80. On the enormous popularity of baseball in twenties Japan, see Richard C. Cradeau, "Pearl Harbor: A Failure of Baseball?," *Journal of Popular Culture* 15 (Spring 1982): 67–73.

12. Emily Rosenberg calls this philosophy "liberal developmentalism." Others, who emphasize its corporate aspects, include Joan Hoff Wilson, *American Business and Foreign Policy, 1920–1933* (Lexington: University of Kentucky Press, 1971), and Hogan, *Informal Entente: The Private Structure of Cooperation in Anglo-American Economic Diplomacy, 1918–1928* (Columbia: University of Missouri Press, 1977).

13. Editorial, *Rotarian* 6 (Feb. 1915): 22.

14. Rotary International, *Proceedings, Tenth Annual Convention, Salt Lake City, 1919*, 24. Wilson describes the impact of World War I on American business sentiment as a whole in *American Business and Foreign Policy, 1920–1933*, 1–30.

15. General discussion of the Rotary international sentiment (and the above quotes) appear in Crawford C. McCullough, "Modern Business and World Progress," *Rotarian* 21 (Mar. 1922): 105–6, and Harry Rogers, address at the 1927 Rotary Convention, Ostend, Belgium, *Proceedings, 1927*, 22–26. Discussion of international organizations, resolutions concerning them, and their ultimate rejection occurred particularly at the overseas conventions. At the Twelfth Annual Convention in Edinburgh in 1921, Rotarian delegates set up a Committee on International Amity but rejected endorsement of arbitration; at Ostend in 1927 they

tabled a resolution concerning international debt (*Proceedings,* 1927, 184–85), and at Vienna in 1931 they took no action after a lengthy discussion on tariff reduction (*Proceedings,* 1931, 219–40). An editorial in the *Rotarian* was typical of the American Rotarian attitude toward the World Court, expressing support but refusing endorsement, and then calling for local Rotary clubs to set up "an informative program to enlighten members" as to the World Court's function. *Rotarian* 26 (May 1925): 32.

16. Charles S. Maier, *Recasting Bourgeois Europe: Stabilization in France, Germany, and Italy in the Decade after World War I* (Princeton, N.J.: Princeton University Press, 1975), 3–15.

17. The European interest in vocational service was evident at conventions, where Europeans such as Anton Verkade (Netherlands) and Sidney Pascall (Great Britain) chaired vocational service committees and tried to push Rotary to greater emphasis on this program, but it was also observed by historians of overseas Rotary. Nicholl, *The Golden Wheel,* 204–9, and Hewitt, *Towards My Neighbour,* 79–81.

18. My impressions and a sampling of rosters of the European clubs are drawn from Nicholls, *The Golden Wheel,* 203–310; Hewitt, *Towards My Neighbour,* 9–46; *Annuario del Distretto Italiano, 1936–37; Annuaire des Rotary-Clubs de France, 1938–39; Histoire du Rotary en France;* Heintel, *50 Jahre Rotary Club Wien, 1925–1975;* and Schler, *25 Jahre Rotary-Club Baden-Baden.*

19. Rotary International, *Proceedings,* 1921, 88; Nicholls, *The Golden Wheel,* 257.

20. Mann's speech was published in the *Rotarian* 37 (Nov. 1930): 9–11, 54–55, incongruously placed before Knute Rockne's article "Footballs or Hand-Grenades." Rockne "respectfully suggest[ed] football as a substitute for bloodshed."

21. Given my limited sources, I would not want to extend my generalizations beyond an explanation of the differences in Rotarian behavior. Three scholars who do, with observations upon which I base my analysis, are Jurgen Kocka, whose *White-Collar Workers in America, 1890–1914* authoritatively establishes the greater importance of "the collar line" in continental Europe; J. Martin Evans, *America: The View from Europe* (San Francisco: San Francisco Book Co., 1976), who comments convincingly on the relationship between the "openness" and "exteriority" of American culture and its candor and informality; and Arthur Marwick, who undertakes an ambitious comparison of class based on images in popular and government usage in *Class: Image and Reality in Britain, France, and the USA since 1930* (New York: Oxford University Press, 1980).

22. "International Roundtable" at Atlantic City, N.J., in 1936. *Proceedings,* 76–89. The Americans' greater stress on community service was also noted by Harris, *This Rotarian Age.* Henri Diffre, *Histoire du Rotary en France,* makes no mention of community service.

23. "History of Lionism," MS, Lions International, 14–60; Moserrate Acosta Ayala, *Historia, Filosofia Y Psicologia del Leonism* (Mayaguez, P.R., 1985); Hapgood, *The Men Who Wear the K,* 97–105.

24. Editorial, *Lion* 9 (Aug. 1926): 14; "History of Lionism," 60.

25. Dedication ceremonies, Harding International Good-Will Memorial, *Kiwanis Activities,* 1925, 5–6; "Report of U.S.-Canada Week," Kiwanis International, *Proceedings,* 1927, 160–61; "Pilgrimage to Harding International Good-Will Memorial," *Proceedings,* 1928; "Rush-Bagot Memorial Tablet Erected by Kiwanis International," *Kiwanis Magazine* 20 (June 1935): 246–47.

26. William Osborne, "Across the Backyard Fence," *Rotarian* 36 (Apr. 1930): 26–27; C. King Woodbridge, "Service Clubs an Aid to International Understanding," Address, Kiwanis International Convention, *Proceedings,* Tenth Annual Convention, Montreal, 1926, 129–37; Leland Case, "Our Expanding Backyard," *Rotarian* 44 (May 1934): 5.

27. Salvador de Madariaga, "The Anarchy in Men's Minds," *Rotarian* 44 (Jan. 1934): 6–8, 54–56; George Pope Shannon, "Peace Follows the Order Book," *Rotarian* 37 (Aug. 1930): 12–14; Frank Miles, "Lionism and World Peace," quoted in "History of Lionism," 60.

28. Quote from discussion of Esperanto at Rotary's Twenty-second Annual Convention, Vienna, 1931. *Proceedings,* 177–84. Frank A. Ninkovich discusses Americans' support for Esperanto in the late twenties and early thirties as symptomatic of the apolitical idealism that dominated American foreign relations in that period. *The Diplomacy of Ideas: U.S. Foreign Policy and Cultural Relations, 1938–1950* (New York: Cambridge University Press, 1981), 20–22.

29. Will Manier, "Rotary—An Adventure in International Understanding and Goodwill," *Proceedings,* Twenty-ninth Annual Convention, Nice, France, 1937, 45.

30. Mitchell Indiana Report to District Governor, Jan. 7, 1931, Mitchell File, Rotary International.

31. J. A. Cage, "Institute of International Understanding," Address, *Proceedings,* 1937, 67–69; Kiwanis International, *Proceedings,* Nineteenth Annual Convention, San Antonio, Tex., 1935, 248. The Fort Madison, Iowa, and Fort Smith, Arkansas, Lions clubs supported children during 1925. "Lions Club Activities," *Lion* 7 (Feb. 1925): 33. The Philadelphia Rotary Club pursued a typical international program. It adopted Nottingham, England, as its sister city in 1921; presented a gavel to the Rome Club made of timber from Independence Hall in 1929; and sponsored exchange students throughout the twenties and thirties.

32. Princeton Club Report, Jan. 7, 1933, Princeton Club Files, Rotary International; "A Night in Bohemia," *Rotary Propeller* (Dec. 7, 1929); similar programs described in *Rotarian* 36 (Jan. 1930): 45.

33. Ernest Stavrum, "Foreign Charms of Mexico Told by Non-Lion," *Lion* (Apr. 1934): 17, 34. Robert O. Mead muses briefly on the inadequacies of tourism and international exchange programs in *Atlantic Legacy: Essays in American-European Cultural History* (New York: New York University Press, 1969), 197–200.

34. Report of Secretariat Field Service, 1932, Elgin Club File, Rotary International; "Nippon Navy Based on Needs Says Miyaoka," Dec. 26, 1934, news clipping, Seattle Club File, Rotary International.

35. Editorial, "The Vienna Verdict," *Rotarian* 39 (July 1934): 34, also *Proceedings,* Twenty-second Annual Convention, Vienna, 1931; Letter, *Rotarian* (Aug. 1934): 40; Editorial, "Rotary in the Orient," *Rotarian* (Oct. 1931): 23.

36. John Nelson, "Rotary Carries on in Germany," *Rotarian* 44 (Nov. 1933): 21. One of the men forced to terminate their membership was Thomas Mann.

37. John Nelson, "Rotary and the State," *Rotarian* 43 (Nov. 1933): 57–59; Maurice Duperrey, "Around the World with Rotary," *Proceedings,* Twenty-ninth Annual Convention, San Francisco, 1938, 9–22.

38. *Proceedings,* 1938 Annual Convention, 9–22, 97, 428–29.

39. Editorial, *Rotarian* 54 (Jan. 1939): 45; W. W. Blair Fish, "From a Rotary Viewpoint," *Rotary Service* 1 (Nov. 1940): 9; Wilifred Andrews, "Rotary and Impartiality—A Lamentable Farce," *Rotary Service* 2 (Dec. 1941): 16.

40. Hapgood, *The Men Who Wear the K,* 144–45.

41. "Lions International in War Time," *Lion* 24 (July 1942): 16–17; Hapgood, *The Men Who Wear the K,* 80–86; Nicholl, *The Golden Wheel,* 220–36; Luis M. Morales, "Mental Hygiene in the War of Nerves," ibid., 13, 54. The majority of speeches before Kiwanis clubs in 1942 concerned morale, closely followed by "youth activities in wartime." Kiwanis International, *Proceedings,* Twenty-fifth Annual Convention, Cleveland, Ohio, 1942, 29.

42. S. Kendrick Gurensey, Inaugural Message, *Proceedings,* Thirty-eighth Annual Convention, San Francisco, 1947, 28–32; Ellis Lovelass, "The Spirit of Lionism Can Cure the World's Ills," *Lion* 28 (Feb. 1946): 15.

43. Rotary International, *Proceedings,* Thirty-seventh Annual Convention, Atlantic City, N.J., 1946, 15.

44. Rotary International, *Proceedings,* San Francisco, 1947, 32.

45. Walker Y. Brooks, "Diplomacy from the Cross Roads," *Kiwanis Magazine* 32 (Nov. 1947): 8–9.

46. Frank A. Ninkovich argues that this view of the U.N. dominated official United States policy as well. He faults the Americans for not recognizing that the United Nations was in fact a political structure dealing with international power politics. While this idealism might have been foolish naivete, Ninkovich thinks that in fact it masked the United States' own drive for power. By making cultural unity as defined by the United States the prerequisite for world order, Americans could pursue their own interests in the name of international harmony. *The Diplomacy of Ideas,* 85–181.

47. Melvin Jones, "World Unity through Mutual Understanding," *Lion* 31 (Apr. 1949): 1.

48. Nicholl, *The Golden Wheel,* 236.

Chapter 7: Serving the Suburbs

1. These fears were first voiced in a *Rotarian* article in 1931. "A Rotarian's Son Predicts" (May 1931): 15–16. Then references to them appeared in most debates about membership restrictions, in particular at the 1937 convention in Nice,

France. *Proceedings,* 321–33. Interestingly, Rotarian concerns about corporate neglect of community welfare were echoed by C. Wright Mills and Melville J. Ulmer in their wartime study of small cities, "Small Business and Civic Welfare," commissioned and published by the Senate Select Committee on Small Business as *Small Business and the Quality of American Life,* 545–83. Although Mills expressed a general contempt for the American businessman, his limited sympathy both here and in *White Collar* definitely lay with the small entrepreneur of the old middle class.

2. Clifford F. Hood, Address, Lions International, *Proceedings,* Thirty-fourth Annual Convention, Atlantic City, N.J., 1951, 133–37; Don Herold, "Meet Yourself, Mr. Reader," *Rotarian* 69 (Jan. 1947): 31–32; Merle H. Tucker, "The Man Who Wears the K," *Kiwanis Magazine* 41 (Nov. 1956): 35–38.

3. J. George, "Corporations 'Join' the Community," *Kiwanis Magazine* 32 (Oct. 1947): 12–13. General studies of corporate executives' involvement in the community took place in the fifties, as sociologists attempted to determine the role of the corporation in the local community power structure. Representative articles include R. O. Schulze, "The Role of Economic Dominants in Community Power Structure," *American Sociological Review* 23 (Feb. 1958): 3–9; N. Long, "The Corporation, Its Satellites, and the Local Community," in D. W. Minor and S. Greer, eds., *The Concept of Community* (Chicago: Aldine, 1959), 163–76; Clelland and Form, "Economic Dominants and Community Power: A Comparative Analysis," *American Journal of Sociology* 69 (Mar. 1964): 511–16; and Phillip Mott, "The Role of the Absentee-Owned Corporation in the Changing Community," in Aiken and Mott, eds., *The Structure of Community Power.* In perhaps the most famous of these studies, Robert K. Merton found that corporate executives, operating on the basis of a "cosmopolitan" frame of reference, were much less inclined to join sociable organizations designed for "making contacts" and tended to join associations based on special skills and knowledge. *Social Theory and Social Structure* (New York: Free Press, 1968), 452–53.

4. "With the Lions," *Life* 27 (Aug. 1, 1949): 25; Oren Arnold, "Clubs are Trumps," *Colliers* 121 (Jan. 1948): 11–13; Jerome Ellison, "The Truth about Service Clubs," *Saturday Evening Post* 224 (Oct. 13, 1951): 38–39. The post–World War II position of small business is described in Steven Solomon, *Small Business USA: The Role of Small Companies in Sparking America's Economic Transformation* (New York: Crown Publishers, 1984): 71–75; Stanley Hollander, "The Effects of Industrialization on Small Retailing in the United States in the Twentieth Century," and Harold Vatter, "The Position of Small Business in American Manufacturing, 1870–1970," both in Stuart W. Bruchey, ed., *Small Business in American Life.* John Bunzel discusses the postwar celebration of small business in *The American Small Businessman.*

5. Walter Williams, "Spectators or Players," Rotary International, *Proceedings,* 1950, 52–59.

6. O. Sam Cummings, "Kiwanians, Champions of Private Enterprise," *Kiwanis Magazine* 37 (Jan. 1952): 10–12.

7. Quote from J. J. Kaufman, "They're Selling Freedom," *Lion* 33 (July 1951): 12–14.

8. This Menckenesque line came from a Soviet journalist observing American life, and apparently it was widely reported in American newspapers. All the service clubs took affront, but none more so than the Lions, who devoted several pages of the *Lion* to responses from around America. One of them came from the *Wall Street Journal,* which condescendingly defended the clubs on the grounds that American democracy "includes the privileges of the citizen to make himself ridiculous if he chooses." "What a Soviet Reporter Said about America—and about Lions," *Lion* 29 (Sept. 1946): 20–21. On anticommunism, see Robert Griffith, "American Politics and the Origins of McCarthyism," in Griffith and Athan Theoharis, eds., *The Specter: Original Essays on the Cold War and the Origins of McCarthyism* (New York: New Viewpoints, 1974). Griffith argues convincingly that the Red Scare owed a great deal to the compromises political leaders made to win support for their particular programs—compromises that systematically weakened liberal opposition and created an environment in which the claims of conservative businessmen's associations, veterans organizations, patriotic societies, and of course McCarthy himself were given a hearing.

9. Milton Lomask, "500,000 Americans Can Be Wrong," *Kiwanis Magazine* 36 (Feb. 1951): 24–25; J. J. McGraw, "Red-Letter Day," *Kiwanis Magazine* 34 (Mar. 1949): 34–35; "Kiwanis Activities," *Kiwanis Magazine* 36 (Oct. 1951): 41.

10. Lions International, *Proceedings,* 1951, 172.

11. Quoted in Griffith, "American Politics and the Origins of McCarthyism," 4.

12. "Lion Fisher's Speech at the International Convention," *Lion* 32 (Sept. 1949): 21; Editorial, *Kiwanis Magazine* 32 (Sept. 1947): 48; Hugh Stevenson, "Why Is Anyone a Communist?," *Kiwanis Magazine* 34 (Mar. 1949): 9–11.

13. S. Robertson, "Indulgent Paternalism," *Rotarian* 76 (May 1950): 57; Wallace F. Bennett, "How Rotary Can Become a Vital Source," Rotary International, *Proceedings,* Forty-second Annual Convention, Atlantic City, N.J., 1951, 37–41.

14. Harry Adams, "Labor's Date with Destiny," *Kiwanis Magazine* 32 (Feb. 1947): 14–15.

15. Blackford, *A History of Small Business in America,* 74–81.

16. Ronald L. Filippelli, "The Historical Context of Postwar Industrial Relations," and Bruce Nissen, "A Post–World War II 'Social Accord?,' " in Nissen, ed., *U.S. Labor Relations, 1945–1989: Accommodation and Conflict* (New York: Garland Publishing, 1990).

17. Sanford M. Jacoby, "American Exceptionalism Revisited: The Importance of Management," in Jacoby, ed., *Masters to Managers: Historical and Comparative Perspectives on American Employers* (New York: Columbia University Press, 1991), 173–200.

18. Nelson Lichtenstein, "From Corporatism to Collective Bargaining: Organized Labor and the Eclipse of Social Democracy in the Postwar Era," in Steve Fraser and Gary Gerstle, eds., *The Rise and Fall of the New Deal Order, 1930–*

1980 (Princeton, N.J.: Princeton University Press, 1989), 122–52; Jacoby, "American Exceptionalism Revisited."

19. Rotary International, *Service Is My Business* (Chicago: Rotary International, 1948), 97; "Human Relations," *Lion* 36 (Nov. 1953): 7, 47.

20. F.B.S., "Pull up a Chair," *Kiwanis Magazine* 35 (Jan. 1950): 56; Rotary International, *Service Is My Business*, 95–126.

21. Ironically, they applied this psychological interpretation to club conservatism. When critics of America's "pseudo-conservatives" in the 1950s sought to explain why apparently irrational views on the "socialistic" tendencies of postwar America had acquired such wide currency, they turned to a sociopsychological explanation. America was at the time experiencing unprecedented prosperity; there appeared to be no legitimate grounds for grievance among the kinds of people that made up the anticommunist bloc. Therefore they argued that behind the conservatives' resentment lay the anxieties of status deprivation. The commentators—among them C. Wright Mills, Richard Hofstadter, and Seymour Martin Lipset—reasoned that, though prosperous, the small businessmen and professionals who made up the old middle class now found themselves on the fringes of society and needed scapegoats for their loss of prestige. These displaced conservatives vented their spleen on labor and big government as symbols of the new order. Their politics expressed frustration and insecurity, and their paeans to free enterprise represented an attempt to recapture their lost status. C. Wright Mills, *White Collar;* essays by the others pursuing the same line of thought appeared in Daniel Bell, ed., *The New American Right* (New York, 1955; republished as *The Radical Right* (New York: Doubleday, 1963).

22. Norman Vincent Peale, "Formula for Great Days Ahead," Rotary International, *Proceedings,* Fortieth Annual Convention, New York, 1949, 67–73; idem, "The Art of Living in Postwar America," *Kiwanis Magazine* 32 (Aug. 1947): 18–19; idem, "How to Find a Richer Life," *Lion* 36 (June 1954): 12–13. For an insightful analysis of Peale and pop psychology in American culture, see Donald Meyer, *The Positive Thinkers: Religion as Pop Psychology from Mary Baker Eddy to Oral Roberts* (New York: Pantheon Books, 1980).

23. See Peter L. Berger, "Toward a Sociological Understanding of Psychoanalysis," in *Facing Up to Modernity: Excursions in Society, Politics, and Religion* (New York: Basic Books, 1977), 23–34.

24. The statistics were compiled by comparing data in the U.S. Bureau of the Census's *County and City Data Book, 1956* and club directories, 1945–55.

25. Herbert J. Gans, *The Levittowners: Ways of Life and Politics in a New Suburban Community* (New York: Pantheon, 1967), 52–67. At Rotary's headquarters most of the paperwork in each club's file concerns elaborate founding procedures.

26. Claude S. Fischer and Robert Max Jackson, "Suburbs, Networks, and Attitudes," in Barry Schwartz, ed., *The Changing Face of the Suburbs* (Chicago: University of Chicago Press, 1976), 279–305; Gans, *The Levittowners,* 135–49.

27. Club Activities, *Kiwanis Magazine* 36 (Mar. 1951): 41; Ruth Wyrick, "Teaching Community Living," *Kiwanis Magazine* 37 (June 1952): 22; John Read

Carel, "Buster's Barbecue," *Lion* 35 (Nov. 1952): 6–8; "They Waded In," *Lion* 35 (June 1953): 17–19; "Project Light Bulb," *Lion* 35 (Feb. 1954): 18–19; "Selling Ac'cent," *Lion* 37 (July–Aug. 1955): 23–25.

28. See Claude S. Fischer, "Ambivalent Communities: How Americans Understand Their Localities," in Alan Wolfe, ed., *America at Century's End* (Berkeley: University of California Press, 1991), 79–90; Albert Hunter, "Persistence of Local Sentiments in Mass Society," in Roland L. Warren and Larry Lyon, eds., *New Perspectives on the American Community* (Homewood, Ill.: Rand McNally, 1983), 178–94; and Warren, "External Forces Affecting Local Communities—Bad News and Good News," *Journal of Community Development and Society* 6 (Fall 1975): 6–21.

29. William Whyte, *The Organization Man*, 359–65.

30. Sam Bass Warner, Jr., *The Private City: Philadelphia in Three Periods of Its Growth* (Philadelphia: University of Pennsylvania Press, 1968), 173–76.

31. Barry Schwartz, "Images of Suburbia: Some Revisionist Commentary and Conclusions," in Schwartz, ed., *The Changing Face of the Suburbs* (Chicago: University of Chicago Press, 1976), 330–32.

32. Basil G. Zimmer, "The Urban Centrifugal Drift," in Amos H. Hawley and Vincent P. Rock, *Metropolitan America in Contemporary Perspective* (New York: John Wiley and Sons, 1975), 23–91; Kenneth T. Jackson, *Crabgrass Frontier: The Suburbanization of the United States* (New York: Oxford University Press, 1985), 257–61.

33. Zane L. Miller, *Suburb: Neighborhood and Community in Forest Park, Ohio, 1935–1976* (Knoxville: University of Tennessee Press, 1981).

34. W. B. Todd, "What Are We Here For?," *Lion* 9 (Oct. 1926): 11, 17; J. O. Tally, Jr., "Message of the President," Kiwanis International, *Proceedings,* Forty-sixth Annual Convention, Toronto, 1961, 38–46; Rotary International, *Proceedings,* Fifty-seventh Annual Convention, 1966, 225–34; "Dialogue on World Community Service," ibid., 201–8.

35. Examples of the linking of voluntarism and independent individualism include Rotary International, *Proceedings,* Fifty-third Convention, Los Angeles, 1962, 250–62; idem, *Proceedings,* Fifty-fourth Convention, St. Louis, 1963, 110–17; Edward M. Lindsey, "The Independent Sector," *Lion* 49 (Oct. 1966): 5–6; Clarence L. Sturm, "Call to Leadership," *Lion* 42 (July–Aug. 1959): 5–6; and "The Future of the Service Club Movement: A Discussion," *Kiwanis Magazine* 53 (Dec. 1967–Jan. 1968): 25–28.

36. W. R. Bryan, "Challenge of the Seventies," *Lion* 52 (July–Aug. 1969): 7–8; Miller A. F. Ritchie, "Pea-Size Colleges Answer the Campus Rebellion," *Lion* 52 (Feb. 1970): 10–12; Panel Discussion on Youth Law and Order, Rotary International, *Proceedings,* Fifty-ninth Annual Convention, Mexico City, 1968, 301.

37. Trutter apparently represented a minority opinion. "Turn On, Tune In, Don't Drop Out," *Rotarian* 117 (Dec. 1971): 22–25.

38. See Jonathan Rieder, "The Rise of the Silent Majority," in Fraser and Gerstle, *The Rise and Fall of the New Deal Order, 1930–1980*, 243–68; J. Bruce

Eure, letter to the *Rotarian* 117 (Jan. 1971): 16. Eure's letter appeared in response to a thoughtful (October 1970) issue of the *Rotarian* on the "World Campus," which carried a wide variety of opinion on student revolts. Predictably, of the many letters commenting on the issue, few showed much sympathy for student protestors. The historian of the Bellingham, Washington, Rotary club notes with regret that while students' activities were viewed with disfavor by Rotarians, "at no time between 1969 and 1973 did Rotarians ever hear a presentation of the student's side of the issue." Keith A. Murray, *The History of the Bellingham Rotary Club, 1917–1981* (Bellingham: Center for Pacific Northwest Studies, Western Washington University, 1981), 51.

39. Address, William E. Walk, Rotary International, *Proceedings,* Sixty-first Annual Convention, 1970, 106; "Club Talk," *Newsweek,* Feb. 15, 1971: 81; Speech of R. P. Merridew, Kiwanis International, *Proceedings,* Fifty-sixth Annual Convention, San Francisco, 1971, 98–104.

40. Key Club president Stephen E. Kolzak, Kiwanis International, *Proceedings,* 1971, 93.

41. The file at Rotary International on blacks and membership makes interesting reading. It contains some eloquent appeals for desegregation from white members dated as early as the 1920s. Here, as in a few other cases, Rotary officials are not revealed in their best light: their replies are often evasive and show more concern about Rotary's organization than Rotary's ideals.

42. "Blacks and Rotary" File, Rotary International.

43. "Court Rules Rotary Must Admit Women," *Los Angeles Times,* May 5, 1987, 1.

44. I do not discount local resistance to change, but I believe the desire to expand membership plus the increasing presence of women professionals and executives will force the issue. Immediately after the U.S. Supreme Court ruling, for example, the Cleveland Rotary Club, the third largest in America, announced it had admitted four new women members.

45. "A New Opportunity to Serve," *Lion* 71 (July–Aug. 1988): 34.

46. Robbins's question brings to mind George Bernard Shaw's remark in response to an earlier club soul-searching: "I know where Rotary is going—it's going to lunch."

47. Dave Smith, "Rotary's True Image," *Rotarian* 158 (June 1991): 36–37, 53; "The Image of Lionism: Planning for the Future," *Lion* 69 (Oct. 1986): 16–17.

48. For an excellent overview of recent sociological study of the contemporary American scene, see Alan Wolfe, ed., *America at Century's End.* Especially relevant for the present discussion are the articles by Claude S. Fischer, "Ambivalent Communities: How Americans Understand Their Localities"; Alan Wolfe, "Out of the Frying Pan into . . . What?"; and Richard Madsen, "Contentless Consensus: The Political Discourse of a Segmented Society." Madsen has a particularly insightful discussion of the debate between "no-growth" and "growth" advocates in a California community—the growth faction was supported by the local Kiwanis club. See also Barbara Ehrenreich's provocative, if unsystematic, study of the

current middle-class scene, *Fear of Falling: The Inner Life of the Middle Class* (New York: Pantheon, 1989). For descriptions of new patterns of middle-class community life, see Joel Garreau, *Edge City: Life on the New Frontier* (New York: Doubleday, 1991), esp. 265–301; and Rob Kling, Spencer Olin, and Mark Poster, eds., *Postsuburban California: The Transformation of Orange County since World War II* (Berkeley: University of California Press, 1991).

49. Austin P. Jennings, "Adaptability: Our Key to Success," *Lion* 71 (July–Aug. 1988): 4–5, 44.

50. Robert Fisher and Joseph Kling, "Community Mobilization: Prospects for the Future," *Urban Affairs Quarterly* 25 (Dec. 1989): 200–211; John R. Logan and Gordana Rabrenovic, "Neighborhood Associations: Their Issues, Their Allies, and Their Opponents," *Urban Affairs Quarterly* 26 (Sept. 1990): 68–94.

51. "Remarks by General Secretary Perry," Meeting of the Executive Committee, Oct. 31, 1941, Perry File, Rotary International. Perry later rewrote his talk under the title "Shall It Be Rotary?," which was published in the June 1942 *Rotarian*.

Bibliography

Primary Sources

Manuscripts

Aurora, Illinois: Aurora Historical Society
Bloomington, Illinois: McClean County Historical Society
Champaign, Illinois: Illinois Historical Survey, University of Illinois
Urbana Association of Commerce Papers
De Kalb, Illinois: Northern Illinois Regional History Center, Northern Illinois University
De Kalb Kiwanis Collection
  Dixon Chamber of Commerce Collection
  Embree Collection
  Smith Oil Collection
  Sterling Association of Commerce Collection
Evanston, Illinois: Rotary International Headquarters
Jacksonville, Illinois: Jacksonville Public Library
  Local History Collection
Washington, D.C.: Library of Congress
  James Davis Papers

Club and Lodge Magazines

American Elk. Detroit. 1906–15
Eagle Magazine. Detroit. 1912–40
Elk News. Detroit. 1904
Elks Magazine. Chicago. 1922–30
Federation Bulletin. Boston. 1903–12
The Friendly Elk. Detroit. 1904–5
General Federation of Women's Clubs Magazine. Boston. 1913–20
Ki-Grams. Washington, D.C. 1921–58
The Kiwanis Magazine. Chicago. 1923–85
The Lion. Chicago. 1919–92
Mooseheart Magazine. Chicago. 1915–29

The National Rotarian. Chicago. 1911–14
The Odd-Fellow World. Aberdeen, S.Dak. 1898–1901
The Pulse. Sacramento. 1920–29
The Rotarian. Chicago. 1915–92
Rotary Service. London. 1942–46
Royal Arcanum Bulletin. Boston. 1893–97

Publications of Club and Lodge Members

Andrews, Thomas G. *The Jericho Road: The Philosophy of Odd-Fellowship.* Oklahoma City: William Thomas Co., 1937.
Arnold, Oren. *The Golden Strand: An Informal History of the Rotary Club of Chicago.* Chicago: Quadrangle Books, 1966.
———. *The Widening Path: An Interpretive Record of Kiwanis.* Chicago: Kiwanis International, 1949.
Ayala, Acosta. *Historia, Filosofia Y Psicologia del Leonismo.* Mayaguez, P.R.: Leons de Mayaguez, 1985.
Beadle, Muriel, and the Centennial History Committee. *The Fortnightly of Chicago: The City and Its Women, 1873–1973.* Chicago: Henry Regnery Co., 1973.
Casey, Robert J., and W. A. S. Douglas. *World's Biggest Doers.* Chicago: Wilcox and Follet, 1959.
Chapelon, Marcel. *Annuaire des Rotary-Clubs de France, 1938–39.* Paris: Rotary International, 1938.
Chapman, Irvin C. *A History of the California-Nevada-Hawaii District of Kiwanis International.* Los Angeles: Kiwanis International, 1981.
Chapple, Joe Mitchell. *Our Jim.* Boston: Chapple Publishing Co., 1928.
Chester, Charlie. *Charlie Chester's Cry Simba!* London: Bachman and Turner, 1977.
Chituin, John. *Rotary Club of Christ Church Golden Jubilee, 1922–1972.* Auckland, NZ.: Whitcombe and Tombs Ltd., 1972.
Cremer, Oliver L. *Rockford Rotary: Fifty Years of Service.* Rockford: Rotary Club of Rockford, 1966.
Croly, Mrs. Jane Cunningham. *The History of the Woman's Club Movement in America.* New York: Nery G. Allen, 1898.
———. *Sorosis: Its Origin and History.* 1886, repr., New York: Arno Press, 1975.
Curry, Elvin J. *The Red Blood of Odd-Fellowship.* Baltimore, Md.: Published by author, 1903.
Davis, James. *The Iron Puddler.* New York: Grosset and Dunlap, 1922.
Diffre, Henri. *Histoire du Rotary en France.* Lyon: BOSC Freres, 1959.
Duncan, Terence S. *The Hub of the Wheel: The Story of the Rotary Movement in Ireland, 1911–1976.* Belfast: Published by author, 1976.
Dunn, E. J. *Builders of Fraternalism in America.* Chicago: Fraternal Book Concern, 1924.

Ellis, Charles Edward. *An Authentic History of the Benevolent and Protective Order of Elks.* Chicago: Published by author, 1910.

Frank, Henriette Greenbaum, and Amalie Hofer Jerome, eds. *Annals of the Chicago Woman's Club, 1876–1916.* Chicago: Chicago's Woman's Club, 1916.

Fraternal Order of Eagles. *Journal of Proceedings.* Thirty-ninth Annual Session of the Fraternal Order of Eagles. Chicago, 1937.

Friday Afternoon Club. *Topics, 1905–1906.* Farmington, N.H.: Privately printed, 1905.

Fuller, Guy H., ed. *Loyal Order of the Moose and Mooseheart.* Mooseheart, Ill.: Mooseheart Press, 1918.

General Federation of Women's Clubs. *Biennial Convention Official Report.* Eighth (1906), Ninth (1908), Thirteenth (1916), Seventeenth (1924), Eighteenth (1926).

———. *Official Proceedings, 1896.* Third Biennial Convention. Louisville, Ky.: John P. Morton and Co., 1896.

Graham, F. Wayne. *Sixty-five Years of Devotion and Accomplishment: A Brief History of the Rotary Club of Morris.* Morris, Ill.: Rotary Club of Morris, 1980.

Green, C. Sylvester. *Fifty Years of Rotary in Greenville, North Carolina.* Greenville, N.C.: Rotary Club of Greenville, 1977.

Green, Harold K., ed. *Rotary Club of Charlotte: Fifty Years of "Service above Self."* Charlotte, N.C.: Rotary Club of Charlotte, 1966.

Guest, Edgar A. *Collected Verse.* Chicago: Reilly and Lee Co., 1934.

Hallock, B. B., ed. *The Odd-Fellows Offering.* New York: Samuel A. House and Co., 1842.

Hapgood, L. A. *The Men Who Wear the K: The Story of Kiwanis.* Indianapolis, Ind.: Kiwanis International, 1981.

Harrell, Rev. T. G. B. *The New I.O.O.F. Monitor and Guide, Containing a History of the Degree of Rebekah and Its Teachings.* Indianapolis, Ind.: Robert Douglas, 1888.

Harris, Paul P. *The Founder of Rotary.* Chicago: Rotary International, 1928.

———. *My Road to Rotary.* Chicago: A. Kroch and Son, 1948.

———. *This Rotarian Age.* Chicago: Rotary International, 1935.

Harter, David W. *Historical Souvenir of the Loyal Order of Moose.* Chicago: Published by author, 1912.

Heintel, Erich. *50 Jahre Rotary Club Wien, 1925–1975.* Wien, Ger.: Rotary Club Wien, 1975.

Hewitt, C. P. *Towards My Neighbour: The Social Influence of the Rotary Movement in Great Britain and Ireland.* London: Longsman, Green and Co., 1950.

Hijmans, Dorr H. *Dertig Jaren Rotary in Nederland.* Haarlem: H. D. Tjeenk Willenk und Zoon, 1953.

Howard, Joseph L. *History of the San Diego Rotary Club 33, 1911–1982.* San Diego: San Diego Rotary Club, 1981.

Hunt, Harold. *The Story of Rotary in Australia, 1921–1971.* Sydney: Halstead Press, 1971.

Hyer, Julien C. *Texas Lions: A History of Fifty Years of Lionism, 1917–1967.* Waco, Tex.: Hill Junior College Press, 1969.

International Association of Lions Clubs. *Lions Stunt Book and Toastmaster's Guide.* Chicago: Lions International, 1950.

———. *Official Directory.* 1925–60.

———. *Official Proceedings.* Annual Convention. 1937, 1951, 1956, 1961.

———. *Report of Melvin Jones, Secretary Treasurer of Lions International, De-livered at the Nineteenth Annual Convention of the IALC, Mexico City, Mex., 1935.*

International Order of Odd-Fellows. *Journal of Proceedings.* Right-Worthy and Sovereign Grand Lodge of the United States of America, 1851–1935.

Irons, Thomas. *A Brief Story of Early Odd-Fellowship Briefly Told.* Philadelphia: John C. Winston and Co., 1925.

Kittler, Glen. *The Dynamic World of Lions International.* New York: M. Vans and Co., 1968.

Kiwanis Club of Columbia. *What Am I Going to Do?* Columbia: Kiwanis Club of Columbia, 1928.

Kiwanis International. *Kiwanis Activities.* Vols. 2–15. Chicago, 1922–36.

———. *Kiwanis at Fifty.* 1965.

———. *Manual for Club Officers.* 1939.

———. *Official Directory.* 1925–60.

———. *Proceedings.* Annual Convention. 1922–71.

Lamb, Frank. *Rotary: A Businessman's Interpretation.* Hoquium, Wash.: Rotary Club of Hoquium, 1927.

Lauriston, Victor. *History of the Sarnia Rotary Club, 1927–1965.* Sarnia, Ont.: Sarnia Rotary Club, 1966.

Lay, Chester F. *Fifty Golden Years: A Brief History of Lakeland Rotary.* Lakeland, Fla.: Rotary Club of Lakeland, 1968.

Lee, Everetts. *The Story of the Kiwanis Club of Schenectady.* Schenectady, N.Y.: Kiwanis Club of Schenectady, 1964.

Lemke, Carl R. *Official History of the Improved Order of Red Men.* Waco, Tex.: Davis Bros. Publishing Co., 1964.

Leonard, Patrick J., ed. *The History of the Braintree Rotary Club—The Founding Years, 1923–1928.* Braintree, Mass.: Braintree Rotary Club, 1978.

Levi, Gilbert. *History of the Rotary Club of San Jose.* San Jose: Rotary Club of San Jose, 1963.

Loesell, Clarence. *A History of Kiwanis in Michigan with Vital Statistics and Statistical Tables.* Charlotte, Mich.: McGrath-Defoe Co., 1956.

Loso, Foster W., ed. *History of the New Jersey Kiwanis District.* Somerset, N.J.: Somerset Press, 1947.

Loyal Order of Moose. *Minutes,* Thirty-fourth Annual Convention of the Supreme Lodge of the World. Mooseheart, Ill., 1922.

———. *Minutes.* Thirty-third Annual Convention of the Supreme Lodge of the World. Toledo, Ohio, 1921.

McCallister, William A. *Forty Years of Rotary in the Marianas*. Agana, Guam: Rotary Club of Agana, 1978.

Meier, Walter F. *The Heart of Elkdom*. Seattle, Wash.: Far West Lithograph and Printing, 1925.

Moffret, Robert W. *The Rise and Progress of the Manchester Unity of the Independent Order of Odd-Fellows, 1810–1904*. Manchester, Eng.: Board of Directors, Manchester Unity, 1905.

Morais, J. Victor. *The Golden Wheel: The Stirring Story of Rotary's Long Journey of Love and Service and of Its Notable Achievements in Malasia, Brunei, Singapore, Thailand, Vietnam, Cambodia and Laos*. Singapore: Rotary Club of Singapore, 1964.

Moss, John H. *We Build: The Story of Kiwanis*. Chicago: John F. Cuneo, 1942.

Mountin, William J. *History of the Rotary Club of San Francisco*. San Francisco: Rotary Club of San Francisco, 1940.

Murray, Keith A. *The History of the Bellingham Rotary Club, 1917–1981*. Bellingham, Wash.: Center for Pacific Northwest Studies, Western Washington University, 1981.

Nicholl, David Shelley. *The Golden Wheel: The Story of Rotary, 1905 to the Present*. Estover, Plymouth, Eng.: McDonald and Evans, 1984.

Nicholson, James R. *History of the Order of Elks, 1868–1952*. Chicago: National Memorial and Publication Commission of the B.P.O.E., 1953.

Nitzsche, George E., ed. *Philadelphia—Guide to a City*. Philadelphia: Rotary Club of Philadelphia, 1920.

Nolan, Raymond A. *History of Rotary International, District 760*. Reston, Va.: Rotary International, 1984.

O'Dell, Richard F. *Reaching Out: A History of the Rotary Club of Marquette, Michigan, 1916–1981*. Marquette, Mich.: Rotary Club of Marquette, 1982.

Oliva, Mariategui Ricardo. *Historia del Rotary Club de Lima, 1920–1955*. Lima, Peru: Rotary Club del Lima, 1955.

Oliver, Warner. *Back of the Dream: The Story of the Loyal Order of Moose*. New York: E. P. Dutton, 1952.

Past Grand Patriarch. *Revised Odd-Fellowship Illustrated: The Complete Revised Ritual of the Lodge, Encampment, Patriarchs Militant and the Rebekah Degrees Profusely Illustrated*. Chicago: Ezra A. Cook, 1886.

Petty, Weston A. *The Big Story of America's Largest . . . The Lubbock Lions Club, 1929–1982*. Austin, Tex.: Eakin Publications, 1983.

Preston, Charles H. *Panorama: Rotary and Allentown, 1914–1964*. Allentown, Pa.: Rotary Club of Allentown, 1964.

Ridgely, James L. *History of American Odd-Fellowship: The First Decade*. Baltimore, Md.: Published by author, 1878.

Ross, Theodore. *Odd-Fellowship: Its History and Manual*. New York: M. W. Hazen, 1888.

A Rotarian. *The Meaning of Rotary*. London: Perry Lund Humphries, and Company, Ltd., 1927.

Rotary Club of Baltimore. *Baltimore and Rotary: A Preachment of Progress.* Baltimore, Md.: Rotary Club of Baltimore, 1917.

Rotary Club of Lancaster. *History of the Lancaster Rotary Club.* Lancaster, Pa.: Rotary Club of Lancaster, 1935.

Rotary Club of Los Angeles. *History of the Rotary Club of Los Angeles.* Los Angeles: Rotary Club of Los Angeles, 1955.

Rotary Club of Minneapolis. *The Story of Minneapolis Rotary, 1910–1935.* Minneapolis: Rotary Club of Minneapolis, 1935.

Rotary Club of Newport Mon, England. *Rotary International Friendships.* Newport Mon: Rotary Club of Newport Mon, 1944.

Rotary Club of Oakland. *Rotarily Yours: A History of the Rotary Club of Oakland.* Oakland, Calif.: Rotary Club of Oakland, 1969.

Rotary Club of Palo Alto. *The First Fifty Years of the Rotary Club of Palo Alto, 1922–1972.* Palo Alto, Calif.: Rotary Club of Palo Alto, 1972.

Rotary International. *Adventure in Service.* 1946.

———. *Annual Report of Officers.* Fifth Convention, 1914.

———. *Fifty Years of Service: Rotary, 1905–1955.* 1954.

———. *Handbook of Entertainment for Rotary Clubs.* 1919.

———. *Manual for Secretaries of Rotary Clubs.* 1918.

———. *Official Directory.* 1920–60.

———. *Proceedings.* Annual Conference of the Second District. Stockton, Calif., 1927.

———. *Proceedings.* Annual Conference of the Thirteenth District. Sacramento, Calif., 1918.

———. *Proceedings.* Annual Conference of the Twenty-third District. Long Beach, Calif., 1921.

———. *Proceedings.* Third Annual Conference of the Twenty-fourth District. Clarksburg, W. Va., 1925.

———. *Proceedings.* Annual Convention. 1916–87.

———. *Program for the 1930 Conference of the Rotary Clubs of the Forty-fifth District of Rotary International.* Murphysboro, Ill.

———. *Rotary Basic Library: Focus on Rotary, Club Service, Vocational Service, Community Service, International Service, Youth Activities, Rotary Foundation.* 1982.

———. *Service Is My Business.* 1948.

———. *The World of Rotary.* 1975.

Rotary Italiano. *Annuario, 1928–29.*

———. *Annuario del Distretto Italiano, 1936–1937.*

Runnals, J. Laurence, ed. *Golden Anniversary History of the Rotary Club of St. Catharines, Ontario, 1921–1971.* St. Catharines, Ont.: Rotary Club of St. Catharines, 1971.

Russell, E. C. *Fifty Years of Rotary in Ottawa, 1916–1966.* Ottawa, Can.: Rotary Club of Ottawa, 1966.

Sackett, M. W. *Early History of Fraternal Beneficiary Societies in America: Origin and Growth, 1868–1880.* Meadville, Pa.: Tribune Publishing Co., 1914.

Schler, Alfon S. *25 Jahre Rotary-Club Baden-Baden.* Baden-Baden, Ger.: Ernst Koelblin, 1955.

Scouller, Mildred Marshall. *Women Who Man Our Clubs.* Philadelphia: John C. Winston Co., 1934.

Sheldon, Arthur F. *The Science of Efficient Service, or the Philosophy of Profit Making.* Chicago: Sheldon Business Schools, 1915.

Smedley, Edward, ed. *Wheels within Wheels: A History of the Rotary Club of Peterborough.* Peterborough, Eng.: Rotary Club of Peterborough, 1964.

The Sons of Malta Exposed: By One Who Was "Sold." New York: Published by author, 1860.

Spenser, Charles Edward. *My Thirty Years in Kiwanis.* New York: William Frederick Press, 1951.

Steele, Helen McKay. *The Indianapolis Women's Club, 1875–1940.* Greenfield, Ind.: Wm. Mitchell Printing Co., 1944.

Taylor, Carl Cleveland. *Urban-Rural Relations.* Chicago: Kiwanis International, 1928.

Thompson, Gordon S. "Bish." *Of Dreams and Deeds: The Story of Optimist International.* Chicago: Optimist International, 1966.

Upchurch, John J. *The Life, Labors, and Travels of Father J. J. Upchurch.* San Francisco: A. T. Dewey, 1887.

Unsworth, J. Lewis, et al. *History of the Trenton Rotary Club, 1914–1969.* Trenton, N.J.: Trenton Historical Society, 1970.

Waitt, Robert W., Jr. *The Glitter of the Golden Years, 1913–1963: The Story of Fifty Years of Rotary in Richmond.* Richmond, Va.: Rotary Club of Richmond, 1963.

Walsh, James P. *The First Rotarian: The Life and Times of Paul Percy Harris, Founder of Rotary.* Shoreham by the Sea, West Sussex, Eng.: Scan Books, 1979.

Wells, Mildred White. *Unity in Diversity: The History of the General Federation of Women's Clubs.* Washington, D.C.: GFWC, 1953.

Wells, Robert W. *Mooseheart: The City of Children.* Mooseheart, Ill.: Loyal Order of Moose, 1965.

Wood, Mary I. *The History of the General Federation of Women's Clubs.* New York: Norwood Press, 1912.

Wysong, Richard. *A History of Kiwanis in Michigan with Vital Statistics and Statistical Tables, 1956–1960.* Charlotte, Mich.: McGrath-Defoe, 1964.

Yates, Keith. *The Fogarty Years: A History of the A.O.U.W.* Seattle, Wash.: Evergreen Printing Assoc., 1972.

Zapffe, Carl A. *Rotary!* Baltimore, Md.: Rotary Club of Baltimore, 1963.

Secondary Sources

Abbott, Carl. *The New Urban America: Growth and Politics in Sunbelt Cities.* Chapel Hill: University of North Carolina Press, 1981.

Adams, Jane. "Creating Community in a Midwestern Village: Fifty Years of the Cobden Peach Festival." *Illinois Historical Journal* 83 (Summer 1990): 97–108.

Aiken, Michael, and Paul E. Mott, eds. *The Structure of Community Power*. New York: Random House, 1970.

Aikman, Duncan. "American Fascism" *Harper's Magazine* 174 (Apr. 1925): 514–19.

Aron, Cindy Sondrik. *Ladies and Gentlemen of the Civil Service: Middle-Class Workers in Victorian America*. New York: Oxford University Press, 1987.

Atherton, Lewis. *Main Street on the Middle Border*. Bloomington: Indiana University Press, 1954.

Bahlke, Howard. "Rotary and American Culture: A Historical Study of Ideology." Ph.D. diss., University of Minnesota, 1956.

Baker, Paula. *The Moral Frameworks of Public Life: Gender, Politics, and the State in Rural New York, 1870–1930*. New York: Oxford University Press, 1991.

Baker, Richard A. *Conservation Politics: The Senate Career of Clinton P. Anderson*. Albuquerque: University of New Mexico Press, 1985.

Baltzell, E. Digby. *The Protestant Establishment: Aristocracy and Caste in America*. New York: Random House, 1964.

Bederman, Gail. "The Women Have Had Charge of the Church Work Long Enough": The Men and Religion Forward Movement of 1911–1912 and the Masculinization of Middle-Class Protestantism." *American Quarterly* 41 (Fall 1989): 432–63.

Bell, Daniel, ed. *The Radical Right*. New York: Doubleday, 1963.

Bender, Thomas. *Community and Social Change in America*. New Brunswick, N.J.: Rutgers University Press, 1971.

Berger, Petei L. *Facing Up to Modernity: Excursions in Society, Politics, and Religion*. New York: Basic Books, 1977.

Binford, Henry C. *The First Suburbs: Residential Communities on the Boston Periphery*. Chicago: University of Chicago Press, 1985.

Blackford, Mansel G. *A History of Small Business in America*. New York: Twayne Publishers, 1992.

Blair, Karen J. *The Clubwoman as Feminist: True Womanhood Redefined, 1868–1914*. New York: Holmes and Meier Publishers, 1980.

Bliven Bruce. "The Babbitt in His Warren." *Scribner's Magazine* 83 (Dec. 1928): 899–901.

———. "Lower 9, Car 26." *New Republic* 41 (June 10, 1925): 72.

Blumenthal, Albert. *Small-Town Stuff*. Chicago: University of Chicago Press, 1932.

Blumenthal, Henry. *American and French Culture, 1800–1900: Interchanges in Art, Science, Literature, and Society*. Baton Rouge: Louisiana State University Press, 1975.

Blumin, Stuart M. *The Emergence of the Middle Class: Social Experience in the American City, 1760–1900*. New York: Cambridge University Press, 1989.

———. "The Hypothesis of Middle-Class Formation in Nineteenth-Century

America: A Critique and Some Proposals." *American Historical Review* 90 (Apr. 1985): 294–338.

———. *The Urban Threshold: Growth and Change in a Nineteenth-Century American Community.* Chicago: University of Chicago Press, 1976.

Bodnar, John, ed., *Records of Ethnic Fraternal Benefit Associations in the U.S.: Essays and Inventories.* St Paul: University of Minnesota Press, 1981.

Boorstin, Daniel J. *The Americans: The National Experience.* New York: Vintage Books, 1965.

Boyer, Paul. *Urban Masses and Moral Order in America, 1820–1920.* Cambridge, Mass.: Harvard University Press, 1978.

Braeman, John L. "American Foreign Policy in the Age of Normalcy: Three Historiographical Traditions." *Amerikastudien/American Studies* 26 (Nov. 1981): 125–28.

———, Robert Bremner, and David Brody, eds. *Change and Continuity in Twentieth-Century America: The 1920s.* Columbus: Ohio State University Press, 1968.

Brandeis, Louis. *Business—A Profession.* Boston: Small, Maynard, and Co., 1914.

Bremer, William W. *Depression Winters: New York Social Workers and the New Deal.* Philadelphia: Temple University Press, 1984.

Brinkley, Alan. *Voices of Protest: Huey Long, Father Coughlin, and the Great Depression.* New York: Vintage Books, 1983.

Brown, Malcolm, and John N. Webb. *Seven Stranded Coal Towns: A Study of an American Depressed Area.* Washington, D.C.: U.S. Government Printing Office, 1941.

Brownell, Blaine A. *The Urban Ethos in the South, 1920–1930.* Baton Rouge: Louisiana State University Press, 1975.

Bruchey, Stuart, W., ed. *Small Business in American Life.* New York: Columbia University Press, 1980.

Brunner, Edmund des. *Village Communities.* New York: George H. Doran Company, 1927.

———, and J. H. Kolb. *Rural Social Trends.* New York: McGraw-Hill, 1933.

Bunzel, John H. *The American Small Businessman.* 1955. Reprint. New York: Arno Press, 1979.

Cantor, Milton, ed. *American Working-Class Culture: Explorations in American Labor and Social History.* Westport, Conn.: Greenwood Press, 1979.

Carnes, Mark. *Secret Ritual and Manhood in Victorian America.* New Haven, Conn.: Yale University Press, 1989.

Carosso, Vincent P., and Stuart W. Bruchey, eds. *The Survival of Small Business.* New York: Arno Press, 1979.

Cavanagh, Hellen M. *Seed, Soil, and Science: The Story of Eugene D. Funk.* Chicago: Lakeside Press, 1963.

Chambers, Clark A. *Seedtime of Reform: American Social Service and Social Action, 1918–1933.* Ann Arbor: University of Michigan Press, 1967.

Clark, S. D. *The Suburban Society.* Toronto: University of Toronto Press, 1966.

Clarke, Ida Clyde. "A Clubless Woman's World." *Century Magazine* 114 (Oct. 1927): 752–59.

Clawson, Mary Ann. *Constructing Brotherhood: Class, Gender, and Fraternalism.* Princeton, N.J.: Princeton University Press, 1989.

———. "Fraternal Orders and Class Formation in the Nineteenth-Century United States." *Comparative Studies in Society and History* 27 (June 1985): 672–95.

———. "Nineteenth-Century Women's Auxiliaries and Fraternal Orders." *Signs* 12 (Autumn 1986): 40–61.

Clelland, Donald A., and William H. Form, "Economic Dominants and Community Power: A Comparative Analysis," *American Journal of Sociology* 69 (Mar. 1964): 511–16.

Coben, Stanley. *The Rebellion against Victorianism: The Impetus for Cultural Change in 1920s America.* New York: Oxford University Press, 1991.

Cochran, Thomas C. *American Business in the Twentieth Century.* Cambridge, Mass.: Harvard University Press, 1972.

Cohen, Lizabeth. *Making a New Deal: Industrial Workers in Chicago, 1919–1939.* Cambridge: Cambridge University Press, 1990.

Conkin, Paul K. *Tomorrow a New World: The New Deal Community Program.* Ithaca, N.Y.: Cornell University Press, 1959.

Costigliola, Frank. *Awkward Dominion: American Political, Economic, and Cultural Relations with Europe, 1919–1933.* Ithaca, N.Y.: Cornell University Press, 1984.

Cott, Nancy. *The Grounding of Modern Feminism.* New Haven, Conn.: Yale University Press, 1987.

Cradeau, Richard C. "Pearl Harbor: A Failure of Baseball?" *Journal of Popular Culture* 15 (Spring 1982): 67–73.

Crunden, Robert M. *Ministers of Reform: The Progressives' Achievement in American Civilization, 1889–1920.* New York: Basic Books, 1982.

Cumbler, John T. *Working Class and Community in Industrial America: Work, Leisure, and Struggle in Two Industrial Cities, 1880–1930.* Westport, Conn.: Greenwood Press, 1979.

Curtis, Susan. *A Consuming Faith: The Social Gospel and Modern American Culture.* Baltimore, Md.: Johns Hopkins University Press, 1991.

Davis, David Brion, ed. *Ante-Bellum Reform.* New York: Harper and Row, 1967.

Dawley, Alan. *Struggles for Justice: Social Responsibility and the Liberal State.* Cambridge, Mass.: Belknap Press, 1991.

Degler, Carl N. *At Odds: Women and the Family in America from the Revolution to the Present.* New York: Oxford University Press, 1980.

Dobriner, William. *Class in Suburbia.* Englewood Cliffs, N.J.: Prentice-Hall, 1963.

Dolce, Phillip, ed. *Suburbia: The American Dream and Dilemma.* Garden City, N.Y.: Anchor Books, 1976.

Douglas, George H. *H. L. Mencken: Critic of American Life.* Hamden, Conn.: Archon Books, 1978.

Douglas, Harlan P. *The Suburban Trend.* New York: Johnson Reprint Corp., 1970.

Doyle, Don Harrison. *The Social Order of a Frontier Community: Jacksonville, Illinois, 1825–70*. Urbana: University of Illinois Press, 1978.

Dulles, Foster Rhea. *The American Red Cross*. 1951. Reprint. Westport, Conn.: Greenwood Press, 1971.

Dumenil, Lynn. *Freemasonry and American Culture, 1880–1930*. Princeton, N.J.: Princeton University Press, 1984.

———. " 'The Insatiable Maw of Bureaucracy': Antistatism and Education Reform in the 1920s." *Journal of American History* 77 (Sept. 1990): 499–524.

Ebner, Michael H., and Eugene Tobin, eds. *The Age of Urban Reform: New Perspectives on the Progressive Era*. Port Washington, N.Y.: Kennikat Press, 1977.

Ehrenberg, Lewis. *Stepping Out: New York Nightlife and the Transformation of American Culture, 1890–1930*. Chicago: University of Chicago Press, 1981.

Ehrenreich, Barbara. *Fear of Falling: The Inner Life of the Middle Class*. New York: Pantheon, 1989.

Ekirch, Arthur A., Jr. *Ideologies and Utopias: The Impact of the New Deal on American Thought*. Chicago: Quadrangle Books, 1969.

Elias, Robert H. *Entangling Alliances with None*. New York: W. W. Norton, 1973.

Engelbourg, Saul. *Power and Morality: American Business Ethics, 1840–1914*. Westport, Conn.: Greenwood Press, 1980.

Evans, J. Martin. *America: The View from Europe*. San Francisco: San Francisco Book Co., 1976.

Faue, Elizabeth. *Community of Suffering and Struggle: Women, Men, and the Labor Movement in Minneapolis, 1915–1945*. Chapel Hill: University of North Carolina Press, 1991.

Feather, William. "The Sire of Kiwanis." *American Mercury* 1 (Mar. 1924): 355.

Ferguson, Charles W. *Fifty Million Brothers: A Panorama of American Lodges and Clubs*. New York: Farrar and Rinehart, 1937.

Ferster, Louise Howard. "Why Be a Clubwoman?" *Forum* 93 (Jan. 1935): 39–41.

Fisher, Robert, and Joseph Kling. "Community Mobilization: Prospects for the Future." *Urban Affairs Quarterly* 25 (Dec. 1989): 200–211.

Forbush, William Byron. *The Boy Problem in the Home*. Boston: Pilgrim Press, 1915.

Fosdick, Harry Emerson. *The Meaning of Service*. New York: Association Press, 1920.

Fox, Kenneth. *Metropolitan America: Urban Life and Urban Policy in the United States, 1940–1980*. Jackson: University Press of Mississippi, 1986.

Fox, Richard W., and T. J. Jackson Lears, eds. *The Culture of Consumption: Critical Essays in American History, 1880–1980*. New York: Pantheon, 1983.

Fraser, Steve, and Gary Gerstle, eds. *The Rise and Fall of the New Deal Order, 1930–1980*. Princeton, N.J.: Princeton University Press, 1989.

French, Warren, ed. *The Twenties: Poetry, Fiction, Drama*. Deland, Fla.: Edward/Everett and Co., 1975.

Fuller, Wayne E. *The Old Country School: The Story of Rural Education in the Middle West*. Chicago: University of Chicago Press, 1982.

Galambos, Louis. "The Emerging Organizational Synthesis in Modern American History." *Business History Review* 44 (Autumn 1970): 279–90.

——. "Technology, Political Economy, and Professionalization: Central Themes of the Organizational Synthesis." *Business History Review* 57 (Winter 1983): 471–83.

Gans, Herbert J. *The Levittowners: Ways of Life and Politics in a New Suburban Community.* New York: Pantheon, 1967.

——, et al. *On the Making of Americans: Essays in Honor of David Riesman.* Philadelphia: University of Pennsylvania Press, 1979.

Garreau, Joel. *Edge City: Life on the New Frontier.* New York: Doubleday, 1991.

Giddens, Anthony. *The Class Structure of the Advanced Societies.* London: Hutchinson University Library, 1973.

——, and David Held, eds. *Classes, Power, and Conflict: Classical and Contemporary Debates.* Berkeley: University of California Press, 1982.

Gilbert, James. *Perfect Cities: Chicago's Utopias of 1893.* Chicago: University of Chicago Press, 1991.

Gilkeson, John S. *Middle-Class Providence, 1820–1940.* Princeton, N.J.: Princeton University Press, 1986.

Goodman, Paul. *Towards a Christian Republic: Antimasonry and the Great Transition in New England, 1826–1836.* New York: Oxford University Press, 1988.

Gosden, P. H. J. H. *Self-Help: Voluntary Associations in Nineteenth-Century Britain.* New York: Harper and Row, 1974.

Greenberg, Brian. "Worker and Community: Fraternal Orders in Albany, New York, 1845–1885." *Maryland Historian* 8 (Fall 1977): 38–53.

Griffith, Robert, and Athan Theoharis, eds. *The Specter: Original Essays on the Cold War and the Origins of McCarthyism.* New York: New Viewpoints, 1974.

Griffith, Sally. *Hometown News: William Allen White and the Emporia Gazette.* New York: Oxford University Press, 1988.

Gundelach, Peter. "Social Transformation and New Forms of Voluntary Associations." *Social Science Information* 23 (June 1984): 1049–81.

Halttunen, Karen. *Confidence Men and Painted Women: A Study of Middle-Class Culture in America, 1830–1870.* New Haven, Conn.: Yale University Press, 1982.

Hammack, David. "Problems in the Historical Study of Power in the Cities and Towns of the United States." *American Historical Review* 83 (Apr. 1978): 323–49.

Handy, Robert T., ed. *The Social Gospel in America, 1870–1920.* New York: Oxford University Press, 1966.

Haskell, Thomas L., ed. *The Authority of Experts.* Bloomington: Indiana University Press, 1984.

——. "Capitalism and the Origins of Humanitarian Sensibility." *American Historical Review* 90 (Apr. 1985): 294–338 (Part I), (June 1985): 547–66 (Part II).

——. *The Emergence of Professional Social Science: The American Social Science Association and the Nineteenth-Century Crisis of Authority.* Chicago: University of Chicago Press, 1977.

Hausknect, Murray. *The Joiners: A Sociological Description of Voluntary Association Membership in the United States*. New York: Bedminster Press, 1962.

Hawley, Amos H. *The Changing Shape of Metropolitan America: Deconcentration since 1920*. Glencoe, Ill.: Free Press, 1956.

――――, and Vincent P. Rock, eds. *Metropolitan America in Contemporary Perspective*. New York: John Wiley and Sons, 1975.

Hawley, Ellis W. "The Discovery and Study of a 'Corporate Liberalism.' " *Business History Review* 52 (Autumn 1978): 309–19.

――――. *The Great War and the Search for a Modern Order: A History of the American People and Their Institutions, 1917–1933*. New York: St. Martin's Press, 1979.

――――. *The New Deal and the Problem of Monopoly*. Princeton, N.J.: Princeton University Press, 1966.

Hays, Samuel P. *American Political History as Social Analysis*. Knoxville: University of Tennessee Press, 1980.

――――. *The Response to Industrialism, 1885–1914*. Chicago: University of Chicago Press, 1957.

Heald, Morrell. "Big Business Thought in the Twenties: Corporate Responsibility." *American Quarterly* 25 (Mar. 1962): 223–46.

――――. *The Social Responsibilities of Business: Company and Community, 1900–1960*. Cleveland: Case Western Reserve, 1970.

Hearn, Charles R. *The American Dream in the Great Depression*. Westport, Conn.: Greenwood Press, 1977.

Higham, John. *Writing American History: Essays on Modern Scholarship*. Bloomington: Indiana University Press, 1970.

Hilton, George W., and John F. Due. *The Electric Interurban Railways in America*. Palo Alto, Calif.: Stanford University Press, 1960.

Hiner, N. Ray, and Joseph M. Hawes, eds. *Growing Up in America: Children in Historical Perspective*. Urbana: University of Illinois Press, 1985.

Hines, Thomas S. "Echoes from 'Zenith': Reactions of American Businessmen to *Babbitt*." *Business History Review* 41 (Summer 1967): 123–40.

Hirsch, Susan E. *Roots of the American Working Class: The Industrialization of Crafts in Newark, 1800–1860*. Philadelphia: University of Pennsylvania Press, 1978.

Hoffman, Frederick J. *The Twenties*. New York: Collier Publishers, 1962.

Hogan, Michael J. *Informal Entente: The Private Structure of Cooperation in Anglo-American Economic Diplomacy, 1918–1928*. Columbia: University of Missouri Press, 1977.

――――. "Revival and Reform: America's Twentieth-Century Search for a New Economic Order Abroad." *Diplomatic History* 8 (Fall 1984): 287–310.

Hoover, Herbert. *American Individualism*. New York: Doubleday, 1922.

Horowitz, Irving L. *C. Wright Mills: An American Utopian*. New York: Free Press, 1983.

Huizinga, Johan. *America*. New York: Harper and Row, 1972.

Huthmacher, J. Joseph, and Susman, Warren I., eds. *Herbert Hoover and the Crisis of American Capitalism.* Cambridge, Mass.: Schenkman Publishing, 1973.

Jackson, Kenneth T. *Crabgrass Frontier: The Suburbanization of the United States.* New York: Oxford University Press, 1985.

Jacoby, Sanford M., ed. *Masters to Managers: Historical and Comparative Perspectives on American Employers.* New York: Columbia University Press, 1991.

Jaher, Frederick. *The Urban Establishment: Upper Strata in Boston, New York, Charleston, Chicago, and Los Angeles.* Urbana: University of Illinois Press, 1982.

Jenkins, William D. *Steel Valley Klan: The Ku Klux Klan in Ohio's Mahoning Valley.* Kent, Ohio: Kent State University Press, 1990.

Jones, John Finbar, and John Middlemist Herrick. *Citizens in Service: Volunteers in Social Welfare during the Depression, 1929–1941.* East Lansing: Michigan State University Press, 1976.

Jordon, Virgil. "The Business Psychle." *Freeman* 8 (Dec. 5, 1923): 293–300.

Kasson, John F. *Rudeness and Civility: Manners in Nineteenth-Century Urban America.* New York: Hill and Wang, 1990.

Katz, Michael B. *In the Shadow of the Poorhouse: A Social History of Welfare in America.* New York: Basic Books, 1986.

Kett, Joseph. *Rites of Passage.* New York: Basic Books, 1977.

Kennedy, David M. *Over Here.* New York: Oxford University Press, 1980.

———. "Revisiting Frederick Lewis Allen's *Only Yesterday.*" *Reviews in American History* 14 (June 1986): 309–14.

Kerber, Linda. "Separate Spheres, Female Worlds, Women's Place: The Rhetoric of Women's History." *Journal of American History* 75 (June 1988): 9–39.

Kling, Rob, Spencer Olin, and Mark Poster, eds. *Postsuburban California: The Transformation of Orange County since World War II.* Berkeley: University of California Press, 1991.

Klingaman, David C., and Richard K. Vedder, eds. *Essays on the Economy of the Old Northwest.* Athens: Ohio University Press, 1987.

Kneoppel, Raymond. "A Member Replies." *Scribner's Monthly* 83 (Dec. 1928): 954.

Kocka, Jurgen. *White-Collar Workers in America, 1890–1940: A Social-Political History in International Perspective.* Translated by Maura Kealey. Beverly Hills, Calif.: Sage Publications, 1980.

Kutolowski, Kathleen Smith. "Freemasonry and Community in the Early Republic: The Case for Antimasonic Anxieties." *American Quarterly* 34 (Winter 1982): 543–61.

Lasch, Christopher. *The Culture of Narcissism: American Life in an Age of Diminishing Expectations.* New York: Norton, 1978.

———. *The New Radicalism in America: The Intellectual as a Social Type, 1889–1963.* New York: Alfred A. Knopf, 1965.

Laski, Harold J. "The American Scene." *New Republic* 53 (Jan. 19, 1928): 16–17.

Lears, T. J. Jackson. *No Place of Grace: Antimodernism and the Transformation of American Culture, 1890–1920.* New York: Pantheon, 1981.

Lemons, Stanley J. *The Woman Citizen: Social Feminism in the 1920s.* Urbana: University of Illinois Press, 1973.

Leiby, James. *A History of Social Welfare and Social Work in the United States.* New York: Columbia University Press, 1978.

Lewis, Sinclair. *Babbitt.* New York: New American Library, 1961.

———. *Dodsworth.* New York: Random House, 1947.

———. *Main Street.* New York: New American Library, 1961.

———. "The Man Who Knew Coolidge." *American Mercury* 13 (Jan. 1928): 5–25.

Light, Martin. *The Quixotic Vision of Sinclair Lewis.* West Lafayette, Ind.: Purdue University Press, 1975.

Lingeman, Richard. *Small-Town America: A Narrative History, 1620 to the Present.* New York: Putnam's, 1980.

Lipson, Dorothy Ann. *Freemasonry in Federalist Connecticut, 1789–1835.* Princeton, N.J.: Princeton University Press, 1977.

Lloyd, Craig. *Aggressive Introvert: A Study of Herbert Hoover and Public Relations Management, 1912–1932.* Columbus: Ohio State University Press, 1972.

Logan, John R., and Gordana Rabrenovic. "Neighborhood Associations: Their Issues, Their Allies, and Their Opponents." *Urban Affairs Quarterly* 26 (Sept. 1990): 68–94.

Lubove, Roy. *The Professional Altruist: The Emergence of Social Work as a Career, 1880–1930.* Cambridge, Mass.: Harvard University Press, 1965.

Lundberg, George, et. al. *Leisure: A Suburban Study.* New York: Columbia University Press, 1934.

Lunden, Rolf. *Business and Religion in the American 1920s.* Westport, Conn.: Greenwood Press, 1988.

Lynd, Robert S., and Helen Merrell Lynd. *Middletown: A Study in American Culture.* New York: Harcourt, Brace and Co., 1929.

———. *Middletown in Transition: A Study in Cultural Conflict.* New York: Harcourt, Brace and Co., 1937.

McElvaine, Robert S. *The Great Depression: America, 1929–1941.* New York: Times Books, 1984.

Macleod, David. *Building Character in the American Boy: The Boy Scouts, YMCA, and Their Forerunners, 1870–1920.* Madison: University of Wisconsin Press, 1983.

Mahoney, Timothy. *River Towns in the Great West: The Structure of Provincial Urbanization in the American Midwest, 1820–1870.* New York: Cambridge University Press, 1990.

Maier, Charles S. *Recasting Bourgeois Europe: Stabilization in France, Germany, and Italy in the Decade after World War I.* Princeton, N.J.: Princeton University Press, 1975.

Marden, Charles F. *Rotary and Its Brothers: An Analysis and Interpretation of the Men's Service Clubs.* Princeton, N.J.: Princeton University Press, 1935.

Marsh, Margaret. *Suburban Lives.* New Brunswick, N.J.: Rutgers University Press, 1990.

Martin, Edward. *H. L. Mencken and the Debunkers*. Athens: University of Georgia Press, 1984.

Martin, Theodora Penny. *The Sound of Our Own Voices: Women's Study Clubs, 1860–1910*. Boston: Beacon Press, 1987.

Martindale, Don, and R. Galen Hanson. *Small Town and the Nation: The Conflict of Local and Translocal Forces*. Westport, Conn.: Greenwood Publishing, 1969.

Marwick, Arthur. *Class: Image and Reality in Britain, France, and the USA since 1930*. New York: Oxford University Press, 1980.

———, ed. *Class in the Twentieth Century*. Worcester, Eng.: Harvester Press, 1986.

Maule, Harry E., and Melville H. Cane, eds. *The Man from Main Street*. New York: Random House, 1953.

May, Henry. *Ideas, Faiths, and Feelings: Essays on American Intellectual and Religious History, 1952–1982*. New York: Oxford University Press, 1983.

———. *Protestant Churches and Industrial America*. New York: Harper and Row, 1949.

Mayer, Kurt. "Small Business as a Social Institution." *Social Research* 20 (1947): 345–50.

Mead, Robert O. *Atlantic Legacy: Essays in American-European Cultural History*. New York: New York University Press, 1969.

Mencken, H. L. *Minority Report*. New York: Alfred J. Knopf, 1956.

———. *Prejudices, Third Series*. New York: Alfred J. Knopf, 1922.

———. *Prejudices, Sixth Series*. New York: Alfred J. Knopf, 1926.

Merton, Robert K. *Social Theory and Social Structure*. New York: Free Press, 1968.

Meyer, Donald. *The Positive Thinkers: Religion as Pop Psychology from Mary Baker Eddy to Oral Roberts*. New York: Pantheon, 1980.

Miller, Perry. *The Responsibility of Mind in a Civilization of Machines*. Amherst: University of Massachusetts Press, 1979.

Miller, Zane L. *Suburb: Neighborhood and Community in Forest Park, Ohio, 1935–1976*. Knoxville: University of Tennessee Press, 1981.

Mills, C. Wright. *White Collar: The American Middle Classes*. New York: Oxford University Press, 1953.

Mintz, Steven, and Susan Kellog. *Domestic Revolutions: A Social History of American Family Life*. New York: Free Press, 1988.

Mitchell, Wesley C., ed. *What Veblen Taught: Selected Writings*. New York: Sentry Press, 1967.

Moline, Norman. "Mobility and the Small Town, 1900–1930: Transportation Change in Oregon, Illinois." University of Chicago Department of Geography, Research Paper No. 132, 1971.

Moore, Leonard J. *Citizen Klansmen: The Ku Klux Klan in Indiana, 1921–1928*. Chapel Hill: University of North Carolina Press, 1991.

Motherwell, Hiram. *The Imperial Dollar*. New York: Brentano's Publishers, 1929.

Muraskin, William N. *Middle-Class Blacks in a White Society: Prince Hall Freemasonry in America*. Berkeley: University of California Press, 1975.

Ninkovich, Frank A. *The Diplomacy of Ideas: U.S. Foreign Policy and Cultural Relations, 1938–1950.* New York: Cambridge University Press, 1981.

Nissen, Bruce, ed. *U.S. Labor Relations, 1945–1989: Accommodation and Conflict.* New York: Garland Publishing, 1990.

Noggle, Burl. *Into the Twenties: The United States from Armistice to Normalcy.* Urbana: University of Illinois Press, 1974.

Oestreicher, Richard Jules. *Solidarity and Fragmentation: Working People and Class Consciousness in Detroit, 1875–1900.* Urbana: University of Illinois Press, 1986.

Ogden, Annegret S. *The Great American Housewife: From Helpmate to Wage Earner, 1776–1986.* Westport, Conn.: Greenwood Press, 1986.

Pells, Richard H. *The Liberal Mind in a Conservative Age: American Intellectuals in the 1940s and 1950s.* New York: Harper and Row, 1985.

———. *Radical Visions and American Dreams: Culture and Social Thought in the Depression Years.* New York: Harper and Row, 1973.

Persons, Stow. *The Decline of American Gentility.* New York: Columbia University Press, 1973.

Popenoe, David. *The Suburban Environment: Sweden and the United States.* Chicago: University of Chicago Press, 1977.

Poppendieck, Janet. *Breadlines Knee-Deep in Wheat: Food Assistance in the Great Depression.* New Brunswick, N.J.: Rutgers University Press, 1986.

Poston, Richard W. *Small Town Renaissance.* New York: Harper Bros., 1950.

Puffer, J. Adams. *The Boy and His Gang.* Boston: J. Houghton Mifflin Co., 1912.

Reichlin, David Smith. "From Civic Duty to Psychological Reward." Ph.D. Diss., University of Pittsburgh, 1981.

Richardson, Anna Steese. "Is the Women's Club Dying?" *Harper's Magazine* 159 (Oct. 1929): 605–12.

———. "Lobbying in Women's Clubs." *New Republic* 63 (June 11, 1930): 91–93.

Riesman, David, with Nathan Glazer and Reuel Denney. *The Lonely Crowd: A Study of the Changing American Character.* New Haven, Conn.: Yale University Press, 1956.

Riley, Thomas James. *A Study of the Higher Life of Chicago.* Chicago: University of Chicago Press, 1905.

Rosenberg, Emily S. *Spreading the American Dream: American Economic and Cultural Expansion, 1890–1945.* New York: Hill and Wang, 1982.

Rosenof, Theodore. *Dogma, Depression, and the New Deal: The Debate of Political Leaders over Economic Recovery.* Port Washington, N.Y.: Kennikat Press, 1975.

Rosenzweig, Roy. "Boston's Masons, 1900–1935: The Lower Middle Class in a Divided Society." *Journal of Voluntary Action Research* 6 (July–Oct. 1977): 119–26.

Ross, Jack C. *An Assembly of Good Fellows: Voluntary Associations in History.* Westport, Conn.: Greenwood Press, 1976.

Rubin, Joan Shelley. *The Making of Middlebrow Culture.* Chapel Hill: University of North Carolina Press, 1992.

Ryan, Mary P. *Cradle of the Middle Class: The Family in Oneida County, New York, 1760–1865*. New York: Cambridge University Press, 1981.

Salmond, John A. *The Civilian Conservation Corps, 1933–1943: A New Deal Case Study*. Durham, N.C.: Duke University Press, 1967.

Salvatore, Nick. *Eugene Debs: Citizen and Socialist*. Urbana: University of Illinois Press, 1984.

Sapin, Ruth. "Babbitt, Jr." *New Republic* 48 (Sept. 8, 1925): 68–69.

Schiesl, Martin J. *The Politics of Efficiency: Municipal Administration and Reform in America, 1800–1920*. Berkeley: University of California Press, 1977.

Schmidt, Alvin J. *Fraternal Organizations*. Westport, Conn.: Greenwood Press, 1980.

———. *Oligarchy in Fraternal Organizations: A Study in Organizational Leadership*. Detroit: Gale Research Co., 1973.

———. "The Unbrotherly Brotherhood: Discrimination in Fraternal Orders." *Phylon* 34 (Fall 1973): 275–82.

Schulze, R. O. "The Role of Economic Dominants in Community Power Structure." *American Sociological Review* 23 (Feb. 1958): 3–9.

Schwartz, Barry, ed. *The Changing Face of the Suburbs*. Chicago: University of Chicago Press, 1976.

Scott, Anne Firor. *Making the Invisible Woman Visible*. Urbana: University of Illinois Press, 1984.

———. *Natural Allies: Women's Associations in American History*. Urbana: University of Illinois Press, 1991.

Sealander, Judith. *Grand Plans: Business Progressivism and Social Change in Ohio's Miami Valley, 1890–1920*. Lexington: University of Kentucky Press, 1988.

Seldes, Gilbert. "Service." *New Republic* 43 (July 15, 1925): 207.

Sennett, Richard. *The Fall of the Public Man*. New York: Alfred A. Knopf, 1977.

Simmel, Georg. *The Sociology of Georg Simmel*. Translated and edited by Kurt H. Wolff. New York: Free Press, 1964.

Sitkoff, Harvard, ed. *Fifty Years Later: The New Deal Evaluated*. Philadelphia: Temple University Press, 1985.

Sklar, Martin. *The Corporate Reconstruction of American Capitalism, 1890–1916*. New York: Cambridge University Press, 1988.

Sklar, Robert. *Movie-Made America: A Cultural History of American Movies*. New York: Random House, 1975.

Smith, Constance E., and Anne Freedman. *Voluntary Associations: Perspectives on the Literature*. Cambridge, Mass.: Harvard University Press, 1972.

Solomon, Steven. *Small Business USA: The Role of Small Companies in Sparking America's Economic Transformation*. New York: Crown Publishers, 1984.

Starr, Kevin. *Inventing the Dream: California through the Progressive Era*. New York: Oxford University Press, 1985.

Steiner, Jesse F. "An Appraisal of the Community Movement." *Journal of Social Forces* 7 (Mar. 1929): 333–42.

Sternsehr, Bernard, ed. *Hitting Home: The Great Depression in Town and Country*. Chicago: Quadrangle Books, 1970.

Stevens, Albert C. *Cyclopaedia of Fraternities*. New York: E. B. Treat, 1907.

Stock, Catherine McNicol. *Main Street in Crisis: The Great Depression and the Old Middle Class on the Northern Plains*. Chapel Hill: North Carolina University Press, 1992.

Sturges, Kenneth. *American Chambers of Commerce*. New York: Moffat, Bard and Co., 1915.

Susman, Warren. *Culture as History: The Transformation of American Society in the Twentieth Century*. New York: Pantheon, 1984.

Tarkington, Booth. "Rotarian and Sophisticate." *World's Work* 58 (Jan. 1929): 41–44.

Thelen, David. *Paths of Resistance: Tradition and Dignity in Industrializing Missouri*. New York: Oxford University Press, 1986.

Thoreau, Henry David. *Reform Papers*. Wendell Glick, ed. Princeton, N.J.: Princeton University Press, 1973.

Trachtenberg, Alan. *The Incorporation of America: Culture and Society in the Gilded Age*. New York: Hill and Wang, 1982.

Trout, Charles H. *Boston, the Great Depression, and the New Deal*. New York: Oxford University Press, 1977.

Tyack, David, Robert Lowe, and Elisabeth Hansot. *Public Schools in Hard Times: The Great Depression and Recent Years*. Cambridge, Mass.: Harvard University Press, 1984.

Ullman, John E., ed. *The Suburban Economic Network: Economic Activity, Resource Use, and the Great Sprawl*. New York: Praeger, 1977.

United States Senate Select Committee on Small Business. *Small Business and the Quality of American Life: A Compilation of Source Material on the Relationship Between Small Business and the Quality of Life, 1946–1976*. Washington, D.C.: U.S. Government Printing Office, 1977.

University of Chicago Social Science Survey Committee. *Rotary? A University Group Looks at the Rotary Club of Chicago*. Chicago: University of Chicago Press, 1934.

Walters, Ronald G. *American Reformers, 1815–1860*. New York: Hill and Wang, 1978.

Warner, Sam Bass, Jr. *The Private City: Philadelphia in Three Periods of Its Growth*. Philadelphia: University of Pennsylvania Press, 1968.

Warner, W. Lloyd, et al. *Democracy in Jonesville: A Study in Quality and Inequality*. New York: Harper and Row, 1949.

Warner, W. Lloyd, and Paul S. Lunt. *The Social Life of a Modern Community*. New Haven, Conn.: Yale University Press, 1941.

Warren, Roland L. "External Forces Affecting Local Communities—Bad News and Good News." *Journal of Community Development and Society* 6 (Fall 1975): 6–21.

———, and Larry Lyon, eds. *New Perspectives on the American Community*. Homewood, Ill.: Rand McNally, 1983.

Wellman, Barry, and Barry Leighton. "Networks, Neighborhoods, and Communities: Approaches to the Study of the Community Question." *Urban Affairs Quarterly* 14:3 (Mar. 1979): 363–90.

Whyte, William. *The Organization Man.* New York: Doubleday, 1956.

Wiebe, Robert H. *Businessmen and Reform: A Study of the Progressive Movement.* Cambridge, Mass.: Harvard University Press, 1962.

———. *The Search for Order, 1877–1920.* New York: Hill and Wang, 1967.

Wilson, James Q. *Political Organizations.* New York: Basic Books, 1973.

Wilson, Joan Hoff. *American Business and Foreign Policy, 1920–1933.* Lexington: University of Kentucky Press, 1971.

———. *Herbert Hoover: Forgotten Progressive.* Boston: Little, Brown and Co., 1975.

———. *Ideology and Economics: U.S. Relations with the Soviet Union, 1918–1933.* Columbia: University of Missouri Press, 1974.

Winks, Robin W., ed. *Other Voices, Other Views: An International Collection of Essays from the Bicentennial.* Westport, Conn.: Greenwood Press, 1978.

Wolfe, Alan, ed., *America at Century's End.* Berkeley: University of California Press, 1991.

Wright, William C., ed. *Urban New Jersey since 1870.* Trenton: New Jersey Historical Commission, 1975.

Zelizer, Viviana A. Rotman. *Morals and Markets: The Development of Life Insurance in the United States.* New York: Columbia University Press, 1979.

Zunz, Olivier. *Making America Corporate, 1870–1920.* Chicago: University of Chicago Press, 1990.

Index